Affordable and Social Housing

Affordable and Social Housing is a candid and critical appraisal of current big-ticket issues affecting the planning, development and management of affordable and social housing in the United Kingdom. The successor to the second edition of the established textbook *An Introduction to Social Housing*, this book includes new chapters, reflecting the focal importance of customer involvement and empowerment, regeneration and the localism agenda that will have radical impacts on housing provision and tenure, as well as the town and country planning system that enables its development. There is also a new chapter on housing law in response to demand for a clear and signposting exposition of this often complex area. Paul Reeves indicates how each theme affects the other, and suggests policy directions on the basis of past successes and failures.

Reeves takes a people-centred approach to the subject, describing the themes that have run through provision of social housing from the first philanthropic industrialists in the nineteenth century through to the increasingly complex mixture of ownerships and tenures in the present day.

The book is ideal for students of housing and social policy, and for housing professionals aiming to obtain qualifications and wanting a broad understanding of the social housing sector.

Paul Reeves has been working in the housing and planning field in local authorities, housing associations and central government as a senior manager, consultant, adviser and trainer since 1982, and is an established academic – currently a Visiting Lecturer at the University of Westminster and other UK institutions.

Affordable and Social Housing

Policy and practice

Paul Reeves

Routledge
Taylor & Francis Group

NEW YORK AND LONDON

First published 2014
by Routledge
711 Third Avenue, New York, NY 10017

and by Routledge
2 Park Square, Milton Park, Abingdon, Oxon OX14 4RN

Routledge is an imprint of the Taylor & Francis Group, an informa business

© 2014 Paul Reeves

The right of Paul Reeves to be named as author of this work has been asserted in accordance with sections 77 and 78 of the Copyright, Designs and Patents Act 1988.

British Library Cataloguing in Publication Data
A catalogue record for this book is available from the British Library

Library of Congress Cataloging-in-Publication Data
Reeves, Paul (Paul F.)
Affordable and social housing : policy and practice / Paul Reeves.
pages cm
Includes bibliographical references and index.
1. Housing policy–Great Britain. 2. Housing–Great Britain. 3. Low-income housing–Great Britain. I. Title.
HD7333.A3R358 2014
363.50941–dc23
2013017032

ISBN: 978-0-415-62855-6 (hbk)
ISBN: 978-0-415-62856-3 (pbk)
ISBN: 978-1-315-88275-8 (ebk)

Typeset in Bembo by
FiSH Books Ltd, Enfield

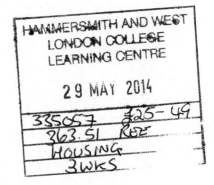

MIX
Paper from responsible sources
FSC
www.fsc.org FSC® C013056

Printed and bound in Great Britain by
TJ International Ltd, Padstow, Cornwall

This book is dedicated to my dear wife, Marlena, whom I love dearly and whose support I value beyond anything else.

Contents

List of figures and tables

Figures

Tables

List of acronyms

ADDR	Adult Disability Dependency Ratio
ALMO	Arms-Length Management Organisation
ARF	Area Regeneration Framework
BME	Black and Ethnic Minority
CCT	Compulsory Competitive Tendering
CDS	Co-Operative Development Society
CIH	Chartered Institute of Housing
CSG	Cost Sharing Group
CSR	Comprehensive Spending Review
DCLG	Department of Communities and Local Government
ECHR	European Convention on Human Rights
EU	European Union
HAG	Housing Association Grant
HCA	Homes and Communities Agency
HHSRS	Housing Health and Safety Rating System
HMA	Housing Market Assessment
HMCTS	Her Majesty's Courts and Tribunal Service
HRA	Housing Revenue Account
JCT	Joint Contract Tribunal
L&Q	London and Quadrant
LDDC	London Docklands Development Corporation
LETS	Local Exchange Trading Scheme
LSF	Labour Force Survey
LSIC	Local Service Improvement Compact
M&M	Management and Maintenance
NHF	National Housing Federation
NHS	National Health Service
OADR	Old Age Dependency Ratio
ONS	Office for National Statistics
PEST	Political, Economic, Social and Technological Analysis
PFI	Private Finance Initiative
PIL	Public International Law
PPS	Planning Policy Statement

PWLB	Public Works Loan Board
RICS	Royal Institute of Chartered Surveyors
RPI	Retail Price Index
RSO	Resident Service Organisation
RtB	Right to Buy
SEH	Survey of English Housing
SORP	Statement of Recommended Practice
SWOT	Strengths, Weaknesses, Opportunities and Threats
TSA	Tenant Services Authority
VAT	Value Added Tax

Preface

The housing scene is always changing, but there are themes which remain constant. These include the fact that everyone needs to live somewhere, in accommodation which suits their needs, and which they can afford. Unfortunately, many households simply cannot afford to compete in the market place – owner-occupied or rental – to satisfy their requirements, which is where the national or local state comes in. Assistance can be provided by reducing the price of the dwelling to that which can be afforded, through personal subsidy in the form of welfare benefits or similar assistance, or by subsidising the cost of building the dwelling which can be reflected in lower rental or purchase prices, or a combination of these.

The UK housing scene provides an interesting case study of how to enable affordable housing, and it is one which has altered significantly in the last few years. Between 2008 and 2011, approximately £8.4 billion was made available to housing providers, mainly housing associations, to help them build property without having to raise loans to meet the entire cost, and therefore to enable them to charge rents which conformed to the rent-restructuring formula – in England – or to traditionally lower rent levels which could be afforded by people on lower incomes across the UK. When the Coalition Government came to power, it made significant cuts in public expenditure, and housing took its share of the cuts, with the capital budget to support development halved, but with similar targets for production as the previous four years. To square the circle, it was decided to encourage providers to charge higher rents in order to raise more of the development finance by way of private sector loans; so there emerged two rent regimes. The first regime was that based on a formula taking into consideration lower incomes and property values compared to the national level, and the second was based on rents being set at up to 80 per cent of market rental values – the so-called affordable rent regime.

Although the financial regime has changed, there are several constants. Housing need will not go away, and has to be measured properly to guide development in terms of degree and location, and there has been considerable emphasis on evaluations of housing markets to assess the degree to which the housing market economy can supply enough of the commodity to satisfy need. Housing management is something which will always be required wherever there are tenancies with rights and obligations, and the style of management has changed over the years from the paternalistic – or maternalistic – model espoused by Octavia Hill in the nineteenth century to more enlightened and legally based alternatives, based on encouraging tenants to take responsibility for their homes and lifestyles. The model of the tenant has changed over the years – from one where housing management had to inculcate good behaviour and responsibility, to the model where tenants are responsible for their own actions and customers in every sense of the word. The advent of localism – devolving power to communities – is another challenge for housing management, and it will be interesting to see how organisations measure up to the challenges that this entails, including enabling tenants and other residents to manage their own homes in a beefed-up version of the Right to Manage which will surely come.

Introduction

Keywords: *the end of social housing; what affordable housing is; overview of key themes by chapter: supply and demand; customer involvement and empowerment; housing management; housing finance; housing law; housing regeneration and development; localism.*

The end of social housing?

'House' is a noun and a verb, as demonstrated in 'to house someone in a house'. This bit of semantics leads to the thought that 'housing' is both a process and an end product; and it is a valuable commodity or service which can be something which meets both essential need and luxury. This book is about both the end product and process of developing, obtaining and managing housing, and is focused on products and services which are oriented towards meeting need or marginal effective demand rather than purely demand or over and above requirement, but we must not lose sight of the essential ambiguity of the term, nor its breadth of definition, as meeting luxury requirements is in fact relevant to the provision of affordable and social housing because the recognition of and the need to meet degrees of aspiration is part and parcel of the product and the service, as will be explained.

Ten years ago, most academics and practitioners would have had no problem with the term social housing, although 30 years ago the term was virtually unknown. I have no idea exactly when the term was first used; a quick survey of papers and books reveals that it was used by Michael Harloe in 1981 in his monograph *The Recommodification of Housing* (Harloe, 1981), and the term was certainly in currency by the early 1990s and indeed formed the main part of the title of my first book on the subject, *An Introduction to Social Housing* (Reeves, 1996). There was little dispute as to what it meant, but some lamentation in the profession and elsewhere that things had got to that pass. It is possible to define the term ostensively (by example) and by dictionary definition, although the former may in fact be easier than the latter, although open to challenge. An ostensive definition might include:

- Housing (houses and flats) built and/or managed for rent by local authorities or housing associations or other registered providers;

- A list of all blocks which are owned and rented out by councils and their agents and housing associations, plus those which are leased from other owners by these organisations would probably constitute the set of social housing, although it is a fuzzy set, as there are arguably dwellings which fulfil these criteria but which are not 'really' social housing. An example is dwellings let out in consequence of employment, and some things which could be construed as social housing but which are not housing in the sense that we might understand the term, for example, a caravan or motor home, or a tent in the context of a disaster zone.

In terms of dictionary definition, there are a number of variants. The *Collins English Dictionary* (2003) defines it as '(Social Welfare) accommodation provided by the state for renting'. That's not bad, but it is inaccurate in that 'provided by the state' would seem to imply that the state (national or local state) is the source of all social housing, which it is not, as housing associations are not part of the state apparatus, even though they may have at some time received public subsidy in some form or another, or some or all of their tenants may or may have been in receipt of personal subsidy, principally some form of housing benefit. A somewhat better definition is that given by the housing charity Shelter on its website: 'Social housing is housing that is let at low rents and on a secure basis to people in housing need. It is generally provided by councils and not-for-profit organisations such as housing associations' (Shelter, 2012). It gives us a start.

Let's consider the dimensions of the Shelter offering. The key elements in the initial part of the definition are: 'low rent(s)', 'secure', and 'housing need'. The scoping element is self-explanatory, and relatively uncontroversial. Notably, the site gives the caveat that the content applies to England only, although I can find no reason to doubt that it would apply to the entire UK.

'Low rent' must be relativised to something, namely the set of all rents, just as it would be impossible to understand what an average car was unless you had some conception of the scope of possible dimensions. Uncontroversially, the rent one might expect to pay for a three-bed flat in London's Knightsbridge is by no stretch of the imagination a low rent, and market rents are generally but not always considerably higher than social rents. In social housing, at least in England, 'low rent' for council and housing association dwellings built before 2011 comes out of a formula which actually entails that social rents are relatively low rents, although they vary across the country and with size, value and the local wage economy. The formula used adjusts the rent to take account of local relative to national average manual wages (accounting for roughly 70 per cent of the formula rent), something that the market does not do, and therefore artificially constrains rent levels. Formula rents are also based on actual average social rents as they were in 2000, adjusted for relative size, value and wages, and social rents at that time were in any case markedly lower than market rents. There will be more about this when we come to discuss housing finance, but it is clear to see that state intervention had in this case given rise to a product which retails below market levels, although this in itself gives rise to the question as to whether there is or can be a market for social rented housing, which will be dealt with when we come to examine choice-based lettings initiatives.

The outcome of using this formula can be illustrated simply by comparing the rent of an ex-local authority flat in Southwark, London, with that of a local authority flat in the same location. A two-bed ground floor flat in Reedham Avenue, SE15 was advertised in January 2012 on the Choice Based Letting site applying to Southwark Council for £95.76 a week (Southwark HomeSearch, 2012). A similar ex-local authority property in SE15 advertised on the property site Rightmove, seen on the same day, was offered at £208 a week (Rightmove, 2012). This was the cheapest comparable property on that site in that location. Admittedly, this is a very small sample, which is purely illustrative, but it does identify the local authority-let property as comparatively low rent, at 46 per cent of the market comparator. It may then raise the question of how the local state can provide accommodation at this comparatively low rent, and indeed why, which leads into a consideration of meeting need, which we will briefly consider before discussing 'secure'.

In a sense, the phrase 'housing need' poses some difficulties. Uncontroversially, everyone needs somewhere to live. Everyone is therefore in need of housing, and therefore it could be argued that the term covers all eventualities. However, the term is somewhat more limited than this. To understand it fully, it is necessary to compare and contrast the terms 'need' and 'demand'. In economic terms, demand, when considered as effective demand, relates to a requirement which can be bid for and obtained using a means of exchange, commonly money, often in competition with others, and therefore 'demand' is usually employed when talking about the market. If we net out market housing from all housing, we are left with non-market housing from which the element of satisfaction through competitive bidding with cash or an equivalent is absent. This gives us a residuum which is allocated according to some other principle, and that may be (but is not necessarily) be on the basis of need. It could be allocated on the basis of favour, for example, a grace and favour apartment given to a senior politician as a consequence of their duties, or Buckingham Palace. If we combine the thought that everyone needs some form of housing (used widely, in the sense of shelter) and that not everyone is in a position to compete successfully for this, then we are left with the idea that housing need is the residuum (in terms of households) left when the market has finished allocating housing on the basis of demand, and it can immediately be seen to be a fluid entity, since the market is always changing in relation to levels of supply and demand. Put simply, we can say that if someone cannot satisfy their housing need through the market place, then they are in a pure state of housing need, just as someone who cannot meet their requirements generally because they do not have enough money to do so can be termed 'needy'. Low-rent housing provided by the state and its agents, and by organisations specifically set up to provide it, can be said to be that aimed at meeting housing need in this sense. Arguably, if everyone could satisfy their housing requirement through the market place, there would be no housing need in this sense, and therefore no need for housing to meet it. Notably, I have used the terms 'need' and 'requirement', and as a presage to what follows in the next chapter, I have done this to distinguish what everyone needs (i.e. a roof over their head), which is 'requirement', from what everyone needs but which some people cannot get through engagement with the market, which is 'need'. A quantitatively simple (and indeed simplistic) way of defining the quantum of housing need would be to subtract everyone who can meet their requirement through market engagement from the total quantum of people who have a housing requirement, and this, crudely, is what housing needs surveys do.

On a logical note, it is often possible to discover the distinction between concepts by considering whether x can or cannot be the case concurrently with y, or vice versa. For example, in the case of housing need and demand. It is certainly possible to demand housing without needing it, as is the case for second-home buyers. Therefore there is a logical distinction between demand and need. It is also possible to need housing without demanding it, in the case that a person has a mental disability which prevents them from realising that they have such a need. This thought also indicates that demand is active and conscious whereas need is a state of affairs not dependent upon activity or consciousness. Another logical test of distinction is to establish whether a contradiction arises by asserting that x is the case and y is not. If a contradiction regularly arises it may be that in fact x means y, or put another way, x and y mean the same thing. If no contradiction arises, then it is usually possible to say that the words represent different concepts, even if there is a relationship between them. So for example, it is possible to have a need but not demand something, and to demand but not to need something, as we have already exemplified. Therefore demand and need represent different concepts, even though there is a relationship between the two.

Before we leave the concept of need, it is worth considering whether it is absolute or relative. According to Bradshaw (1972), there are at least four ways of classifying need. Normative need is need which arises from comparison with a standard set out by someone or somebody, usually regarded as an expert or authority (for example, the state). Comparative need is sometimes known as relative need, and is determined by trying to establish a pecking order of need – for example by comparing all estates in the country and distinguishing those that are in the worst condition, or looking at all incomes and determining the lowest quartile. Felt need is subjective need, that is, it exists where people feel that they are in need – if everyone else you know has an iphone then you may have a felt need for one. Finally, expressed need is the need which people say they have, for example, a need to go to the pub; clearly it is possible to feel a need which is not expressed, and vice versa.

In my view, expressed need and felt need are psychological states, the former verbalised, and may have no basis in fact, and would be very hard to use in assessing need in a rational way which would justify state expenditure on relieving it. Normative need can arise from a consideration of comparative need, and vice versa, and at the heart of both is the notion that there is some fact of the matter which can be discovered and which would make a normative judgement true or reasonable. So my money is on a hybrid of normative and comparative need. To look at it another way, without forgetting the above mixture of reasoning, we can talk about absolute and relative need, which are fairly well entrenched sociological concepts, and usually expressed in terms of defining poverty. Seebohm Rowntree (1901) defined absolute poverty as being below a subsistence line, a minimum standard needed to live. P. J. Townshend (1979) defined relative poverty as 'the absence or inadequacy of those diets, amenities, standards, services and activities which are common or customary in society' (Townshend, 1979). Need can be substituted for poverty in the above without lack of sense. Everyone needs to consider which camp they fall in as regards definitions of need, but the current state position seems to be normative, comparative and relative, and it seems reasonable. One can imagine that someone could get by for a while without shelter at all, living under bridges and under the pier but against the background of what is considered reasonable in today's society, it would be hard to sustain the argument that that person is not in fact in housing need. This argument would be supported by considering the medium- to long-term consequences for the health of that individual were this homelessness and rooflessness to continue, which may well be death. The absolute definition therefore captures too little in our quest to define need in a way which is useful to our ends.

We can now move on to the term 'secure'. The term has been used to define specific arrangements within the rental tenure, when capitalised. Secure tenancies came about as a result of the 1980 Housing Act, as will be discussed in the chapter on housing law, and were applied to local authority and housing association tenancies in England and Wales and in a modified format elsewhere in the UK. They are still the main form of tenure in the council sector, although the assured and assured shorthold forms of tenancy are those used by housing associations following the 1988 Housing Act. However, at this point, it is necessary only to compare the concept of a secure tenancy and one which is not secure. Unmet housing need will re-arise where tenancies are in some way not guaranteed or secure. Assured shorthold tenancies are not secure in that they can be determined at any time after a minimum period, generally six months, on service of appropriate notice. If the point of social housing is to provide accommodation with security, then the assured shorthold tenancy would not be a good candidate. What 'secure' means is that as long as the tenant abides by the conditions of the tenancy, including paying rent when required and behaving reasonably, they can generally stay there for as long as they want. This is in fact a major distinguishing characteristic from the 'affordable' tenancy arrangements which are coming in at the time of writing, especially in their conditional tenancy manifestation.

Putting it all together, we have a concept of social housing which is low rent compared to market-sector housing – else otherwise it would be beyond the reach of those unable to compete effectively in the market place – which is (therefore) there to meet housing need as opposed to effective demand, and which is relatively secure, as if it were not, unmet housing need would recur. This is both a definition and an answer to the question 'What is the end (as in purpose) of social housing?'. It is a reasonably coherent and clear concept which more or less reflects the reality of the arrangement, and which in fact generates arguments in favour of another form of housing – affordable housing – which is distinct in both logical form and purpose from social housing, but can be provided by the same agencies as the former.

What is affordable housing?

We now turn to affordable housing. The concept at first sight seems to be absurd or obvious, until the context of use is made clear. All housing is affordable to someone. If

I were a billionaire, I could probably afford to buy and run any sort of house I wanted or that existed which was potentially or actually available for purchase. So what is the point of appending 'affordable' to 'housing'? We can get somewhere if we consider affordable as a relative term. What may be affordable to x may not be affordable to y, so the question is, when we are talking about affordable housing, to whom are we relativising the housing cost? It may be that the answer is that it is relativised to those who cannot afford to compete in the market place to obtain housing which would reasonably meet their needs. However, that delivers more or less what is meant by social housing, and surely there must be some difference that makes a difference, otherwise why use two terms where one might do? Another way to try to distinguish between the terms affordable and social housing is that affordable housing is housing which people can afford regardless of their need and the security of tenure of the property whereas social housing must fulfil all the other criteria which have been set out. However, this definition does not seem to capture enough – it would also lead to unwanted conclusions. For example, if all someone could afford was a bedsit, and they had a family of three, they would have affordable housing, but it would be totally inadequate to meet their needs, which is hardly a laudable or in fact an actual social policy objective. Enough has been said to suggest that in the absence of definition by *fiat* (imposition or rule), the term is hard to resolve.

The reality of the matter is that the term has arisen for largely ideological reasons bolstered by judgements about how much the nation can afford to subsidise non-market housing and macroeconomic worries in general. It can be traced back to the start of the fixed housing association grant regime in 1989, following the 1988 Housing Act. Prior to the act, housing associations received capital grant aid from the state to ensure that they could meet management and maintenance costs from a fixed 'fair rent' assessed by a rent officer (a local authority official) based on a formulaic assessment of amenity, size and other factors but not scarcity, which is a prime determinant of market rents. In many cases, the proceeds from fair rent would only just cover management and maintenance (M&M) costs, meaning that only a small amount was left over which could service a loan which could be raised to help meet development costs. Essentially, the capital grant (known as housing association grant (HAG)) was broadly equivalent to reasonable development costs minus the loan which could be raised on the basis of the residual income after M&M costs, and in many cases, the percentage of development costs covered by the grant was in the high 90s. In 1988, the decision was taken to radically reform the HAG regime in an attempt to rein in public expenditure whilst forging ahead with housing association development as an alternative to municipal programmes. The system was turned on its head – instead of rents determining grant levels, grants were fixed at around 75 per cent of reasonable development costs, and rents had to be set to cover M&M and the cost of servicing a loan to meet the difference between grant levels and total development costs. This meant that post-1988 Housing Act rents for similar properties were considerably higher in most cases for similar properties than for those developed before its implementation. Despite this, assurances were given by government ministers that resulting rents would still be affordable, although no hard and fast definition of the term was forthcoming. A consultation paper published by the Department of the Environment in 1987,

Finance for Housing Associations: The Government's Proposals, said that one of the objectives of the proposed fixed-grant regime would be 'to target grant accurately whilst still taking into account scheme costs and ensuring that rents are kept within the means of tenants in low paid employment', which was a definition widely accepted for some years, and used as a guiding principle to inform the rent restructuring proposals which came to fruition some 16 years later.

Having entered the language, the term persisted. By the late 1980s many local authorities were able to set rents at far below market levels due to having discharged housing debt and through the contribution of interest from council house sales receipts under the right to buy to their housing revenue accounts (HRA), and in some cases through policies of subsidising the HRA from the rates, a practice which was outlawed in 1990. This gave rise to the observation that surely tenants could afford higher rents than those levied, and that they were getting an easy ride compared with folks who were renting privately or paying mortgages. Similar observations were made in relation to housing association fair rent tenants, fuelled by the differential between fair rents enjoyed by secure tenants and post-1988 Housing Act 'affordable' rents paid by assured tenants, a differential which accelerated in the early 1990s when grant rates started to fall significantly as a percentage of development costs, and new rents started to rise considerably.

To a certain extent, the argument about what was and was not an affordable rent was temporarily laid to rest with the introduction of a formulaic approach to rent-setting in the social rented sector, the so-called rent restructuring regime which applied to housing associations and local authorities in England and in a modified form in Wales, but not Scotland and Northern Ireland. The idea was that by 2012, all social housing tenancies in the same area would have like-for-like rents regardless of whether they were council or association owned, and that they would all be affordable due to the formula factor which related roughly 70 per cent of the 'target rent' in 2012 to the relativity between local and national lower quartile incomes, so that rents would be lower in poorer areas than richer ones.

In the late 2000s a completely different perspective on affordability took over, this time driven by macroeconomic woes. This time, personal affordability was overtaken by national affordability. How would it be possible to control national expenditure at the same time as delivering a reasonable quantum of social housing? The 1988 Housing Act regime had in a sense answered this question – get the grant down, make housing associations charge higher rents, and let the tenants (and the housing benefit budget) take the strain. The rent restructuring approach, with its limitation on rent increases and rent caps, and dysfunctionality in relation to inflation rates, subverted this intention. Quite simply, it became apparent that driving down housing capital expenditure through the spending review mechanism was ultimately incompatible with the formulaic approach adopted. Things came to a head in October 2010, with the first comprehensive spending review of the Coalition government, when the budget for social housing grant was slashed from £8.4 billion to £4.3 billion, with no change in projected output – around 150,000 affordable rented and low-cost ownership homes over the three-year spending review period from 2011. Inevitably, this meant lower grants and higher rents to pay for the increased borrowing which would be needed to supplement state capital assistance. To enable this, the government proposed that new housing association rents would be set at up to 80 per cent of market rent levels, outside the rent restructuring regime, which to many signalled the end of social housing as it had been known. Interestingly no one claimed that the 1988 Housing Act regime which departed from fair rents signalled the end of social housing. This is because social housing had, since 2003, been directly associated with rents informed by that formula.

Affordable housing is, therefore, housing which receives some form of state subsidy which it is deemed that the nation can afford. And what the nation can afford is rents which are set at up to 80 per cent of market values. The question is, can the nation afford the increase in housing benefit which will be payable in respect of these higher rents? There appears to be an answer to this one. In April 2013, a universal benefit will be introduced which will replace housing benefit along with a myriad of other social security benefits phased in gradually, and be capped at around £26,000. There is, at the time of writing, debate in the House of Lords over the Welfare Reform Bill, especially over the impact on housing cost assistance and the impact of the regime on people with disabilities, but it seems that affordability will relate not just to the nation's capital resources but also to what is deemed reasonable in terms of revenue expenditure. As will be seen, this links directly to the conditional tenancy regime introduced by the Localism Act 2011, which will see the introduction of five-year fixed term tenancies for new housing association and local authority lets and re-lets – initially discretionary – and the transformation of social and affordable housing into welfare housing.

Key themes

The book covers seven key themes, each discussed in detail in its own chapter.

Supply and demand

One of the key challenges of the state is how to ensure that its citizens are enabled to live in reasonable circumstances, and to ensure that everyone is able to contribute to the health of society. Hobbes said, in his *Leviathan*, that without some form of government, life would be nasty, brutish and short (Hobbes, 1651). This has been an accepted philosophy since his day, and rather implies some form of duty to ensure that society is governed and sustained by that governance. Mrs Thatcher, prime minister of the UK from 1979 to 1991, famously declared that 'And, you know, there is no such thing as society' in an interview with *Woman's Own* magazine in 1987, but certainly did not imply that there was no need for some form of government, and seemed to be arguing that people saw society as some kind of object which it wasn't, as opposed to a dynamic between individuals and the expression of collective respon-sibility composed of obligations and entitlements, which she seemed to lean towards in that article. The Coalition government and Mr Cameron, the prime minister at the time of writing, certainly seem to believe that there is such a thing as society, and a Big One at that, so the problem of whether there is a society seems to have been resolved for the moment, and where there is society, there must, it seems, be government.

One of the things that government is there to do is to ensure that society remains stable. It does so through the exercise of law, enacting legislation to regulate behaviours which society, or at least the more powerful or vocal parts of it, proscribe offensive or irksome, and to encourage behaviours which meet with its approval. One of the ways to ensure that society remains stable is to endeavour to influence the supply of housing in relation to demand. Since housing is an essential, serious malfunctions in its supply would inevitably give rise to general misery and discontent, and Mrs Thatcher's statement might become literally true due to the anarchy which would almost certainly result from the radical failure of supply.

Since 1957, local authorities have had a duty to evaluate housing need within their areas. They have done so by conducting analyses of housing supply and demand, and projecting need over five years. Since 2007, they have also been preparing strategic housing market assessments, which look at effective demand as well as need to give a holistic picture of the housing requirement in the area of their jurisdiction, in liaison with other authorities and supplier bodies. Several consultancy firms have emerged over that time to provide this analysis, and to an extent the methodology has become standardised. The approaches are relatively straightforward, although the detail and output varies considerably depending on who conducts the exercise, and what the authorities wish to show. It is clearly important to have a view of supply and demand over the medium to long term to ensure that development and allocation policies and strategies performed directly or through partners (for example housing associations) are properly targeted in quantity and market segmentation, as well as to inform planning strategy in relation to bringing enough land forward to assist in meeting targets for provision. In simple terms, a housing needs survey will look at demand arising from newly forming households in the district through natural increase and division of existing households, projected in-migration and subtract from this the number of households expected to leave the district through out-migration and dissolution (for example through deaths). It will then look at projected supply in terms of all tenures, both within and on the borders of the district, based on past production and variables such as the local and national economy. The key to a successful survey is to establish the degree of affordability of housing which is likely to be produced in relation to actual and projected ability to purchase or rent, as this will affect the level of supply to be fed into the analysis. The quantum of housing need is roughly equivalent to the shortfall between total requirement and market supply. By way of illustration, suppose the expected five-year requirement is 4,000 units, and the expected supply of market housing is 3,000, based on housing land availability in the planning system, trends in residential new-build and conversion planning applications, and past construction trends. There is a crude deficit of 1,000 dwellings. Now suppose that 3,000 out of the 4,000 projected households requiring housing over that period can afford to satisfy their need through the market. That means that, all other things being equal (which they never are), the quantum of below-market housing required would be 1,000, which is 4,000 minus 3,000. This can be represented in the formula: total requirement minus effective demand.

The projected market supply figure can then be compared to the effective demand projection. If it is lower, then this indicates a need for additional provision to meet market demand, and if higher, a support for an argument to restrict market supply through planning policy. This does not affect the 'need' figure, which is logically independent of that for effective demand and market supply. A refinement of the model is to endeavour to quantify the number of units for need which are planned to be built over five years by type and size, and then to subtract this from the quantum of unmet requirement. So, if there are 500 units planned to be built, then all other things being equal, there will be a deficit of (1,000 minus 500) units available to meet projected need. That will be the quantum which the local authority will seek to enable through partnership working, with a contingency in the case that real need exceeds that which has been projected. This approach makes perfect logical sense, although it is not an exact science, and there is absolutely no guarantee that development output will in fact be sufficient to meet the total requirement or its market and non-market components. For example, it does not matter how refined the housing targets emerging from planning are, or the how robust are the intentions of developers to produce dwellings, if there is a financial crisis of 2007–2008 proportions and lending is tight or non-existent, development programmes will founder and supply will fall short of requirement. There are many variables which impinge on plans of this sort, only a few of which can be directly controlled and/or predicted with any certainty whatever. The credit crunch of 2007–2008 was a major blow to development, and was relatively unpredicted but it happened anyway.

It is worth pondering why the market cannot or does not seem able to deliver sufficient housing to meet the total requirement, or whether this is inevitably the case. Is it a matter of fact or a matter of logic? If it is a matter of fact, then it may be possible to intervene in the market to the extent that eventually it could meet all requirement without the need for non-market solutions. If it is not, it would be impossible in principle and we would forever be committed to the task of producing non-market housing for those who are unable to engage in it. We will examine the view taken by the Barker report in 2004 (Barker/ODPM, 2004), updated in 2006, that market adjustments are possible and can reduce levels of unmet need. To simplify, this is the classical economic view of supply and demand that if you increase supply and effective demand remains stable, the price of the commodity will stabilise or decrease, so that more people would be able to satisfy their housing requirement through the market than otherwise. One can imagine a situation which is far from that obtaining in the UK in 2012 where there is full employment, and that wages have stabilised at a relatively high level universally. One can also imagine a situation where people are completely flexible in terms of where they want to live, and where labour is therefore perfectly mobile. It is also possible to conceive of a situation whereby housing developers supply so much accommodation – for rent and for sale – that its scarcity reduces radically, and its price therefore falls in relation to effective demand, so that everyone can eventually either rent or buy privately. This is unlikely to happen, but it does not seem to be logically impossible. Now, under these circumstances, there would be no need for state intervention to provide non-market housing for those unable to satisfy their requirement through this mechanism. The kernel of this argument is, the more of something that is produced, the cheaper it should become, provided that there is no corresponding increase in the market for it, and therefore more people will be able to afford to buy it than otherwise. This is surely reasonable – intuitively, the more expensive something is, the fewer are those that can afford it, and the reverse also seems to be true. There are obvious constraints on this logic which limit the effectiveness of using market supply to meet entire requirement – it costs something to build houses, and no rational developer will sell a property below the cost of building it. The building cost plus acceptable profit may well be beyond the means of a segment of the population, unless wages increased massively. Second, it is most unlikely that there will ever be full employment. There never has been in the history of the UK. Therefore there will always be those who cannot compete in the market place for goods and services unless the state meets the cost, which is unlikely to be a feasible option. Therefore, whatever the size of the development programme, it is unlikely that this strategy will ever meet all requirement, and therefore there will always be a need for non-market housing either produced as such or converted into this form. However, it is entirely reasonable to advance that increased residential building levels will have an effect on market prices and could make a measurable contribution to reducing the quantum of housing need. The question is, to what extent?

The question remains as to whether meeting housing requirement through market mechanisms is *logically* sound, rather than in fact very difficult. That is, will the poor always be with us in this respect? There is a semantic argument which can be dismissed relatively easily. Housing need is a component of housing requirement, and is critically defined in terms of not being able to meet one's housing requirement through market mechanisms. Therefore to suggest that you could meet the total housing requirement through market forces would drive you to a contradiction – that those who cannot meet their need through the market can. Therefore the proposition that you can is logically false, i.e. impossible. This is a word game, which relies on the acceptance of truth *by definition*, that housing need is an essential part of what housing requirement is, just as the concept of number is part of the concept of number two. One could equally argue that housing need arises through a dysfunction in the operation of the housing market, but if this were corrected, then so the dysfunction and housing need, in the sense that we have used it, would not, or would, have to be redefined. In this case, there is a logical link between the concept of market and that of housing need, and its contribution to the concept of housing requirement is therefore contingent. I cannot find any other persuasive arguments which would suggest that there is a logical problem with the market meeting housing requirement, and so am driven to the conclusion that it must be a matter of fact – but I am of course willing to be challenged on this view.

So how in fact does the state intervene to meet housing need? The fact is that it has done so for many years, currently does, and is likely to continue to do so into the distant future for as long as the market fails to provide affordable housing for all. It does so in a number of ways, ranging from intervention in crisis situations to influencing and enabling other bodies to provide non-market housing directly or indirectly, and to providing a legal and procedural framework within which housing is provided and allocated according to its view of need both in type and degree. Homelessness is perhaps the most acute type of housing need, and legislation in some form or other has been in existence since the Poor Law of 1536, which made rudimentary provision for vagrants and beggars, refined somewhat in the reign of Queen Elizabeth 1 in 1601, which provided for 'indoor relief' – very rudimentary accommodation – for destitute people of the parish, paid for from the local rates. This was commonly known as the workhouse, which, as the name suggests, entailed some form of labour to justify such assistance. The system was once more refined in Victorian times in the form of the Poor Law Amendment Act of 1834, and was abandoned only in the second half of the nineteenth century. The modern approach to dealing with homelessness dates from the National Assistance Act 1948, which introduced the modern form of social security along with a duty for councils to house certain categories of people who were judged to be too infirm or otherwise needy to secure their own accommodation. The first piece of legislation dedicated to dealing with homelessness as such was the Housing (Homeless Persons) Act 1977, which imposed a duty on local authorities to secure accommodation for homeless households who were judged to be in a priority need category, not intentionally homeless and with a local connection, the last element derived from the Poor Law system. This legislation has since been incorporated into other acts of parliament, and the two main laws which govern the approach in England and Wales are the Housing Act 1996 and the Homelessness Act 2002. Note everybody qualifies for assistance with housing under this regime – only those with a priority need, for example, households with dependent children, the aged and sick, and the punishment for having made yourself homeless is temporary respite only, even if regarded as a priority case. The local connection element still exists, except where there is none. We will explore this regime in greater detail in the next chapter and that on housing law, but it does raise some interesting questions which centre largely on desert.

It is clear from the legislation that some homeless people are more deserving of assistance than others, and there is a complex means of assessing this through priority categories. So, for example, a healthy person under retirement age without dependents is assumed to be able to fend for themselves, whereas someone who has the right to live with their family but who cannot find suitable housing for everyone to be together may be in a priority category for housing. The only relevant difference here is that this person has dependents, even if they are unable to support them. Similarly, a pregnant woman who is homeless has a priority need, whereas one who isn't and is otherwise fit and healthy does not. This is a direct reflection of the way society values family life, but is culturally relative. The other strand to the deserving versus undeserving aspect of the legislation is the assumption that by doing something that led to homelessness, this makes it all right for society to make only temporary provision for that unit, whereas if you really couldn't help it, the safety net is somewhat more enduring. Objectively speaking, though, homelessness is homelessness, and in a temperate climate, everyone needs a roof over their head, so this treatment might be regarded as somewhat harsh. If there were a limitless or much larger supply of social housing, it is unlikely that these strictures would apply; because they do, it justifies maintaining restricted social housing provision.

As we shall also discover, social and indeed affordable housing is strictly rationed or allocated on the basis of a complex assessment of household need. The general philosophy is that if you can rent or buy privately, you shouldn't have the choice of social or affordable renting, and if you can afford to buy the whole property with a combination of savings and mortgage finance, you shouldn't get shared ownership. The 1996 Housing Act and the Localism Act 2011 are fascinating guides to the framework of allocations policies for local authorities and indirectly for housing associations. Patience and virtue are added to need – the Localism Act encourages councils to reinvigorate the element of time served on the housing register, which reinforces the good old British respect for queuing. The only exception to this policy, which is common throughout Europe, is where there is low or no demand for social housing, and in these areas the trend for some time has been to knock it down or to try and ship households from higher-demand areas to such districts and to almost certain unemployment. Prior to the Localism Act, once you obtained a social home on the basis of need, tenure for life was virtually guaranteed. This gave rise to the observation that people were inhabiting homes they no longer needed to, in the case that they could afford to rent or buy privately, which was not the purpose of social housing. This has now been 'righted', at least for many tenancies granted in the sector since the passage of the Localism Act, in the form of five-year conditional tenancies which can be brought to end at the close of a fixed-term period if the occupants are deemed to be able to sustain non-social or affordable housing. This means that in the future, all social and affordable housing for rent will be welfare housing for the relatively poor, with perhaps an escape ladder in the form of progression via shared ownership to full ownership, bolstered by well-meaning back to work or economic betterment initiatives. This has led some to predict that council and housing association estates will become dreadful enclaves of hopeless cases like the worse sort of American project housing, which will stigmatise and disempower those within them, although others believe that such estates should be seen rather as a rite of passage territory where you do your time before amassing enough to make your own arrangements, which is neither stigmatising nor depressing, but supportive. Time will tell whether this social engineering experiment will yield one or the other result.

Customer involvement and empowerment

We now turn to a major theme of the last 20 years or so in social housing across Europe – that of the role of the customer apart from his or her legal obligations to the landlord or (in the case of leaseholders) the freeholder. The view that those who inhabit social and affordable housing should be actively involved in formulating and scrutinising the policies of their supplier is largely accepted by most housing organisations, at least formally if not in spirit. Legislation and regulation seeks to ensure that this is the case, and there have been various government initiatives in the UK since the 1990s to move the agenda on. But what is the point? After all, housing organisations employ managers and repairs operatives to make sure that properties are kept in good condition, and if so, why should any tenant want to get involved in the provision of basic services to them? They pay rent for someone else to do these things; standards are guaranteed by law or regulation, and as long as the service is provided at a reasonable level, it might be assumed that there is little reason for the end user to get involved unless things go wrong, and then the complaints system swings into operation. The provision, management and repair of reasonably well-appointed accommodation that suits the needs of those living in it is not an inherently complex business, and it should be well within the powers of professionals who have been trained in these things to make a good fist of things. The reason why resident participation has become such an important part of the housing scene is to be found in the concept of the 'active citizen', which emerged in the 1980s. There are many examples of people who have sought to establish communes or cooperatives to increase the degree of control they have over their lives. The democratic tradition – of voting for representatives to ensure that the peoples' wishes are taken into account in governance, and of standing for elected bodies in order to make a difference to society or to help ensure rational and fair treatment – is well established in many countries, and the concept of the active citizen is linked to these features of modern society. The concept of active citizenship is not new – Alexis de Tocqueville (1835), in his seminal work *Democracy in America*, gave the opinion that the real power of the American nation as a people lay with voluntary association. He believed that the freedom of individuals would be safeguarded if social problems or issues could be resolved voluntarily rather than through government intervention. This is similar to the 'rights and responsibilities' agenda popularised by the Labour government of 1997–2010, especially in the area of social security, where rights are balanced by individual responsibilities. For example, although people may have a right to state support, they have a responsibility to endeavour to support themselves and should not rely upon social security as a mainstay.

The active citizen is therefore someone who takes responsibility for their own welfare within the framework of rights conveyed upon them by the state. In the early 1990s there was a campaign by the Conservative government under John Major to promote 'active citizenship'. Largely as a result of successive spending crises in the 1970s, successive Conservative administrations (1979–1997) sought approaches to reducing crime levels and public expenditure in general which involved lower levels of government intervention. One solution was to suggest that responsibility for society's problems did not lie within the government but with the whole community, leading to the popularisation of the concept that everyone in the nation has a responsibility to solve society's ills. To flesh this out, the Conservative Prime Minister John Major launched the Citizen's Charter initiative in 1991. We will examine this in detail in the chapter on resident participation and involvement, but one of the six principles enumerated below clearly relates to resident involvement and participation in housing:

1. Setting, monitoring and publication of explicit standards.
2. Information for and openness to the service user.
3. Choice wherever practicable, plus regular and systematic consultation with users.

4.   Courtesy and helpfulness.
5.   Well-publicised and easy-to-use complaints procedures.
6.   Value for money.

Choice implies the power to choose, for example between different ways of providing services, and regular and systematic consultation would be pointless unless it informed policy and practice. So resident involvement and empowerment is a development from this early 1990s' agenda.

Resident involvement can be illustrated in a number of ways. Most councils and housing associations involve residents in formulating key management policies in order to ensure that they are on-side with changes and that the service provides a good fit with expectations. Logically, if a service meets expectations, it should result in fewer complaints and therefore less need for continuous adjustment than one which falls short in this respect, so the service provider and consumer should benefit from customer involvement in specification. This is not dissimilar to the reliance on customer panels and focus groups in manufacturing and service industries. If car manufacturers who are highly profit motivated continually use focus group feedback to guide the design of automobiles to get an edge on their competitors, there must be some commercial benefit to customer involvement. The same is true for not-for-profit organisations who wish to run their services as efficiently and effectively as possible given the financial and regulatory constraints under which they labour. This logic works at formulative and evaluative stages. It makes sense to measure satisfaction if you are in the business of delivering a service to satisfy needs and wants, to see if you are actually meeting the mark. There is also the reasonable proposition that people are entitled to value for their money, and that they are the best judges of whether they are getting a good service. It is also a way of ensuring that people are involved in solving issues rather than sitting on the sidelines and carping. The philosophy of resident involvement sits well with the business planning approach, which has been around since the mid-1980s, of involving employees in designing processes to achieve required outcomes in the public and commercial sectors, an approach which has reduced worker–management tension in several sectors and enabled the improvement of business systems and outcomes through 'ownership' of changes and progress, if not the means of production.

Resident empowerment goes somewhat further than involvement, and encompasses tenant management, where customers actually take control of the means of production and direct employees to carry out their aims and objectives. This has found expression in housing cooperatives since the mid 1970s in Europe, and in the form of statutory right to manage tenant management organisations in the local authority housing sector since 1994 in the UK. It also includes management boards which are partnerships of residents and local politicians, the devolution of budgets to tenants' organisations to spend on environmental improvements to estates, local employment initiatives steered by residents' forums and tenants' and residents' associations, and the fostering of resident service organisations to deliver grounds maintenance and repairs on a contractual basis to the landlord. There is evidence that customer satisfaction ratings under self-management are far higher than otherwise, although care must be taken to ensure that management agreements are well negotiated, those running them have the capacity to do so and are properly trained, and that there is a genuine consultative relationship between the boards of such bodies and the residents whose interests they represent and from whom their legitimacy is derived, especially where they are the consultative body on major projects (for example regeneration) which will change the lives of those who look to them for democratic leadership and influence, as well as quality management and maintenance services. Resident involvement and empowerment is a changing field, with the scrutiny function in the ascendancy and the impact of the localism agenda on self-management.

Housing management and maintenance

Housing management concerns the supervision and maintenance of stock and tenants (including leaseholders), and aims to ensure that estates are reasonably pleasant places to live on as well as maintaining the value and utility of the property for future use. It is complex in detail, due mainly to the raft of legislation which applies to the area and the many facets of the management task, which combines effectively dealing with the needs and aspirations of people as well as the specific requirements of properties and related assets.

The philosophy of housing management has changed radically over the last hundred years. This is due to a number of factors, including the development of the active citizenship concept discussed in the previous section. Others include the increased diversity of housing management agencies, ranging from councils, housing associations, specialist providers, arms-length management organisations (ALMOs) and tenant management organisations (TMOs). Technological change has also has its part to play in such change, as well as financial constraint and the influence of commercially led initiatives systems thinking and business planning. The product is also more diverse than it was, with different sorts of tenancy, low-cost home ownership, leaseholds, and care services. As already mentioned, the legislation which applies to this area has burgeoned, creating its own problems and complexities. However, at root, the task is not complex and is at best relatively low interventionist.

In this chapter, housing management is used generically to include tenancy management and maintenance, as good property management is inimical to tenancy supervision. The approach stems from the oft-stated remark that what tenants value most is an effective and efficient repairs service. This came across in the results of the Tenant Services Authority's (TSA) Existing Tenant Survey conducted by the survey firm MRUK between August and October 2008 (TSA, 2008), which together with the results of the 'national conversation' with tenants helped to inform its regulatory standards, as published in April 2010. Thus it is reasonable to suggest that tenant satisfaction with the landlord is determined largely by the quality – perceived or actual – of the repairs service. Considerable efforts have been undertaken in the last decade to improve the repairs service of social housing organisations using business improvement techniques, such as systems thinking and 'Lean' (the object of Lean thinking is to maximise the value to customers at the same time as minimising waste in operations), in connection with asset management strategies designed to improve the stock to Decent Homes standards in the face of capital shortfalls. The challenge of carrying out effective and efficient repairs has intensified with the new imperatives introduced by HRA self-financing from April 2012, when essentially councils have to live solely on their rent income. The connection between repairs service quality and maximising income collection from satisfied tenants is underscored from then onwards.

A central question in contemporary housing management is whether these functions are best carried out by the provider (for example the local authority or housing association) or by another body. The issue has been tested over the years ever since the implementation of compulsory competitive tendering (CCT) into local authority housing in England following the Local Government Act 1988, as modified by the Local Government Act 1992, as replaced by Best Value in 1999 by the Local Government Act. The initial idea behind CCT was to endeavour to reduce the unit cost of local authority functions across the piece (with a few exceptions, such as planning) by exposing the in-house provider to commercial competition, with price and quality as the principal determinants of winning the contract. In practice, in the vast majority of cases the in-house provider won, although councils then divided their operation into client and contractor divisions, and the discipline of CCT arguably led to the fostering of a performance culture, with financial and performance monitoring akin to that employed in the commercial sector being used extensively for the first time in this part of the public sector. The CCT regime was abandoned (at least in housing) largely because of the low take-up of contracts by the private sector, and Best Value was less prescriptive and therefore more welcome to the local authority sector. As will be discussed, Best Value encouraged councils to test and challenge the quality of their directly provided services against those of external organisations, and to learn how to deliver services to better effect as a result, while remaining in charge of strategy and direction. The concept of testing and challenging service delivery in this way has been an abiding feature of the housing management scene since the 1990s, and the option of delivering Decent Homes improvements as well as housing management through ALMOs is a manifestation of this. Externalisation – this is the term used for contracting out services – has also been pursued by housing associations, which frequently engage specialist care providers to deliver management services to extra-care and 'sheltered' housing schemes, funded partly or wholly through Supporting People grant made available from the state via certain classes of local authority.

Another form of externalisation is enabling estate residents (secure tenants and leaseholders) to manage all or some functions through TMOs. This was put on a statutory footing in 1994 through Right to Manage regulations under the 1993 Leasehold Reform Housing and Urban Development Act, and has met with variable success since then. According to the Office of the Deputy Prime Minister's publication, *Tenants Managing: An Evaluation of Tenant Management Organisations in England* (ODPM, 2002), there were in that year 202 established TMOs across 53 local authorities and 81 TMOs in development, covering roughly 84,000 homes. The majority (66 per cent) of TMOs were (and continue to be) in London, with most of the remainder in the North West (18 per cent) and the West Midlands (8 per cent), mainly in larger urban areas. They ranged in size from 12 to 9,760 properties with an average size of a little over 400 homes. The study found that most TMOs were performing well, although it also observed that the strengths of TMOs are hard to capture. This is because they are a very diverse group, with varying approaches to local management and governance. As will be seen, there is evidence that satisfaction levels are higher than in comparable local authority-managed estates. One of the main strengths is that TMOs are focused on local estate issues which may be missed by an organisation attempting to manage a wider area, and another is that they are directly accountable to residents through the initial ballot and five-year vote of confidence, as well as through elections to the board at annual general meetings. They are an expression of localism – and, if properly governed and in listening mode, excellent advocates of local sentiment in relation to regeneration issues and other local authority proposals which will affect the life chances of individuals in their management area. Housing associations can also establish resident management organisations, but are not compelled to do so by law.

The management task will be examined in detail, but it is wide ranging. Although founded on the enforcement of tenancy agreement obligations and ensuring that the landlord complies with his or her obligations, it is rather wider than this. Its complexity lies in the variety of housing types and households, which are its objects and subjects. The allocation of social and affordable housing for rent is firmly based on relieving housing need which finds its expression in the reasonable preference categories found in Section 166a of the Housing Act 1996, and confirmed in the Localism Act 2011. This includes giving relief to those who have been homeless, badly housed, those who need to move on medical or welfare grounds, and others with urgent housing needs. Housing need can arise for a variety of reasons, and is often the effect of other circumstances which may require specialist attention (for example a severe disability which prevents someone from earning enough to rent privately or to buy), discrimination (which is pernicious, even though outlawed) or infirmity by virtue of age. The list is large, but the common denominator – even more so from the introduction of conditional tenancies – is that the individuals – at the point of entry, at least since the early 1990s – are likely to be those who have been marginalised by the market for some reason, and who may have multiple needs. We will examine whether this is generally the case, and the diversity of housing management niche markets which exist as a result, including the reasons for marginalisation where it occurs.

In relation to property management, this text does not pretend to be a guide to how to undertake repairs and maintenance to properties, but it is essential to examine the key drivers to such activities. We will therefore start by considering the impact of the Decent Homes programme on planned and responsive (day-to-day) maintenance, and the importance of asset management strategies and plans in setting an overall context for the delivery of property services. The Decent Homes programme arose for the 2000 Housing White Paper and extended across council and housing association homes in England and Wales, with an equivalent standard in Scotland – predictably, the Scottish Housing Standard. The aim of this programme was to ensure that, by 2010, all socially funded homes for rent met minimum standards of modernity in terms of facilities and amenities (for example in respect of bathrooms and kitchens), repair and comfort, although the target has drifted since inception and at the time of writing there remains a backlog of around 8 per cent, only partially funded by additional capital grant advanced by the government in April 2011. The premise is that a Decent Home will require less reactive maintenance than a non-decent one, and so be more cost-effective to maintain, with consequently better tenant satisfaction. In addition to capital grant being disbursed through ALMOs to support the programme (since 2011 also available directly to councils), the government included an element in HRA subsidy known as the major repairs allowance, intended to help local authorities keep their stock in the same condition over a 30-year period – a depreciative approach rather than a stimulus to improve the dwellings. An asset management plan is essential to guide reactive and planned maintenance and improvements for a number of reasons. First, due to the scale of the enterprise – a landlord may have many thousands of properties in different states of repair and investment requirement, which implies prioritisation for works which would not be possible without an overarching plan. Second, capital is often made available through grant or loan finance over a number of years, so it makes sense to plan a programme over the life of such resource availability to ensure that it is efficiently and effectively disbursed. Third, from 2012, local authorities are required (as are housing associations) to keep a balance sheet showing their assets and liabilities, so it makes sense to plan to ensure that housing assets retain their value and that a positive balance can be shown on a year-on-year basis, especially if it is proposed to secure borrowing against their value.

When discussing repairs systems, much will be made of systems thinking improvements made in the 2000s to delivery, which is timely in the light of increased concern over customer satisfaction with repairs (as already highlighted in relation to the TSA's regulatory standards which are on ongoing feature of the landscape) and the financial disciplines imposed by HRA self-financing and material cost inflation. Systems thinking was popularised by John Seddon (see for example Seddon, 2008) and first used to streamline car production systems at Toyota. It was applied to the public sector from the early 2000s. Essentially, it entails reducing the influence and size of back-office functions (filing, assessing, processing) and transferring more responsibility to the front office (the actual repair operative, the person at the counter) to ensure shorter end-to-end process times and therefore the minimisation of error or even failure, which tends to increase with distance from the customer. Getting it right first time is calculated to please, if not surprise, the customer, and would in itself reduce the back-office complaints bureaucracy.

Finally we examine the staffing of housing organisations, and methods of recruitment and retention in the light of recent management science theory. Housing organisations are at root customer-facing, and person-to-person transactions are by far the more significant activities both in volume and importance, and so we will examine the distinctive features of people-centred organisations and how they can be involved in their destiny via business planning as a corollary to being appraised against them. Change has been something of a constant in the housing world ever since, and an understanding of change management, along with coping strategies related to change curve management, is an essential part of modern housing personnel management.

Housing finance

Housing policy has been driven by government macroeconomic policy since at least 1976, but probably before that, and macroeconomic policy has been driven by cash limits since then (Premchard, 1983). So operating within strictly limited public finance has been a way of life for social and affordable housing organisations for very many years. The spending review is a prime example of cash limiting, defining as it does both welfare and development budgets which inform the national Affordable Housing Programme, resources intended for housing associations (in the main) to deliver a given number of affordable homes for rent and for sale over a three-year period. So, in a sense, is the constraint on rent levels – on both affordable and social homes – implied by governmental formulae. This, combined with the return of strict controls on housing borrowing following the redistribution of debt in 2012 and the liberation of councils from the 1989 Act HRA subsidy regime, means that the entire social housing system, both in terms of capital and revenue activity, can be said to be cash limited in the strict sense.

Housing finance is often viewed as abstruse and colourless, because it is equated with learning the rules of accountancy. This is not an accountancy primer, and the text deals with the big-picture issues which are common to a range of housing products and services. It is therefore essential to set it in the context of big-picture government macroeconomic policy, including primarily the spending review cycle and annual budgetary decisions. It is important to understand that there is no particular ideological opposition to the creation and management of housing for those less able to compete in the market than others, and that there is cross-party support for this form of support. Nor is there any opposition to making capital support available to create such homes. Most sensible politicians would agree that there will always be the need for some form of safety-net housing provision along with welfare support which guarantees freedom from absolute want without providing an alternative lifestyle choice. The big divides are of degree. There has been a remarkable consistency of housing finance policy over the past 20 years, as well as a strong degree of consensus on welfare benefits arrangements.

One of the big divisions made when examining housing finance is the distinction between capital and revenue finance, that is, between investment to create, improve or enhance the value of assets and expenditure from current income to manage and maintain them. The approach to financial management varies between local authorities and housing associations significantly – the main reason for this being that housing associations are significantly reliant on the banking sector to obtain development loans and are used to a supplementary capital grant regime, whereas local authorities, although they have recently obtained grant and will be able to borrow from more sources than hitherto in the future, are more revenue oriented. When considering the difference between capital and revenue operations, it will be necessary to contrast the affordable and social rented sectors. In this context, the affordable for-rent sector is defined by those dwellings built during the 2011–2014 Affordable Housing Programme let at up to 80 per cent of market rent, and the social rented sector is defined as those dwellings whose rents are determined by the rent restructuring/rent influencing regime. In the former case, the influence of private borrowing is vastly more significant than in the latter, and the risk element much higher, with a need to consider creative ways of reducing the capital element, for example through planning deals delivering free or cheap land and cross-subsidy from for-sale schemes.

No book of this size can do justice to the entire range of issues in housing finance, and so I will confine the discussion to the key elements. One of the major features of the social housing landscape from 2012 is the switch from a 20-year-old subsidy regime to HRA of local authorities to HRA self-financing, where councils will have to live on their rents. In 1990, a system of subsidising local authority housing revenue activities was imposed which looked formulaically at what councils should be spending on running their housing tenancy M&M operations and what they should be receiving mainly by way of rent and interest on sales receipts. Councils, where the formula showed a notional deficit between income and expenditure, received HRA subsidy, and those where the opposite was the case had to pay a sum equivalent to the notional surplus to the Treasury, which was recycled to those deemed to need subsidising. Towards the end of the 2000s, most of those authorities receiving HRA subsidy did so because of the size of their housing debts, the interest on which attracted support, and most of those having to pay into the system were either low debt or debt free. Cross-party support had emerged by the end of the decade that the HRA subsidy system no longer worked efficiently, and it was decided to end it by removing some or all of the debt from with-debt authorities which would remove the notional deficit on their HRAs, and reassign this debt to those without it and so eliminate the notional surpluses they had, as they would now be liable for interest payments. The idea was that this reassignment would completely eliminate the need for subsidy, and from thenceforth councils would be fee to keep all of their rental income, but would have to live on it. This new approach – HRA self-financing – also eliminates the absurd situation which had arisen by the end of the decade that the HRA subsidy system was massively in surplus due to the interaction of relatively stable expenditure assumptions in the formula and rapidly rising rents, as they climbed to meet their target levels implied by the rent restructuring formula.

So what will self-financing look like, and is it a reasonable strategy? The learning curve for housing personnel will be steep. There will be no safety cushion for poor expenditure decisions and a lack of robust income management. The HRA remains ring-fenced and cannot carry forward losses over more than a year. 'Ring-fenced' means that it is unlawful to pay non-housing receipts (for example council tax income) into the HRA or to transfer housing revenue receipts (mainly rent) into the HRA, although legitimate recharging – for example where the HRA performs services to the community in general or to non-tenants such as grass-cutting on a mixed-tenure estate – is quite in order. HRAs will have to generate sufficient income to manage and maintain council housing, to repay new loans and to maintain a prudent margin. In other words, they will have to be run on business lines. Councils are permitted to undertake trading activities, and it is likely that very many will scope out the possibility of more commercial activity to generate money from HRA assets to guarantee a balancing account or even a healthy surplus, as they are able to use such resources to finance development and improvement. They will also have to consider (as some authorities already have) disposing of more expensive-to-maintain properties in order to reduce costs and to generate finance to undertake major works if specific capital grants are unavailable or in short supply.

Turning to reforms in capital finance, it is necessary to examine the possible impact of allowing councils to reinvest all of their sales receipts from land and housing. Currently they are only able to retain 25 per cent of right to buy sales receipts and 50 per cent of housing land receipts – the rest goes to the Treasury – but in the future, this is likely to be relaxed. Right to buy sales have dwindled over the years, although at the time of writing the government wishes to revive the scheme, and so the contribution of sales money may yet become a significant once again, as it was in the 1980s and early 1990s. In the 1980s some councils could have afforded to charge a zero rent due to the size of interest income from sales balances. It is unlikely that this will ever happen again, but it cannot be entirely discounted.

Turning next to housing association capital finance, we will examine the impact of the post-2011 Affordable Housing Programme and scope for further reform. Housing associations are now highly commercial, with many having developed subsidiary companies which produce outright-sale homes in order to generate a surplus to subsidise affordable housing for rent, and it is entirely possible to envisage a situation whereby they become market leaders in this area, which might (in some cases) mean that they lose reliance entirely on any government subsidy or even cheap or free land from planning deals or undervalue land from public authorities. If successful, they would be able to develop high-quality homes for rent at significantly below 80 per cent market rents, and if this came to fruition, we could see the emergence of a new low-rent sector which could become once again a genuine alternative choice to private renting or purchase. Given the continued demand for owner-occupation, the challenge for housing associations is to develop businesses which can meet market demand, although this strategy is not without risk and depends on the availability of mortgage finance, which cannot be guaranteed, witness the credit crunch of 2007–2009.

Finally we will examine the impact of the new universal credit regime on social and affordable housing customers and providers. In 2012, there were over a hundred individual benefits that can be claimed, including Housing Benefit and Local Housing Allowance, all of which have slightly differing rules and which as a whole represent a structure akin to a building which has been extended and embellished according to the fashion of that time and which therefore has no coherency. Over the years, attempts have been made to simplify the system, but without a great deal of success. The proposals will entails the replacement of these separate benefits with a universal credit capped at a level roughly equivalent to average lower quartile net income. The executive summary of the White Paper *Universal Credit: Welfare that Works*, published on 11 November 2010, says that:

> Universal Credit is an integrated working-age credit that will provide a basic allowance with additional elements for children, disability, housing and caring. It will support people both in and out of work, replacing Working Tax Credit, Child Tax Credit, Housing Benefit, Income Support, income-based Jobseeker's Allowance and income-related Employment and Support Allowance.
>
> (DWP, 2010, p. 3)

For customers, it means that they will have a lump sum with which to pay for all their outgoings, and this will entail careful budgeting. There will also be enhanced work incentives, provided they can find any work. For providers, it will mean that they will have to deliver careful budgeting advice at the point of entry to and during conditional tenancies, should they decide to adopt them, in order to maintain cash flow. One big area of debate is whether the system will allow for direct payments to the landlord, as is the case for council tenants universally, and for housing associations if they elect for this option. If not, the risk of reduced income to landlords will increase, with greater levels of nervousness for lenders. It is therefore essential that any reform takes lender sentiment on board, and it remains to be seen whether the direct payment option will materialise either initially or in the long-term.

Housing law

Housing tenure is regulated by statute and case law, and it is essential that students and practitioners of housing have a good grasp of its essentials. When a tenancy is taken on, the occupant takes on a contract with rights and obligations. Basically, the right is to live in the property for the term specified in the tenancy agreement and to receive management services and enjoy repairs to the property, and the obligation is to pay rent and other charges and to behave in a 'tenant-like' manner, respecting the property and neighbours. The tenancy can be forfeited by breach of obligations, although the courts have discretion in some cases as to whether to grant possession to the landlord. In the private sector, the tendency has been to restrict the rights of tenants through the assured shorthold tenancy arrangement, and to remove rent restrictions which formerly enabled tenants to fix a rent below market levels, in order to foster a continuous supply of private renting.

This tendency has since been extended to the social and affordable housing sectors in a number of ways. Since 1989, as a consequence of the 1988 Housing Act, the default form of housing association tenancy has been the assured tenancy based on the model adopted in the private rented sector, although rents were subsequently regulated by the rent influencing regime also applied to local authorities. The Localism Act has extended the ability of housing associations to grant assured shorthold tenancies more generally than before, in the light of the conditional tenancies that councils can now grant under the same act.

Regardless of this major change, the secure and assured tenancy forms will continue to be the staple arrangements, together with introductory and probationary tenancies, and their terms and conditions form the heart of housing management. It is also essential to understand the nature of repairing obligations both on landlords and tenants, as this is the major area of dispute between parties, and remedies for unfitness as contained in the 2004 Housing Act. The chapter will bring clarity to these issues, and signpost readers to primary and case law to assist them in their decision-making.

Housing regeneration and development

The development of social and affordable housing has long been controversial, and not without its critics, but dwellings built to house those in need have often been well constructed: estates have often been thoughtfully planned to ensure that those living on them are reasonably safe, can easily get to where they need to be, and often well integrated into other facilities such as play areas, health centres and shopping. Mass social housing was first built in the 1920s, following on from housing association block development in the nineteenth century, often at the behest of industrial philanthropists such as Peabody and Guinness, and was poles apart from the squalid private rented accommodation that was the lot of poorer working people at the beginning of the twentieth century. Mistakes have been made along the way – sometimes estates were built at too high a density and in inconvenient locations, and at other times structural problems compromised health and safety. Tower blocks are often held to be prime examples of ill-advised social housing development, although in some cases unfairly. Where space is at a premium, and land costs are high, it may often make economic sense to build up rather than along, and provided that lifts work and allocations are performed appropriately and sensitively, flats in such blocks can make spacious homes, with excellent views. However, recent disasters mainly related to fire have given such developments a bad name, and many have been demolished over the past 30 years. Yet others have been successfully refurbished, and are once again popular destinations – witness Trellick Tower in North Kensington, London, which was turned around from a sink-block known for drug peddling and anti-social behaviour into a much sought-after address. As a counterbalance to the legendary unpopularity of towers and higher-density developments in particular, there are many examples of low-rise relatively low-density estates which have not worked well, sometimes down to the way they have been allocated and in other cases to monotony, poor location and infrastructure.

Not all the ills of social housing development can be laid at the feet of designers and a lack of resident consultation to find out what people really value about their homes, although this is fair comment in many instances. It should be remembered that local authorities and housing associations are required to obtain planning permission before they build, and therefore some responsibility lies with planning professionals. Planning has changed significantly over the last few years in England and Wales. The Localism Act 2011 has made further changes which have the potential to increase resident involvement in this area through neighbourhood development planning, although it remains to be seen whether local people will either take up these challenges or be taken seriously when they devise plans for their areas. At this time of change, it is therefore essential to have a grasp of planning law and practice, which is what this chapter will deliver.

Although much will be said about construction methodology and the way on which development contracts are brokered and progressed, attention will also be focused on the importance of creating truly sustainable communities. It is hard to give an exact definition of this term in context, but it broadly means to create properties and environments which address the economic and social needs of those living there, as well as taking heed of environmental opportunities and constraints and ensuring that dwellings are relatively easy and cost-effective to manage and maintain from the organisational and user viewpoint. In terms of social sustainability, much has been written about the supposed advantages of creating mixed-tenure development – broadly, ensuring that homes for rent and for sale, on a low- and full-cost ownership basis, are created in the district (for example, Hills, 2007). It has been held that this reduces social polarisation and leads to more stable communities, avoiding the sink-estate ascription which is often unfairly given to some estates where worklessness dominates (or seems to). It will be interesting to see how the introduction of conditional tenancies will interact with these intentions, as it is unlikely that they will be allocated unless people cannot satisfy their need in the market. Where they can, it is likely that, after the minimum fixed term, such tenancies will be determined. It is therefore hard to see how mixed, sustainable and relatively stable communities, containing non-working people and those in work who could potentially afford to pay a higher rent and who wish to stay in the area, will be maintained in the long run.

There have been several guides on how to produce social and affordable housing which is fit for purpose in terms of sustainability in the senses used above, following on from the Parker Morris Report of 1961, *Homes for Today and Tomorrow*, which based its recommendations at least in part on a survey of potential users' lifestyles and the need to ensure that modern appliances could fit in dwellings. An example is the *London Housing Design Guide* (LDA, 2011) which specifies design standards which must be adhered to by registered providers building with the aid of Affordable Housing grant and which give guidance to planners when considering proposals. This is firmly based on the lessons of the past and the aspirations and needs of modern households, as well as on environmental and ecological imperatives and the need to ensure that dwellings can meet the needs of households throughout their lifecycle. It makes sense to build homes which will stand the test of time; otherwise the risk is that the bulldozer will be employed even before they are paid for, as has frequently been the case in the past.

Regeneration has been a major trend in capitals and other urban areas throughout the world for several decades. It goes hand in hand with development but has a wider meaning. The term raises the issues of what is to be regenerated, why and the vision which those responsible for such plans have for the future of areas. Not to regenerate is often not an option at all; there have been significant changes in the economic and social geography of urban areas over the past decades, with the reduction in the significance of manufacturing and associated industrial processes with market changes.

Sometimes technological changes have caused such an economic decline, as in the case of the introduction of containerisation as the preferred method of moving freight by sea to gain economies of scale. The sheer size of such vessels has made river-ports all but redundant in many countries – witness the decline of the London docklands as a major port of entry from the 1970s. Coastal ports with deepwater harbours are now preeminent, which leaves the question of what the fate for redundant docklands and the communities which once looked to them for employment and secondary trade is or should be. In the case of London docklands, central government set up the London Docklands Development Corporation (LDDC) in 1981 under s.136 of the Local Government, Planning and Land Act 1980 to consider the future for the area and bring in investment. It took over the planning powers of the local authorities in the area, and enabled offices, new dwellings and infrastructural improvements – major road and rail projects – to ensure that the area was accessible for commercial activity. The result is a high-profile mixed residential/commercial development which is still being progressed on the fringes, and arguably a commercial counter-magnet to the City of London. It is characterised by the iconic Canary Wharf, with its iconic One Canada Square tower. Spin-off advantages have included the leverage of private financial investment into improving municipal blocks and infrastructural facilities for residents. Similar if smaller projects have been undertaken in other UK cities, such as Liverpool, which suffered a similar dockland decline to that of London, and many of the developments bear a striking similarity to each other.

On another scale, and perhaps more related to the main subject matter of this book, there have been significant estate regenerations in Western Europe which have changed the social character of such districts. Some of these have been associated with the drive to ensure that Decent Homes standards are met, but not exclusively, and in many cases, such regenerations have increased the private ownership and rented component of neighbourhoods. When major regenerations are proposed, it is important to consider the existing communities which have in many cases been there for a considerable length of time, and how their aspirations and requirements as long-time users of the homes and infrastructure of the affected areas can be taken into account, and, indeed, whether wholesale regeneration is necessary at all. The issues of resident involvement in regeneration, the quality of advice given to local people, and best practice in ensuring that their views are taken into account in the form of a jointly agreed charter of rights on where they will live and involvement in development briefs to make sure their aspirations for design and layout are taken into account should they wish to remain in or return to their home area will be thoroughly explored by case study in this chapter.

Localism

Localism is a major theme in the development and delivery of social and affordable housing policy and practice, and rightly so. Localism is the idea that communities should have a major influence on the way that local authorities and other influencers deliver their policies and services, and that they should be able to shape their local environment in ways which meet their aspirations. Much of the Localism Act is about how planning policy should be devolved to communities as far as possible, as well as giving councils more scope to act innovatively as custodians of the local realm. It draws on the concept of the Big Society popularised by the UK Coalition government's Prime Minister David Cameron, and fits in well with the choice and responsibility agenda already outlined, as well as endeavouring to encourage volunteering. In the context of housing, the relevant elements are planning localisation and housing delivery. It remains to be seen as to the extent to which central powers can be effectively devolved to local administrations and communities, as the matter of how such enterprise can be financed is a major issue in the economic context of the age, and issues relating to spatial equity and fairness are also present, but it looks as though the tendency is here to stay, so it must be examined. In its raw form it does raise some interesting questions. In terms of housing management, TMOs are at least in theory excellent expressions of the localist philosophy, in that they are the locus of power in terms of the delivery of M&M services which matter and which have a direct bearing on day-to-day lives, and the question is to what extent is this true and is there scope for extending their remit to other local governance areas such as the provision of social care and support, education and employment? Local involvement in planning is another area which needs to be examined, building on the preceding chapter. Localism implies that local communities should have a say in the nature and form of development in their areas. If so, what will be the result of neighbourhood planning in this form? Will some communities endeavour to exclude social or affordable housing development on the grounds of lifestyle incompatibility, perhaps bolstered by concern over property values, and if so, what will be the impact on the life chances of those seeking affordable housing in areas close to their work or kinship groups which they value? How will a balance between the needs of an area seen from a sustainable and objective viewpoint and the aspirations of existing residents be maintained, and can it without alienating one group or another? Additionally, to what extent is it fair, just and reasonable to enable local authorities to develop policies and practices which may result in spatial inequality over the wider area? And to what extent is localism affordable locally and nationally? These questions will be examined in depth, as well as early outcomes of the project as they affect the housing field.

It is hoped that this book will stimulate thought about the future of housing policy as well as promote reflection on what is and has been in the sector. The past is never a wholly reliable guide to the future, but as the philosopher and poet Georges Santayana (1863–1952) rightly said, 'Those who do not learn from history are doomed to repeat it', and perhaps this in itself justifies the writing of this book.

References

Barker, K./ODPM (Office of the Deputy Prime Minister), (2004) *Delivering Stability: Securing our Future Housing Needs*. Final Report, March. London: ODPM.

Bradshaw, J., (1972) A taxonomy of social need, *New Society* (March): 640–3.

Collins English Dictionary, (2003) Availabe at: www.thefreedictionary.com/Social+housing, viewed 12 January 2012.

Department of Environment, (1987) *Finance for Housing Associations: The Government's Proposals*.

London: DoE.

DWP (Department of Work and Pensions), (2010) *Universal Credit: Welfare that Works*. London: DWP.

de Tocqueville, A., (1835) *Democracy in America*. London: Saunders and Otley.

Hills, J., (2007) *Ends and Means: The Future Roles of Social Housing in England*. London: Centre for Analysis of Social Exclusion (CASE).

Harloe, M, (1981) The recommodification of housing, in Harloe, M. and Lebas, E. (eds) *City, Class and Capital*. London: Edward Arnold.

Hobbes, T., (1651) *Leviathan, or the Matter, Forme, and Power of a Commonwealth*. London: Ecclesiastical and Civil.

LDA (London Development Agency), (2010) *London Housing Design Guide*. London: LDA.

ODPM (Office of the Deputy Prime Minister, (2002) *Tenants Managing: An Evaluation of Tenant Management Organisations in England*. Norwich: HMSO.

Parker Morris Committee, (1961) *Homes for Today and Tomorrow*. London: HMSO.

Premchard, A., (1983) *Government Budgeting and Expenditure Controls: Theory and Practice*. Google ebook, available at: http://books.google.co.uk/books?id=FrKid1w4eNUC&dq =cash+limits+system&source=gbs_navlinks_s

Prime Minister's Office, (1991) *The White Paper: The Citizen's Charter: Raising the Standard*. London: Prime Minister's Office.

Reeves, P., (1996) *An Introduction to Social Housing*. London: Edward Arnold.

Rightmove, (2012) Location identifier, availabe at: www.rightmove.co.uk/property-to-rent/find.html?locationIdentifier=OUTCODE per cent5E2315&insId=1&sortByPrice Descending=false&sortByRelevance=false&minBedrooms=2&maxBedrooms=2&display PropertyType=flats&oldDisplayPropertyType=flats, viewed 12 January 2012.

Rowntree, B. S., (1901) *Poverty: A Study of Town Life*. London: Longman.

Seddon, J., (2008) *Systems Thinking in the Public Sector*. London: Triarchy Press.

Shelter, (2012) What is social housing?, available at: http://england.shelter.org.uk/campaigns/housing_issues/Improving_social_housing/what_is_social_housing, viewed 12 January 2012.

Southwark HomeSearch, (2012) Homesearch, available at: www.southwarkhomesearch.org.uk/Data/ASPPages/1/111.aspx?PropertyID=128428, viewed 12 January 2012.

Townsend, P., (1979) *Poverty in the United Kingdom*. London: Penguin.

TSA (Tenant Services Authority, 2008. *Existing Tenants Survey 2008: Tenant perspectives on social landlord services*. London: TSA.

Woman's Own, (1987) Margaret Thatcher PM interview. *Woman's Own*, 31 October.

1 Supply and demand

Keywords: *economic concept of supply and demand, application to housing markets; Barker Report view of reducing price of housing through increasing supply across tenures; defining affordable housing; effective demand and need; acute housing need; overcrowding; the management of housing need; supply issues; areas of over-supply; postscript to Chapter 1: can planning reforms solve the problems of supply and demand?*

Introduction

If demand meant the total quantum of housing required, and if supply was exactly balanced with this quantum in relation to number, location, household size and personal resources, there would be no housing need, as it would be met either immediately or in short order. You cannot be in need of what you have, or of what would be made available the moment you require it. Of course, the moment before you obtain something which is necessary to you, you need it, but in the context of housing, we are talking about a lack of some duration. In the real world, however, there is not a balance between housing demand, used broadly, and supply, and this imbalance gives rise to distressing human circumstances such as homelessness and rooflessness which, sadly, are far too common across the world.

Why is this? Or what gives rise to this imbalance? This can be answered on many levels. One answer, which is not generally applicable spatially or over time, is that it might be believed that the human population has grown, or tends to grow, at a faster rate than the discovery or production of available resources and if housing is a (secondary) resource, demand will therefore inevitably outstrip supply. This was the view proposed by Thomas Malthus in the eighteenth century, and has been immensely influential in social and economic theory since propounded in his *An Essay in on the Principle of Population* published in 1798 and reissued in six editions to 1826 (Malthus, 1798). Essentially, he suggests that the growth of human population tends to be geometric (1, 2, 4, 8, 16, 32, etc.), as opposed to the increase in resource exploitation which is likely to follow at best an arithmetic progression (1, 2, 3, 4, 5, 6, etc.), so that ultimately, population growth exceeds the means to support it, resulting in war, famine and disease. This is a very gloomy picture of human societal development redolent of an apocalyptic horror movie, but may very well end up being verified, as human population growth has indeed followed a geometric progression over recorded history. Yet there is no evidence that it is remotely true for human society in developed Western countries. There is plenty of vacant land available on which housing could be built, and many empty dwellings which could provide shelter and sustenance. There is a crude surplus of agricultural production over consumption in Western economies, and a seemingly limitless supply of natural resources, sustainable and even fossil, to support human life to a reasonable standard even at present growth rates. Additionally, although the world population appears to be growing exponentially, the same is not true of many individual developed nations, and so whereas eventually we may globally outstrip the means of sustenance, there is no reason to think that we will do so here and in the near future.

Another thought is that there is something inevitable about unmet housing need, which arises from the operation of laws of economics, and which leads to the necessity of state intervention if it is believed that housing is basic to human survival, and that the promotion of human survival is a basic mark of a civilised society and we wish to promote civilisation. This arises from the observation that housing costs something to produce and maintain, and that providers will seek to recoup their outlay plus a profit for supplying it to reimburse their effort. It also proceeds from the observation that it is not in the interests of producers to manufacture or make available unlimited quantities of what they make, or even enough to meet actual demand, by which (in this context) I mean total unmet requirement.

To understand why unmet housing need might be seen to be inevitable, we need to consider the 'laws' of supply and demand propounded by classical economists. The model is that the price of anything will be determined by the interaction of supply and effective demand, which means demand from consumers who are willing and able to pay for something. The idea is that, in a competitive market situation, the price of a product or service is the result of the price which consumers are willing to pay meeting the price at which the vendor is willing to sell. Consumers may start by bidding too low – in this case, suppliers will not make the goods available. Alternatively, suppliers may price their products too high to attract consumers, in which case they will have to come down. The idea is that eventually the product attains its equilibrium price, where the price offered by consumers meets that at which suppliers are willing to make the good available. Within this generalisation, four laws are recognised by many economists. Simplifying, they are:

1. The equilibrium price and quantity will increase where demand increases and supply is level.
2. Equilibrium price and quantity will decrease if demand decreases and supply is level.
3. Where supply increases and demand is level, the equilibrium price will decrease and quantity will increase.
4. If supply decreases and demand is unchanged, this will lead to higher prices and lower quantities.

These laws are often attributed to Adam Smith, which considered the dynamics of price in his seminal work, *The Wealth of Nations* (Smith, 1776), and have long been accepted as a basis for pricing theory, although they have been varied and refined over the years. On the basis of these 'laws' we can deduce that there will always be some consumers who are unable to bid for the 'equilibrium price' – if all could, it would mean that the price of the product would probably be far below the cost of producing it, even in the case of very cheaply produced housing. It is also obvious that those with very low resources or none would be outbid by other consumers, since the supply of the product is limited, if only by the capacity of producers to develop housing.

That said, it should be possible to reduce the price of the product by influencing effective demand levels, and by increasing supply. If effective demand for housing in an area drops, the price decreases, although interestingly enough, because the market is segmented (for example between private renting and owner-occupation), a falling housing market for sale may well lead to the withdrawal of owner-occupied products from the market and an increase in the availability of private rented accommodation, as people have to live somewhere. It is no accident that in areas where house prices are high in relation to wages, there is often a buoyant rental market, as in many parts of London. Here again, rental prices may be high due to increased demand resulting from the former factor, and in this case, many households will be excluded from the owner-occupier and private rental market.

The influence of classical economic thinking has had a marked effect on national housing policy in England since the 2000s, when Kate Barker produced her seminal report on how to assist in meeting future housing needs by market intervention or stimulus in 2004 (Barker/ODPM, 2004). In essence, the analysis is straightforward. Housing need (by which I mean housing requirement which is unmet by the market) is not uniform across the country. This can be deduced purely on the basis of homelessness statistics – looking at the numbers of homeless acceptances by local authorities per 1,000 population. According to the Department for Communities and Local Government (DCLG) housing statistics in Table 772 on statutory homelessness: households accepted by local authorities as owed a main homelessness duty, by region, 1998 to 2011, the acceptance rate in London was 0.9 in quarter three of 2011, compared to 0.4 in the less economically vibrant North East, and against a national figure of 0.6. The rate in London has been consistently higher than nationally since the statistical series was started in 1998, sometimes by a factor of two, and also has outperformed less economically active regions such as the North East and North West at least since that date. If homelessness can be taken as a surrogate for housing need used in the sense of unmet requirement, we can reasonably infer that housing need is relatively higher in London than elsewhere (see Figure 1.1).

The overall reduction in numbers per 1,000 is due largely to changed government policy in the form of the encouragement of prevention strategies and housing options services to deflect housing need away from the social housing sector since around 2003. The relevant aspect of Figure 1.1 to note is the regional relativities in rate at any one time. How, then, is it possible to increase supply relative to demand in areas of most acute housing need?

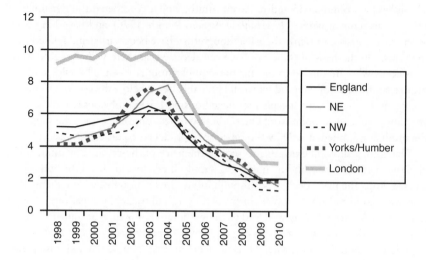

Figure 1.1 Trends in homelessness acceptances by region, 1998–2011 (number/1,000 households by year)

Source: CLG, Table 772, available at: www.communities.gov.uk/housing/housingresearch/housingstatistics/housingstatisticsby/homelessnessstatistics/livetables/, viewed 21 January 2012.

The Barker review, *Delivering Stability: Securing our Future Housing Needs* (Barker/ODPM, 2004) was commissioned April 2003. Its terms of reference were to conduct a review of issues underlying in the lack of supply and responsiveness of housing in the UK, to examine the role of competition, capacity, technology and finance of the house-building industry, and to establish the interaction of these factors with the planning system and the government's sustainable development objectives. The review concluded that, taking as the baseline the level of private sector build in 2002–2003, 140,000 gross starts and 125,000 gross completions, reducing the trend in real house prices to 1.8 per cent would require an additional 70,000 private sector homes per annum; and to reduce the trend in real house prices to 1.1 per cent, an additional 120,000 private sector homes per annum would be required.

It also concluded that an increase in supply of social housing of 17,000 homes each year was required to meet the needs among the flow of new households, and that there was a case for providing up to 9,000 a year above this rate in order to make inroads into the backlog of need. If all of the additional build were carried out in the South East, an additional 120,000 homes per year would take around 0.75 per cent of the total regional land area. One wonders how this would fit in with the localism agenda on planning!

Increasing land availability through the planning system was thought to be the prime mover for this quantum increase:

> Central to achieving change is the recommendation to allocate more land for development. This certainly does not mean removing all restraints on land use, on the contrary the review advocates more attention be given to ensuring the

most valuable land is preserved. But house-builders would have greater choice as to which sites to develop, increasing competition. And it would also allow a quicker and more flexible response to changing market conditions on the upside ... This calculation assumes that 60 per cent will be built on brownfield sites, and that dwellings will be built at a density of 30 per hectare. It also includes an allowance for related infrastructure.

(Barker/ODPM, 2004, p. 6)

This sounds excellent in theory, at least as a way of stabilising house prices so that more people can afford to buy rather than rent, and possibly reducing the call on the social or affordable housing sectors. However, it does presuppose the capacity of developers to produce homes in the quantity required, and the notion that 60 per cent of new homes should be built on brownfield sites deserves attention. Brownfield sites are those which have already been developed but where the initial use is redundant, so permitting redevelopment. Generally, they are within urban contexts, with the advantage of proximity to infrastructure, but in many cases such sites are expensive to prepare for development due to the need for decontamination (more so in the case of severely polluted 'redfield' sites). The corollary of this is that around 40 per cent of new provision should be built on greenfield (previously undeveloped) sites. The vast majority of these sites are in rural locations. If house price stabilisation in areas of high demand is a key objective, this will inevitably mean building in relatively sacred environments such as the Green Belt, close to centres of economic prosperity, and not in locations in the middle of nowhere where arguably the environmental and social impact might be somewhat less.

The Barker approach is also rather simplistic in that local housing market dynamics are affected by many other factors than supply. Regional income profiles vary significantly, while labour is not perfectly mobile. There is also the negative feedback aspect of development: build more houses in an area and its attractiveness as a destination may decrease, with the consequence that it may not be possible for those putting money into such schemes to realise their investment quickly enough, or at the level required. Then there are the vagaries of local economies: there have been well-observed general trends in the rise and decline of regional economies, and the underlying factors are relatively well known. The economic decline of the North East, for example, between 1950 and 1980 was a product of the loss of key multiplier industries such as shipbuilding, steelworks and coal mining, whereas the economic growth of London and the South East is largely down to the burgeoning finance and information industries and location vis-à-vis Europe's golden triangle. It could therefore be predicted that this would stimulate a migration of working-age people from the North East and other declining peripheral regions to the South East, with consequent increases in demand for housing in the recipient area. But how permanent is such a trend, and what technological or other changes in the market may intervene both within and between regions to alter this? And should a housing market stimulation policy be based on economic trends which may well reverse with the development of the location-less information economy which is just as at home in Newcastle as it is in London?

However, it should be admitted that supply of market housing is an important factor in attempting to deal with the knotty question of how much affordable housing should be provided, where and when, hence the growing significance of housing market assessments in examining the strategic housing requirement at a variety of spatial levels, from the local authority to the national level, and it is to these that we now turn.

Housing needs surveys and housing market assessments

Housing needs surveys

Local authorities have had a duty to assess housing need in their area since 1957 as part of their strategic housing function. This does not mean that they have to meet that need themselves, and in fact they are (given the current financial climate) incapable of doing so. What it does mean is that they have to work with others, including housing associations and private developers, to plan how to meet that need.

Essentially, the task of a housing needs survey is to estimate amount and type of housing needed, consider the cost of providing for households which will not be able to meet their requirements through the market, identify how much land is required in the right areas to meet the implied targets, and to determine the most cost-effective way of supplying good quality housing. The definition of housing need used here accords with the DCLG's third planning policy statement (PPS) (DCLG, 2010, p. 15) which is 'the quantity of housing required for households who are unable to access suitable housing without financial assistance'.

In this book, it will not be possible to consider all the approaches to estimating housing need. There are several approaches and some contradict others. However, there are a few common factors which are present in all such surveys, and which can be laid out in a logical if abbreviated fashion. It makes sense to express the need for housing as a number of homes at various points in time which will be required to meet need, broken down by type and size, and area, justified in terms of an estimate of household types and numbers which will require them.

In headline terms, a basic approach to establish housing need levels is first to establish the amount of housing required regardless of ability to pay, and then to net off that which can be met through the market place. The essential formula to determine housing requirement is:

> new households forming minus households no longer requiring housing plus inflow (in-migrating households) minus outflow (out-migrating households plus households no longer requiring housing)

The *affordable housing requirement* can be summarised as: (A) the number of new and existing households whose requirements cannot be met through the owner-occupier market can be assessed by estimating the number of households whose incomes plus savings cannot support the purchase of the cheapest available housing; and (B) the number of households also excluded from private renting on the basis of income.

Crudely, A + B equals the number of households needing 'affordable housing'. This can also be broken down by household size and therefore can be used to inform the proportion of bed-sizes needed as well as quantity.

Detail

First, then, what is the nature of the population which gives (or will give) rise to the requirement? Over a given time period, households will enter an area, through natural formation and in-migration, and others will leave through dissolution and out-migration.

FORMATION OF NEW HOUSEHOLDS

New households will form in a number of ways, through marriage or cohabitation, divorce or separation, and through children leaving the family home to set up on their own. Note that we are primarily concerned with household not population growth, although there are links. Fertility and mortality rates vary between countries and even within them, but knowing these alone would not enable prediction of growth or decline of household numbers in an area. Much depends upon custom and economic realities. In the West, there has been a tendency over at least the past 50 years for households to get smaller. This can be attributed to younger members of families wishing to move out and lead independent lives at an earlier age than hitherto. The Joseph Rowntree Trust Housing and Neighbourhoods Monitor gives an interesting insight into demographic trends between 1981 and 2008 which backs this contention. The publication suggests that household numbers in Great Britain have shown a continuous trend of growth from 20.3 million in 1981 to 25.7 million in 2006 (a 26.6 per cent increase) with a further projected increase to 33 million in 2031 (a 28.4 per cent increase from 2006). It also suggests that the average household size in England and Wales will decrease from 2.32 and 2.30 in 2006, to 2.13 and 2.03 respectively. Taken together, this means that we are likely to see an increasing number of smaller households produced into the future, with clear implications for housing policy, although the regional and sub-regional trends are by no means uniform. It is this sort of data that is required to inform sensible housing needs projections.

It is also necessary to look beneath the raw trends to find possible explanations for them. The increase in the number of households and their reduction in size may be attributable to a number of factors, of which affordable housing availability is one. For example, the increased availability of higher education which comes with opportunities to move to independent accommodation, and the availability of work in an area which will enable people to move into their own home. Therefore a housing needs survey must also examine the state of the local economy and those in areas surrounding it, along with its prospects. It is also necessary to examine divorce and separation rates to establish likely trends in the formation of additional households from existing ones. According to the Office for National Statistics (ONS) (ONS, 2011), the divorce rate in 2009 in England and Wales was 10.5 per 1,000 of the married population, a decrease of 36.7 per cent from a high point recorded in 1993. As before there will be variations at regional and local levels, and trends are available at this level from the ONS. Figures on separation trends are somewhat harder to ascertain, since this is not officially recorded, and it is necessary to endeavour to establish this through primary survey and secondary research.

Once these tasks have been performed, it should be possible to establish a reasonable baseline and projection trend for the formation of new households in an area. It is then necessary to examine trends in the reduction of households to establish a net figure – new household formation minus household reduction. Factors influencing the latter trend will include mortality rates, which vary considerably across countries and even in localities. One way to gain an appreciation of such variation is to examine the ONS data in its online publication, *Key Population and Vital Statistics* (ONS, 2007). Table 4.1b of that publication shows numbers and standardised mortality rates in the UK, and there is a considerable variation. The UK as a whole is standardised at 100, and England at 97. The North East records 109, with an equal level for males and females, whereas London records an overall 92, with a variation between inner and outer London (95 and 91 respectively) and between the sexes (93 males, 91 females). More rural districts in the relatively affluent South record yet lower mortality rates (for example Surrey at 88). There may be a correlation between economic wellbeing and mortality, which could be useful when assessing the rate of household increase and decline.

MIGRATION

The other big factor in predicting housing need and demand increases is migration rate, which varies considerably over space and time. Turning again to the ONS data (ONS, 2007), Table 3 gives the relative rates alongside natural increase and decrease, over the periods 1996–2006 and 2006–2007 on the basis of population mid-year estimates. It can be seen that, between 1996 and 2006, the major factor influencing change in the UK population was migration, adding around 1,478,000 people, whereas natural change added around 945,000, to give a total population increase of 2,433,000 to 60,587,000. Again, there are regional variations which need to be taken into account, with some areas showing an absolute decline population numbers accounted for by natural decrease and out-migration (for example Tyne and Wear, decreasing from 1,117,000 in 1996 to 1,088,000 in 2006 (rounded up to the nearest 1,000), largely as a result of out-migration to the tune of an estimated 22,000 persons). Other areas showed an increase due to positive migration and natural increase, for example, the South East as a whole, which increased from 7,800,000 to 8,238,000 largely as a result of the in-migration of 312,000 people. Clearly it is necessary to translate these trends into household sizes and numbers, and to analyse the resultant figures by age and other demographic characteristics, but the implications for housing policy are clear in that the statistics reveal areas which are losing population and households and those which are gaining.

INCOME AND WEALTH

Having established the demographic changes above, it is then necessary to examine variations in income and wealth on a spatial and temporal basis to help establish the potential for households to afford market accommodation, before examining the range of market housing prices for rent and for sale in each area.

The above considerations should give a local picture of household size, composition and wealth over a time series, along with the components of each.

HOUSING MARKET

The next task is to estimate the market price of housing, by size and regional variation over an equivalent time and at the same level of geographic resolution. The exact methodology is beyond the scope of this book, but the principle is clear. For any given area, it should be possible to determine by household type the average income and compare this to house rents and prices to determine a price to income ratio, which can then be used to estimate the number of households priced out of the market who stand in need of social housing.

MODELS OF HOUSING NEED

We have examined some of the variables which are taken into account in assessing housing need spatially and over time. Much complex modelling has been undertaken to simulate housing need patterns for policy reasons. One example of this is the DCLG's Estimating Housing Need simulation model based on 2007 data (DCLG, 2010). The (key) variables employed include:

- Previous tenure composition – that is, tenure composition in the baseline year.
- Changes in household composition due to in situ changes, household formation, dissolutions, and migration.
- Mobility rates by tenure for previous and current year.
- Predicted tenure transitions to buy or to social rent by new households and mover households in each tenure, for previous and current year.
- Net migration and Right to Buy rates.
- Long-term trend in household composition.
- Calculations involved in adjusting and controlling in situ changes in household composition.
- Low-cost home ownership impact calculations.

This combinatorial model used 150 variables to endeavour to predict housing need patterns over 15 years from 1997, using actual data from the Survey of English Housing (SEH). The survey examines housing type data for 20,000 households a year. Labour Force Survey (LFS) data is also used to examine socioeconomic variables such as income and wealth: data for 1992 to 2008 was used. The SEH makes use of similar data, but that in the LFS proved to be far more comprehensive and therefore was judged to be a better sample on which to base inferences.

The model also uses econometric trends to predict ability to buy; for example Council of Mortgage Lender data on gross mortgage lending and lending for house purchase between (in this case) 2007 and 2010. This shows a fall from £25 billion in the UK to around £8 billion at the end of 2009, with a low point of around 2.2 billion in February 2009. The availability of mortgage finance clearly impacts on the potential for low-cost home ownership to reduce unmet need, and is therefore a very important factor in modelling it.

Housing need survey outputs

To take the Estimating Housing Need model outputs as an example, the quantum of housing need in England (expressed as a backlog) is predicted to vary between just under 1.4 million and just below 2 million by 2022, from a base of just over 1.2 million in 1999 (DCLG, 2010, Figure B). The scenario generating the highest need figure assumes a more needs-based allocation as a general housing policy, and the lowest need figure arises from a scenario of less credit rationing (in the sense of rationing finance to borrow to buy). Mid-level outputs arise from lower net migration and increased low-cost home ownership opportunity. This makes intuitive sense. However, the old adage that the more the variables in any model the less faith can be held in the predictions arising from it holds as true for housing need models as for others, as does the view that the further one endeavours to look into the future, the less certain is the prediction, where uncertainty increases directly in proportion to the number of factors used to explain the trend. The reason this is that the trends which emerge from models of this sort are of necessity probabilistic, as the data used to generate them are neither accurate nor complete, and errors are additive over time. If you add one probabilistic trend to another in a model and project it forward, the error factor bells out so that at some point, any outcome would be compatible with the model's predictions. Systematic uncertainties of this sort probably justify having a modicum of faith in such outputs over a five-year period maximum!

Housing market assessments

If housing needs surveys are about estimating the requirement for social or affordable housing over a period of time to help inform local, regional and/or national housing supply policies, housing market assessments (HMAs) take a more holistic view of housing requirement and are used to generate targets for planning in relation to housing of different tenures. Housing needs surveys are driven by housing policy and strategy needs, whereas HMAs are driven by town and country planners' desire to know how much land to allocate to housing over a given period of time. There is no necessary contradiction between their aims or the use to which they are put – a good HMA will contain a housing needs survey, as it is necessary to estimate the quantum of non-market housing required to ensure that enough land can be identified for its market counterparts. There is also little point in duplication of effort if one can contain the other, and many local authorities have decided to major on commissioning HMAs for this reason.

There is no doubt that HMAs can provide valuable insights into how housing markets now and in future. They can, if conducted in a sound manner, provide a fit-for-purpose function basis to develop planning and housing policies by considering characteristics of the housing market, how key factors work together and probable scale of change in future housing need and demand.

The general outputs of a HMA include the identification and definition of housing market areas, the percentage of market housing over all provision required, including low-cost homes ownership, and the percentage of affordable housing required, divided into social rented and intermediate housing (in this context, housing for rent at 80 per cent of market value).

Data used

A HMA will utilise primary and secondary survey, with the latter as the main supporting source. Primary data (for example, a survey of house prices in an area gathered from estate agents) will generally be used to validate and further explain the information and assessment obtained from secondary data (for example, house price index trend information aggregated at a borough or regional level). Examples of primary data used are, in the case of that used to estimate levels of housing need, overcrowding levels, the need for adaptations, numbers of hidden homeless (for example sofa surfers), etc. Local affordability information will include that on income, savings, etc., and the aspirations, preferences and concerns of local residents are useful in trying to establish the extent to which low-cost home ownership or innovative rental products will meet housing requirements and possibly reduce the quantum of housing need. Private rented sector rent levels will also be relevant to determine the degree of exclusion from the market assessed against income and wealth data.

Secondary date will be of greater use to support demographic and household types analysis relevant to estimating current housing need, and will include census data, population mid-year estimates, National Health Service (NHS) registration data and social trends data (from the ONS). This will help provide a picture of population by ethnicity, age and numbers of households by type (for example families, couples, lone parents, etc.), tenure and household representative rates and migration estimates.

A well-wrought HMA will be invaluable in helping to inform housing and planning policy and strategy, and annual updates to inform forward housing and planning strategies. Under the government's third planning policy statement (PPS3), local planning authorities and regional planning bodies must consider housing market information when developing policies in local development framework and regional spatial strategies, hence the need for robust HMAs and updates. Notably, planning authorities must regularly monitor trends and activities in housing market areas reflecting the 'plan, monitor, manage' approach to planning for housing.

An excellent text which goes into the principles and details of HMAs is the DCLG's publication, *Strategic Housing Market Assessments: Practice Guidance* (DCLG, 2007), which clearly sets out the required data and best-practice methodology which should be used and followed in undertaking and commissioning them.

ACUTE HOUSING NEED

Estimating housing need and requirement is essential, but having done so, it is necessary to decide which element of need should be dealt with as a matter of priority. This should surely be informed by the acuteness of that need – but what is acute housing need? Several candidates come to mind. Surely, homelessness, living in insanitary or overcrowded housing, and a property which the occupants cannot afford to heat and light must figure must form part of the ostensive definition. We shall consider the so-called 'reasonable preference' categories of need and how they influence allocation systems in greater detail in the housing law and management sections of this book, but the function of this part is to examine their constituents and try to explain how they arise in a so-called civilised society.

By way of background, in considering the sort of housing need local authorities should consider when allocating accommodation directly or (more commonly now) indirectly via nomination arrangements to registered providers such as housing associations, it is instructive to consider what the 'reasonable preference' categories are as a preamble to considering their significance.

The 1996 Housing Act defines the reasonable preference categories for local authority housing allocation in Section 167 (2) as follows:

Councils must give 'reasonable preference' in allocations directly or via nominations to:

- People who are *homeless* – this includes people who are intentionally homeless, and those who do not have a priority need for accommodation.
- People in *insanitary* or overcrowded housing or otherwise living in *unsatisfactory housing conditions*.
- People who need to move on medical or welfare grounds, including disability.
- People who need to move to a particular part of the council's area, where failure to meet that need would cause hardship (to themselves or to others).

Councils can now also take account of the need to attract workers to an area or financial means when allocating properties. Also, it should be noted that the law does not confer any particular weighting to any particular category, nor are they now regarded as additive in defining comparative levels of need.

Let us now examine these categories one by one, as the basis for the rest of this chapter.

Homelessness

Homelessness is perhaps the most acute form of housing need. Legally, it does not equate to rooflessness, although someone who is roofless would fall within this category unless they had a right to occupy accommodation but chose not to exercise it. It is possible to occupy shelter but still be technically homeless if you have no legal right to stay where you are. In England and Wales, homelessness and the rights and duties which appertain to it are laid out in Part VII of the Housing Act 1996, as modified by the 2002 Homelessness Act and marginally by the Localism Act 2011. Essentially, to qualify for housing, which may or may not be provided by a local authority and could be temporary or permanent, it is necessary to satisfy a number of criteria. The detail of the law will be considered in Chapter 5. In this one, we are more concerned with the underlying principles. The first of the qualifying principles is having no right to accommodation. The Human Rights Act 1998 is silent on rights to housing as such, which may strike readers as odd, since without some form of accommodation it is virtually impossible to retain dignity, to function as a member of society, or to exercise other rights which this Act seeks to guarantee, so it might be thought that the right to a home would be foundational. Consider the number of things which are either impossible or very hard to sustain without having a secure home. Normal family life presupposes that adequate housing conditions exist in which to conduct these activities. Cooking, sleeping, eating and washing are basic prerequisites for any sort of civilised existence and are next to impossible without the resource of somewhere settled to stay. Maslow's hierarchy of needs (Maslow, 1943) indicates that property security in his 'safety' tier comes just above basic physiological needs (for example breathing, food and water) is therefore a precondition to be able to enjoy any higher activities such as work or education or features of family life, and so without some form of security in this sense individuals and households are in a sense doomed because they are unable to thrive and progress. These points are so obvious that it seems immoral or unethical that there is no general right to housing. It also seems to be economically, societally, psychologically and environmentally absurd that this is not the case. If individuals are unable to take part in economic activity, they cannot contribute to the wealth of the nation and in crude terms are therefore economic liabilities, assuming they could make a potential contribution. Thus by denying someone a home, society as a whole suffers through the reduction of tax income, and incurs unnecessary expenditure in making available welfare payments for temporary shelter (or other benefits).

Why, then, is there any argument about whether people should or should not have anywhere to live? If it is that basic, surely the question would have a similar status to that asking whether people should have a right to eat, sleep, or even a right to life, since it is almost that primary. The right to life is well established: many countries have now abolished the death penalty, or justify it only on the basis that by murdering someone, or through committing some other heinous act, the offender has forfeited their right to life. This is clearly a very serious matter, and not taken lightly, otherwise the offence of murder would not have the status that it does, and it is unlikely that there would be much distinction between this and, say, manslaughter; but there is. Starving is generally disapproved of, and there is a safety net in most civilised countries which provides a basic minimum in terms of sustenance or the means to obtain it which will prevent starving. Sleep deprivation is only practiced by nations who are not signatories to human rights treaties. However, the question of whether people have a right to a home is, it seems, more open than these issues.

There appears to be international support of some gravitas for such a right. Article 25 of the United Nations General Assembly Universal Declaration of Human Rights of 1948 (United Nations, 1948) states that:

Everyone has the right to a standard of living adequate for the health and well-being of himself and of his family, including food, clothing, housing and medical care and necessary social services, and the right to security in the event of unemployment, sickness, disability, widowhood, old age or other lack of livelihood in circumstances beyond his control.

Regrettably, this clause has not been reflected within the Human Rights Act 1998.

The state of play in the UK as regards a right to housing is that it is caveated by judgement as to whether the individual or household is deserving or undeserving. This is reflected in current legislation and practice, and originates in the Elizabethan Poor Law arrangements which were summarised in the Introduction. In essence, at that time, parishes had a duty to offer support to destitute people of the parish, including rudimentary shelter. During Elizabeth I's reign, the state introduced registers of the poor for each parish and in 1597 justices of the peace were commanded to raise funds locally for the relief of the poor, who were placed into three categories:

1.   *The able-bodied and deserving poor* – those who could work, but had none. They were to be assisted either through 'outdoor relief' or by being given a paid job. In this context, 'outdoor relief' meant financial or in-kind assistance to stay in their homes, including a 'dole' of money as a primitive form of social security.
2.   *The idle poor* – those who could work but would not. They were whipped through the streets in public until they reformed.
3.   *The impotent and deserving poor* – those who were too old or ill to work. They could be housed in almshouses – for elderly people, in 'poor houses' or hospitals, and children of such people were given an apprenticeship so at least they had a chance of work when they reached maturity.

In order to administer the system, two 'overseers of the poor' were elected by the parish, and were charged with estimating the cost of providing poor relief and collecting the local tax to pay for it. Other duties included dispensing food, and supervising the local poor house. There was a codification of these strands in 1601, with the Poor Law of that year.

There are similarities in philosophy between the Elizabethan system and the current (2012) attitude to welfare provision which is highly geared to incentivising work through 'carrot and stick' measures, although mercifully whipping through the streets has long been abolished! The key point to note is that there was a clear categorisation between deserving and undeserving, that accommodation was a central aspect of the regime, and that people had to show that they were willing to do something in return for assistance. It is also notable that such relief was provided on a local (parish) basis – local people supporting other local people – which finds its echo in the 'local connection' aspects of modern homelessness legislation, and also in contemporary approaches to housing allocation.

Another feature of the Poor Law approach is that it essentially related to the settled poor of the parish, and not to travelling people, or 'sturdy beggars' as they were sometimes termed. The 1601 legislation was amended in 1607 to provide for parish 'houses of correction', where wandering vagabonds could be housed and made to work, and were separate from the poor houses which were reserved for the settled poor. This is perhaps the earliest expression of localism. During the later seventeenth century, some parishes combined poor houses with houses of correction in the form of workhouses, which provided rudimentary accommodation in return for labour.

This system basically continued until the 1832 Royal Commission into the Operation of the Poor Laws. The Commission's report resulted in the Poor Law Amendment Act 1834, which significantly modified the previous regime. It was an attempt to streamline the administration of the Poor Law by amalgamating parishes into unions for this purpose, to abolish outdoor relief and to establish a very deterrent and basic form of workhouse as a central plank of assistance, but only for the deserving poor. It also set up the Poor Law Board. Staffed by Poor Law commissioners based in London who would endeavour to standardise the approach country-wide. This approach continued until after the First World War (1914–1918) but it failed to reduce pauperism. Again, it is possible to discern the deterrence which still exists within the legal approach to homelessness in the UK in the finding of 'intentional homelessness' under part V11 of the 1996 Housing Act, and the desire to seek economies and efficiencies through administrative reform is a perennial concern of government.

The Poor Law system was abolished after the Second World War though the National Assistance Act 1948. As well as establishing a social security safety net through the payment of benefits, it also gave councils a duty to provide accommodation for people who were judged to be in need of care and attention. The act was in many ways the forerunner of modern legislation, but carried forward certain features of the Poor Laws which remain today. These include:

1.   Distinguishing certain classes of homeless people from others in considering assistance to be given. Section 21 (1) explicitly mentioned the qualifiers of age, illness and disability, although it did refer to 'any other circumstances' and the whole section is caveated by saying that this duty only extended to cases where care and attention was 'not otherwise available to them' – for example, provision by family members or friends. The current priority needs categories reflect these qualifiers, although they have been added to over the years.

2.   21 (1) (aa) also gives priority to 'expectant and nursing mothers' who needed care which was not otherwise available to them. Notably, it made no provision for their partners, and councils would often discharge this duty by placements into a 'mother and baby home'. This has changed in that assistance is now extended to households rather than the vulnerable individuals within them, but this category is still reflected in modern legislation. The implication is, following the Poor Law philosophy, that those partners who cannot support their pregnant or nursing dependents fall squarely into the category of the undeserving poor and should at best be confined to a workhouse (for which read hostel!), if anywhere at all.

3.   Section 21 2A states that in considering whether care and attention is available, certain elements of the applicant's resources should be disregarded. Thus

assistance was effectively means tested. This is a direct reflection of the Poor Law philosophy that only the poorest should receive central or local state relief, and that levels of assistance, as well as the means test, should be in the gift of the secretary of state.

4.   The issue of 'local connection' is covered in Section 24, which states clearly that assistance should be given to people ordinarily resident in the area, and that if that person had no settled home and was not ordinarily resident in any other area, they should be dealt with by the receiving authority. This is essentially the case today, and directly reflects the localism of the Poor Laws in discouraging 'wandering vagrants'.

There are other continuities which the reader may wish to research by reading the text of the 1948 Act in comparison to more recent legislation. The act is available on the legislation.gov.uk site (UK government, no date).

The 1948 Act should be seen as essentially a social assistance rather than a housing assistance provision. The stress is on ensuring that vulnerable persons are accommodated, not on families and other forms of supportive households, and there is no mention or indeed intention of permanency in the law, as was the case under the previous regime. These points are well made in the seminal television play *Cathy Come Home* (1967) which tells a very sad story of a young couple in an initially stable relationship, who loose their modern home when Reg is injured in an industrial accident and becomes unemployed. Eviction follows, and after a series of temporary accommodation arrangements including Cathy being placed in a mother and baby home, Reg ends up in a hostel and Cathy's children are removed from her by social services. *Cathy Come Home* was instrumental in raising the profile of homelessness as a matter affecting households as well as individuals, although it was made at a time when the production of social housing by local authorities was at a high point, so it must have met with scepticism in some quarters. The influence of the play on bringing about subsequent legislation has been questioned, although it is tempting to imply a cause and effect relationship in retrospect. It certainly led to a publicity and awareness campaign which led to the formation of the charity Crisis in 1967, which still exists, and must have given some impetus to the formation of Shelter, the UK-wide charity supporting the homeless and badly housed through practical housing aid and advice and through lobbying, which was launched shortly after the play was released, in December 1966. One of the direct outcomes of the play was to influence councils in the direction of providing accommodation for family units rather than just for individuals, which should not be downplayed, and which is an enduring feature of the system.

As already suggested, the 1948 Act regime and its practical operation – through social services departments – indicates that homelessness was seen as a social problem or malaise rather than one of accommodation shortage as such, and that it was something about the individuals concerned which led to their situation rather than the economic environment. This is to a certain extent understandable in the context of the 1960s in Britain and much of the Western world, where full employment was widely believed to exist, and where as has been stated, there was a vibrant social housing development programme. That said, care should be taken to qualify the term 'full employment'. According to Tucker, 2011, 4 per cent or less unemployment was regarded as full employment in the 1960s in the UK and US, shifting to 6 per cent in the 1980s and around 5 per cent in 2011. The reason for the apparent shift is due partly to the increased participation of women and those under 25 in the labour market, which increases supply without directly affecting demand for employees, and controversially and arguably, the availability of welfare benefits which ensures that people can at least exist without work.

It took ten years for any form of legislation which recognised homelessness as a housing rather than primarily social issue to be passed in the form of the Housing (Homeless Persons) Act 1977, as a result of hard campaigning by Shelter, Crisis and similar organisations, and the government of the day taking over a private member's bill which looked to embarrass it. There is considerable academic (for example de Friend, 1978) and other support for the paradigm shift suggested here, although it is hard to explain and as has already been said, features of the Poor Law approach remain. The time delay between popular sentiment and legislative change is often in direct relation to the effect of the situation to hand perceived by those in charge. The longer the reaction, the less the perceived seriousness. To illustrate, terrorism is perceived as a very serious threat to the integrity and safety of society. Examples are legion: the Prevention of Terrorism (Temporary Provisions) Act 1974 was approved after just 17 hours of debate in the House of Commons in response to an upsurge in 'the troubles' in Northern Ireland and related events in the rest of the UK, principally a bombing in a pub in Birmingham that year. Another example is the publication of the Offences Against the State (Amendment) Bill in the Irish parliament, the Dial, on 31 August 1998, just two weeks after the Omagh bombings, and its signature following a debate in the Seanead on 3 September. This is also illustrated by the response of the US legislature following the events of 9/11, which gave rise to the 2001 USA Patriot Act (Thomas, 2002).

The current state of play with homelessness is more or less unchanged from the 1977 legislation, with the only significant changes being the widening of the priority needs category, a concentration on eligibility and restrictions on accommodation provision duties. Essentially, in the UK, local authorities have a duty to secure accommodation (directly or indirectly) for persons and their dependants found to be homeless and in a priority category (including those with a disability, by virtue of age, having children of dependent age living in the household, a member of the household being pregnant, etc.), with caveats on whether this should be temporary to give a respite to find somewhere else to live or not depending on whether the household is judged to have made themselves homeless by an act or omission ('intentional homelessness') and local connection by way of previous or current resident, work or family connection. More detail on the law is given in Chapter 5. There is a comprehensive Code of Guidance and mountains of case law to assist councils in conducting their duties, and they rely significantly on partner organisations (principally housing associations, who have a duty to cooperate with them – for example via nomination agreements).

In terms of judgement on priority, it is instructive to look at some of the categories to see if there is really any common thread, or whether in fact the classification is more a result of history than logic. Essentially the 'priority need groups' include households with dependent children or a pregnant woman and people who are vulnerable in some way for example, through mental illness or physical disability. The order made under the 2002 Homelessness Act under Part V11 of the 1996 Housing Act extended the priority need categories to include applicants aged 16 or 17 and applicants aged 18 to 20 previously in care; those considered vulnerable through time spent in care, in custody or in the armed forces; and those who are vulnerable through fleeing their home due to violence or the threat of violence. The golden thread running through this is that of being judged less able to look after accommodation needs than others, and the consequences which would follow if some form of help were not extended. So, for example, someone with a physical disability might be less able to obtain a reasonably paid job than others, and therefore be less able to secure suitable housing, and the consequence of homelessness may well be greater physical deterioration than for a more 'able-bodied' person. If households with dependent children are not housed, the children would suffer physically and mentally, which would run counter to the societal view that since children are future citizens who will potentially contribute to society's good and stability, it makes sense to ensure that their welfare (including housing) is secured. If people who are aged are not housed, they are more likely to become ill and possibly die more rapidly than others who are younger, which would be unacceptable. If young people are not given some sort of accommodation where they have none, it will impact on their ability to become useful and productive members of society, which is not a welcome consequence of inaction, and so forth. The implication is that uncorrected homelessness for others – for whom 'appropriate advice and assistance' (which does not mean making accommodation available) is the official remedy – would not have particularly serious societal consequences or reflect particularly badly on societal morality.

Trends in homelessness

Whenever social trends are published, examined or cited to support an argument, it is very important to determine whether a consistent definition has been used to select the figures, and what the underlying causes of any variations might be, having adjusted the trend for any definitional changes. For example, if further priority categories are added, it is likely that this will result in an increase in the rate of homelessness applications, acceptances and re-housings. If there is a policy change which emphasises preventative measures, which there has been since the mid-2000s, it might be expected that the rate of homelessness would drop; and if policy changes direct homeless households towards the private sector, the number of social re-housings might fall.

With this in mind, it is notable that the rate of homelessness acceptances appears to have fallen over the past ten years, according to official statistics, as shown in Figure 1.1 of this chapter. This is also reflected in trends in homelessness re-housings, as shown in Figure 1.2.

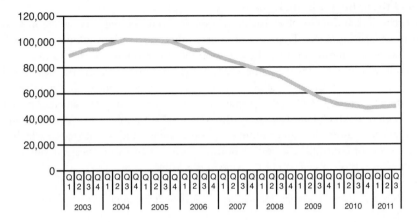

Figure 1.2 Homeless households in temporary accommodation, England and Wales, Q1 2003–Q3 2011

Source: DCLG, Table 783, available at: www.communities.gov.uk/housing/housingresearch/
housingstatistics/housingstatisticsby/homelessnessstatistics/livetables/

It would, then, be wrong to deduce that homelessness as expressed through official statistics has fallen between 2003 and 2011 as a result of increased accommodation provision of improving economic circumstances in the country. Neither has been the case. The explanation lies in the reorientation of housing policy and strategy in this area towards preventative work, including deflection to the private rented sector and in some cases the low-cost home ownership sector.

Homelessness and banding

Homelessness has a high pecking order in allocation systems, as it is one of the reasonable preference categories and has long been regarded as one, if not the most serious expression, of housing need. Crudely, banding is a way of assigning priority for re-housing to a category of households sharing similar housing need character-istics. Several distinct categories of housing need might be assigned to one band, and trump other needs groups assigned to lower bands when it comes to the allocation of scarce social housing. The chances of re-housing within a given time might therefore depend on the band the household is assigned to, along with time waited in that band, a factor which has recently been given more emphasis as a result of the Localism Act 2011. Those in higher bands bidding under choice-based lettings systems will generally find that they are richer in terms of the currency of need than those in lower bands, and therefore more likely to get what they bid for, subject to their skill in participating in the process and information available to them. Readers are invited to visit a range of local authority and housing association sites to find out how such systems are actually constructed and operated and the matter of choice-based letting is fully dealt with later in this chapter.

Final thoughts on homelessness

Is it fair, just and reasonable that homelessness should be regarded as the highest form of housing need? There are of course other very serious conditions which should be given attention by those responsible for rationing social housing, but without a home it is virtually impossible for people to engage in any meaningful sense with society in terms of education, welfare, employment or any number of goods which most people take for granted. It is up for debate as to whether or not the degree to which fault is a part of the way in which homelessness is viewed and dealt with is justifiable – and its influence is pervasive – and the degree to which it is a means of controlling access to housing rather than its justification, but such discussion is probably beyond the scope of this book.

People in insanitary or overcrowded housing or otherwise living in unsatisfactory housing conditions

Looking at the history of social housing, one of the key drivers behind its development was the relief of housing squalor. It is hard to imagine the housing conditions which many had to endure in the early industrial ages in the mature industrial economies, although those which still exist in some developing countries which are undergoing rapid urbanisation might be a reasonable guide. It is worth reflecting that insanitary and squalid housing conditions not only affect the mental and physical health and safety of their occupants but also those of others in the vicinity. With this in mind, it is interesting to probe some of the reasons why social housing was developed in London in the nineteenth century, alongside the rationale employed by more enlightened industrialists of the Victorian era when they decided to build model settlements for their workers close to their factories.

Edwin Chadwick (1800–1890) was a reformer in Victorian England whose views reflected many other socially concerned people of the day on the housing conditions of poorer people, especially those in developing industrial towns. In 1832, he was employed to examine the way in which the Poor Laws operated, and at the same time, collaborated with Dr Thomas Southwood Smith to look into the relationship between health and economic productivity, which resulted in Chadwick's famous treatise published in 1842, *The Sanitary Condition of the Labouring Population* (1842). An extract demonstrates his belief in the causal link between poor housing conditions and bad health:

> That the various forms of epidemic, endemic, and other disease caused, or aggravated, or propagated chiefly amongst the labouring classes by atmospheric impurities produced by decomposing animal and vegetable substances, by damp and filth, and close and overcrowded dwellings prevail amongst the population in every part of the kingdom, whether dwelling in separate houses, in rural villages, in small towns, in the larger towns — as they have been found to prevail in the lowest districts of the metropolis.
>
> (Chadwick, 1842, pp. 369–72)

He supported this contention by case study, and his conclusions proved cause for concern, leading to public health legislation which gave rise to the earliest form of social housing in later nineteenth-century England. The conclusions included that those living in insanitary or overcrowded conditions were likely to live eight to ten years shorter than others; that deaths relating to these conditions in the home and workplace exceeded those from death or wounds in recent wars; that younger people brought up under such conditions were likely to be far less healthy than their counterparts, that education suffers under such circumstances, and that current laws were totally ineffective in dealing with any of this.

Some of his other conclusions reflect the temper of the age and may prove amusing to modern readers. They include the deduction that since those in poor living conditions are less likely to benefit from education, they are therefore likely to be less economically productive than their peers, as well as being more likely to be improvident, reckless and intemperate with a greater predilection for sensual gratification than others! He also supposed that, in insanitary districts characterised by high mortality rates, the birth rate would be higher and population pressure in relation to resources therefore greater than in more healthy areas. This may well be the case, but in other parts of his report, he comments that infant mortality is far higher in such areas than in others, so it is at least on first reading hard to see how this would not counterbalance higher relative fertility rates.

His suggested solutions have a modern ring to them and proven relevance, and are based on case study and are laced with not a little moral philosophising. For Chadwick, the most important measures to take to relieve the adverse health and productivity of the 'labouring poor' were the removal of rubbish from dwellings and streets, proper sewerage (which would also obviate the need for labour-intensive removal) and fresh water supplies piped directly to dwellings. He also suggested that a medical officer be appointed in districts to ensure that such measures were taken – the forerunner of environmental health officials – and that works should be conducted by 'responsible' and qualified civil engineers. He compared the situation in England to that in Sweden, where there had been a move to rectify the ills he described, and stated that if his measures were introduced, it could add 13 years to the average life expectancy of 'the labouring classes'. He also concluded that the interventions suggested would also give rise to the moral improvement of such classes, following on from his earlier observation that physical filth is causally related to physical and moral illness, not to mention unrefined manners.

Some industrialists of the day demonstrated practical agreement with Chadwick, whether or not they followed his writings, in the belief that a healthy workforce is a productive one, and that health and housing are causally related. Examples of such industrialists include Sir Titus Salt, a Yorkshire entrepreneur who built a village near Shipley, modestly named Saltaire, for his wool workers. It is now a UNESCO world heritage site, and visitors can see not only relatively spacious and well-constructed artisan's homes but infrastructure such as a reading room, library, concert hall, billiard room, science laboratory and a gym, as well as a surgery, hospital and allotments. Other examples of enlightened provision for workers include Port Sunlight, near Liverpool, developed by William Lever (1851–1925) for his soap workers between

1899 and 1914. As well as around 800 spacious workers' homes to accommodate around 3,500 people, it provides schools, an art gallery, swimming pool, hospital, concert hall, church and a temperance (no alcoholic drinks served) hotel. The thinking behind these developments was incorporated into the garden cities built in the early to mid-1900s, and influenced the design of social housing constructed by councils between 1919 and around 1930.

Modern connections

More recent research has underscored the linkage between insanitary and otherwise unsatisfactory housing and life chances, and initiatives have been developed to address specific elements of this, as well as more targeted legislation.

Overcrowding

There are clear links between overcrowding and disadvantage, including educational life chances. An influential report by Shelter, *Toying with their Future* (Shelter, 2004) makes the links dramatically and through case study and is particularly clearly written. An ODPM research publication, *The Impact of Overcrowding on Health and Education: A Review of the Evidence and Literature*, makes a similar point (ODPM, 2004). Both are worth reviewing.

The government-sponsored initiative to tackle overcrowding and under-occupation in the social housing sector between 2007 and 2009 exemplifies a policy based on the acceptance of the link between cramped housing, bad health and reduced life chances. The estimation of quantity depends on how overcrowding is measured, but using the most recent criteria, a TSA/DCLG (2009) report draws on the Survey of English Households to suggest that there were at the time of its production some 565,000 overcrowded households in England alone, of which 234,000 were in the social rented sector, and that just over one third of these (34 per cent) were in London. This contrasts with the figure measured under the old standard which would have reduced the total figure to around 20,000. The essential reason for this is that the old method counted all habitable rooms as available for sleeping in, but the new one counts only bedrooms. Initiatives which are suggested include incentivising under-occupying tenants to swap with over-occupiers; ensuring that the allocations system gives a reasonable degree of priority to overcrowded households both within the stock and awaiting housing; undertaking or facilitating conversions for example from flats back to houses in the case of street properties to provide larger accommodation; internal modifications to dwelling layouts to create extra rooms or work/study space within them; and practical advice to relieve the educational disadvantage associated with overcrowding, such as routing to homework clubs.

One of the biggest obstacles to relieving overcrowding is the reduced size of the national affordable housing programme. There is no sign of reduction in unmet housing need, and it seems logical that in the absence of suitable alternatives which have convenient locations, many households who would otherwise have been moved into more suitably sized housing will have to occupy their first-allocated property for longer than convenient, while the nature of the tenure security arrangements for the bulk of the social housing stock currently provides no particular incentive to downsize. Indeed, if a place has been your home for most of your life there may well be a psychological and emotional attachment to it and the memories it represents which may frustrate the most well-meaning endeavours to release it for an overcrowded family, and who is to say that this is wrong?

Relieving insanitary conditions

As previously identified, the link between insanitary conditions in the broadest sense (including health and safety considerations) and poor educational and work performance, as well as disease and mortality rates, is well established. Local authorities in the UK have for a long time had the power to close dwellings judged to be unfit for human habitation on the basis of these connections in the public interest. Public health legislation has a reasonable pedigree – the first act of significance was the Public Health Act 1875, which required all new-build homes to have running water and sewerage. It should be remembered that the awareness of the seriousness of water-borne disease, and even the fact that disease could be water-borne, was relatively fresh in the minds of Victorians following the discovery by Dr John Snow that the cholera outbreak in London's Soho in 1854, which claimed 616 lives, was due to the contamination of a well and spread through the primitive water supply system. This probably gave impetus to the legislation, as well as the stink from the Thames from raw sewage which gave politicians in the Houses of Commons and Lords something to consider. Safety concerns were reflected in the requirement that all streets in urban areas should have lighting and pavements. Safe passageway, lighting, proper sanitary arrangements and water supply all feature in the Housing Health and Safety Rating System (HHSRS) provisions of Section 9 of the 2004 Housing Act which replaced the old fitness standard in 2006 with one which examines the conditions of dwellings in relation to their occupants to determine whether or not a dwelling is hazardous to health.

Plenty of dwellings in the private sector exhibit one or more of the 29 hazards under the HHSRS (ODPM, 2006), and could be closed down by environmental health departments, although the question of re-housing then arises. It should be noted that overcrowding is one of those hazards, as are each of the defects already mentioned above. The list of hazards reflects much of what has already been said on this subject in the previous pages and includes:

A Physiological requirements

- Hygrothermal conditions
  1   Damp and mould growth
  2   Excess cold
  3   Excess heat

- Pollutants (non-microbial)
  4   Asbestos (and manufactured mineral fibres)
  5   Biocides
  6   Carbon monoxide and fuel-combustion products
  7   Lead

8   Radiation
9   Uncombusted fuel gas
10   Volatile organic compounds

B   Psychological requirements

* Space, security, light and noise
  11   Crowding and space
  12   Entry by intruders
  13   Lighting
  14   Noise

C   Protection against infection

* Hygiene, sanitation and water supply
  15   Domestic hygiene, pests and refuse
  16   Food safety
  17   Personal hygiene, sanitation and drainage
  18   Water supply

D   Protection against accidents

* Falls
  19   Falls associated with baths etc.
  20   Falling on level surfaces etc.
  21   Falling on stairs etc.
  22   Falling between levels

* Electric shocks, fires, burns and scalds
  23   Electrical hazards
  24   Fire
  25   Flames, hot surfaces etc.

* Collisions, cuts and strains
  26   Collision and entrapment
  27   Explosions
  28   Position and operability of amenities etc.
  29   Structural collapse and falling elements

People living under these conditions should be considered under the reasonable preference arrangements mentioned when being considered for the allocation of social or affordable housing, for all of the reasons already adduced.

People who need to move on medical or welfare grounds, including disability
There is a crossover between this and the previous reasonable preference category. Someone may need to move due to medical grounds because of some deficient aspect of the accommodation, for example, it may be damp which may aggravate respiratory problems. However, there are other conditions which can be aggravated

by the layout of accommodation which do not relate to insanitariness or overcrowding, or any of the issues already discussed. For example someone who has suffered a heart attack may not be able to climb stairs of a given steepness or flight due to the danger that overexertion of the heart may cause its failure. A person who suffers from severe sciatica may be unable to negotiate stairs at all or steps leading to a dwelling without extreme pain, and progressive Alzheimer's disease may necessitate a move from independent to 'sheltered' or supervised accommodation if peripatetic care is either unavailable or inappropriate. In the past, those suffering from a medical condition who could not fend for themselves and find a carer or somewhere appropriate to live were often warehoused into so-called Part Three accommodation (named after Part Three of the National Assistance Act) – essentially, supervised clustered residential accommodation under one roof consisting of flatlets with communal facilities and medical, social and related care on-site, or in some cases penned in hospital wards set aside for that purpose. Since the Care in the Community initiatives of the 1980s, the emphasis has been to endeavour to provide care for people in their own homes, which strengthens the need to take this reasonable reference category seriously, since a move to more suitable accommodation in the community, with visiting care where needed, may be a much better solution than to remain in the existing home, without institutionalisation. Care in the Community is often thought to be a Thatcherite invention, but actually it dates from at least 1956, where it was presented as a preferred option to institutional housing for older people (for example geriatric wards) in the Guillebaud Committee report of that year, which suggested that policy should aim at making adequate provision wherever possible for the care and treatment of old people in their own homes, and that the development of domiciliary services would save state resources as well as being a humanitarian measure enabling people to lead the life they much prefer. The Griffiths Report, *Community Care: Agenda for Action*, which was published in 1988 as a Green Paper, is generally regarded as the main spur to community care. It made six main recommendations, of which the two most relevant to providing care services to people in situ were: first, council social services departments rather than the health service should assess local care needs, implement bureaucracy to assess individuals' care needs, and design flexible packages of care to address them; and second, to roll back direct state provision through social work departments contracting with the voluntary and private sector to deliver care services.

This is the state of play today, with minor modifications. We will discuss the funding and delivery of special care packages in later chapters, but in essence, the move towards in situ caring has provided challenges to housing providers in provision, design and management terms, not assisted by previous changes in the accompanying financial regimes.

The ageing of the population provides a further challenge: a proportion of this growing group will be unable to sustain themselves in their existing homes and will look to the local state for assistance, and the question arises as to whether enough resources will be made available to meet this need. The demographics are clear, although the inferences in relation to dependency and state funding requirements less so. According to UK Parliament (no date) there will be 5.5 million more people over the age of 65 in the UK in 2032 with a total cohort of around 19 million by 2050, which will account for one in four of the population. The inference regarding the need for more accommodation to assist older people in relation to their possible medical and related needs is difficult, as evidence suggests that people are healthier for longer than in the past, so there may be no correlation between the rate of growth of the over-65 population and the need for specialist housing or specific care arrangements. Indeed, there has been much recent criticism of the traditional method of assessing the economic requirement on the state to provide for ageing, the old age dependency ratio (OADR), used by the United Nations and governments. Critics are academics in the US and Australia who have proposed a new index, the adult disability dependency ratio (ADDR), which endeavours to measure the relationship between those who give care and those who need it. Applying this to demographics, Sanderson and Scherbov (2010) claim it reduces ageing dependency by four-fifths compared to the OADR. This approach may well be a better way of informing estimates for specialist housing provision, adaptations and peripatetic services to the elderly than a rather more crude approach based on slicing the population by age, projecting it forward, and assuming uniform increases in dependency (Sanderson and Scherbov, 2010). It also sits well with the proposed and actual increases to the qualifying age for the old age pension in the UK and other developed world countries. The ageing of the population could be seen as generating an inconvenience in terms of providing for newly arising need. If people are living longer, they will remain secure tenants for longer. There is, at the moment, no way of forcing people out of their homes due to under-occupation by virtue of age or any other factor, although the employment of conditional tenancies by local authorities and increased use of assured shorthold tenancies by housing associations following the Localism Act may provide some flexibility here. Currently, local authorities and other registered providers frequently endeavour to tempt older under-occupying residents out of their homes into smaller housing to make more rational use of stock, but this has met with a variable response, for reasons outlined earlier in this chapter. There are real ethical issues associated with incentivising or pressurising older members of society to give up their homes and move elsewhere just because delivering new provision to meet newly arising need from younger family-sized households seems to be difficult at this time.

People who need to move to a particular part of the council's area, where failure to meet that need would cause hardship (to themselves or to others)
This category is rather harder to define than the previous ones, although examples can readily be given. There are many reasons why someone might need to move for one area of a district to another, for example, to take up employment without excessive transport costs or associated travel time; to care for a dependent relative or to be cared for; to attend an educational establishment to meet special requirements; to be close to a medical or other care facility; to move away from a perpetrator of domestic violence, and so forth. The has been much talk of job-related housing offers recently (2011/2012), and some councils have endeavoured to prioritise those taking up jobs within the reasonable preference bands which are given significant

weight under the Localism Act, or outside them, which is permissible as long as this does not dominate the 'reasonable preference' allocations. In practice, it is not necessary to invent new categories as the existing ones have proved to be fairly adaptable, and this one is no exception.

The provision of housing in a given part of an authority's area on the basis of employment is partly related to the decline of tied accommodation. The author has fond memories of attending social functions at the Nurses' Hostel in St Albans, Hertfordshire, England, which was in the grounds of the City Hospital. At that time, in the 1970s, this form of provision was more or less universal, providing somewhere relatively affordable and secure, convenient to the place of duty, but it has declined since then, and relatively few hospitals now have any provision for staff accommodation, other than in exceptional cases where there is a training facility or university associated with the institution, and even in these cases the level of provision may be quite inadequate. This divestment has been driven largely by economic reality – the drive from the mid-1980s to sell public assets including buildings for conversion or demolition to the private sector for housing or commercial uses. The same is true for many other public sector relatively low-paid professions, such as the fire and police service, and in the education sector. The question then arises as to how to ensure that there are sufficient public sector workers to fill essential roles, although this is less of an issue in the depths of a recession or in the context of public sector cutbacks. The fact that it has proved a thinking-point is evidenced in the 2000s, when there were several initiatives designed to attract so-called key workers to public sector jobs in shortage areas, including 80 per cent market rent 'intermediate rent' schemes run by housing associations and targeted low-cost home ownership offers. The idea has since been largely abandoned, largely through lack of take-up, although some authorities and associations still run equivalents. It may be that the tradition of providing in-service housing has simply died the death, along with live-in servants and the local bobby with a house provided by the parish.

More will be said about how housing needs are defined and met in Chapters 3 and 5, but it should be remembered that the reasonable preference categories as defined in the 1996 Housing Act and modified by the 2002 Homelessness Act are the guiding principles behind allocational priority in social and affordable housing for rent, and that they are reasonably all-encompassing.

Supply

The supply of social and affordable housing to meet need and elements of demand has posed seemingly intractable problems over the past decades. Since the creation of social housing in the mid-nineteenth century, in the UK as a direct result of public health legislation, the assumption has been that it is somehow necessary for the state to provide housing either as a genuine tenure choice, which it sometimes has been viewed as, or as housing of last resort – a form of welfare housing redolent of that provided in the US. There are two extreme views which almost nobody holds these days: one is that the state should always provide housing and the second is that it should never do so. The middle view is that the state should sometimes provide it, and there are endless arguments over how much should be provided, where, who should pay for it and how much.

We are not in this chapter concerned with the mechanism of development, nor how it is financed. Rather we are concerned with what should be supplied, and who should supply it. Let us first look at the proposition that the state should supply all social housing. If it is held that housing is a basic human right, or at least a requirement for a stable society on a par with welfare benefit, it would be wholly reasonable to hold this view. In essence, the most persuasive case for major state intervention in housing is that the market cannot by itself either provide an adequate stock distribute it fairly (for example Lansley, 1979). There are international examples where the state does indeed supply the bulk of social housing, but they are relatively few, with even China, Russia and other state-dominated and formerly communist (or communist in name only) regimes opting for a mixed economy in this area. The retreat from a state monopoly in providing social housing is perhaps indicative of a global shift towards market economics, accompanied by the fragmentation of state capitalist empires as in the case of the break-up of the USSR, and a belief that other organisations can do the work of states at arm's length in many cases more effectively and efficiently than central bureaucracy. It may also be an expression of a perceived lack of consent that the state should provide housing on the scale it used to, due to the emergence and proliferation of the 'choice and responsibility' agenda. Arguments against the state supplying all or most housing in the UK were deployed in the 1980s by Conservative ministers. William Waldegrave MP, a housing minister in the Thatcher administration, famously stated in relation to council housing that 'There should not be much of it' when supporting the growth of housing association development backed by private development finance following the initiation of the 1988 Housing Act finance regime. A common view seemed to be that the state and its agencies were not the most efficient providers of goods and services, as indicated by the performance of some of the nationalised industries of the time, and that the market place (albeit in some cases with a degree of intervention) would allocate even social goods more efficiently. This was the thinking behind compulsory competitive tendering introduced into local authority housing management in the early 1990s. This view was carried forward at least in spirit through the Best Value regime from 1997, which encouraged public providers to contrast and compare their in-house offer with private or voluntary sector providers, if only to challenge their own operations. The same thinking has not been extended to the distribution of welfare benefits, which could theoretically be done through private sector organisations, although some of the processing has been outsourced.

Is this reasonable? Arguably, there would be less risk of misallocation if the state took direct control not only of the funding but also the production of housing to meet need. Reliance on market mechanism alone would be unlikely to deliver the desired result, as investments generally seek optimum returns and the rents which are required to do so far exceed those which lower income households could afford without substantial assistance from the state in the form of benefits. Arguably, therefore, there would be no guarantee that the housing need which statute says must be met would be met. If private enterprise were to deliver and manage all housing, it would be necessary to monitor its operations and output carefully to ensure that it delivered the correct quantity and quality of housing, which would in itself entail considerable bureaucracy and cost, and since private enterprises are essentially independent of the state, enforcement would be cumbersome indeed. The mixed-economy approach which exists in the UK is probably more satisfactory than the private sector alternative as it avoids some of the pitfalls identified above, and at least allows for reasonable and economical regulation, but there is still the risk that production will not keep pace with targets due to factors beyond the control of the state – for example, the banks' willingness to lend for development and the vagaries of the for-sale market which produces finance used by many housing associations to cross-subsidise rental and low-cost home ownership products, and peaks and troughs in planning application activity which can play havoc with business plans which assume availability of land and housing at undervalue arising from Section 106 deals or (latterly) proceeds from the Community Infrastructure Levy. This is not to say that the operation of market forces cannot positively influence the meeting of housing need: as we have already discussed, the Barker review (Barker/ODPM, 2004) premise that by increasing the supply of land for housing for sale, the price of owner-occupied housing might reduce or stabilise, mitigating an (unknown) element of demand for affordable housing as more households would be able to satisfy their requirement through the market than otherwise, but the effect is truly unknown and very hard to predict in practice.

It is, however, unlikely that the satisfaction of housing need will ever be undertaken solely by the state, for the reason that it will always be held that the country cannot afford it. The monetarist argument followed in the 1980s that public expenditure in itself fuels inflation through increasing the velocity of money in circulation has lost some of its former force, especially since the excursions into quantitative easing in the late 2000s to attempt to ease the credit crunch in Western Europe and the US, although the influence of the cash limits system of determining production on the basis of a financial limit rolls on and on, rather than first deciding on a programme and then finding the means to finance it. It is therefore likely that we will continue to expect non-market housing producers endeavour to meet centrally set targets or aspirations through reliance on private market-place funding and reducing central allocations unless supply simply grinds to a halt, and then there will be probably be a big rethink, but well after the release of this book.

Postscript to Chapter One: Can planning reforms solve the problems of supply and demand?

The Localism Act 2011 introduced significant planning reforms in the form of local empowerment of communities who now have more influence over the quality and location of development but not its quantity. It also abolished regional spatial strategies as a cost-saving measure, and introduced the Community Infrastructure Levy, a development betterment tax on the basis of the increased value of land with planning permissions attached, which has already been referred to. None of this will make any impact whatsoever on supply and demand. The reforms are not designed to do this.

There are, however, ways in which planning can make a significant impact on the problems of supply and demand. Planning exists mainly to regulate the quantity and nature of development, to make sure that the amenity and utility of existing uses are not compromised by new development, and to ensure that there is some democratic control over the quantity and quality of whatever is proposed by those who wish to build. One of the ways it does so is to use land-use classifications to restrict or permit the development of certain types of development – for example residential, industrial, leisure – in certain areas defined essentially by a land use map. It also does so by imposing regulation and control on the form of building that can be erected. A free-for-all in any of these aspects would probably result in disaster – unrestricted development in areas of outstanding natural beauty, the loss of delicate and precious habitats forever, incompatible land uses next to each other with health and safety, not to say aesthetic, implications. Clearly there needs to be some control over what can be developed for the public good. But it is a matter of priorities. What matters most? That people should be decently housed in affordable accommodation, or someone's countryside view? That sites should be preserved for retail or industrial uses by the whim of some planning committee, or that there should be a presumption in favour of affordable housing development on any and every site which can take it, where there is need for it, where it could be economically developed, and where the health and safety of the occupants would not be compromised by proximity to incompatible (for example, polluting) uses? It comes down to the nature of society's value system.

In the view of the author, in addition to such a presumption, there should also be an absolute relaxation on the conversion of existing buildings to residential of all classes. That is, if a developer wishes to convert a building of any other class to residential, they should be permitted to do so if it would add significantly to the housing stock of the area, and that preferential permission should be granted to developers who intend to earmark some or all such dwellings for affordable use, perhaps further incentivised by a tax break on such development. There should also be a relaxation on density guidelines: good interior design can often offset the relative lack of space, as can be witnessed in the more fashionable quarters of most great cities, and it should not beyond the wit of creative architects to square this circle.

There is also a case for imposing a planning requirement on all public land disposals that planning permission be restricted to residential use including a mandatory amount of affordable housing dictated by the outputs of the housing needs survey or HMA for the area, subject to location. That is, if there is a deficit of such housing and the land is located in close proximity to employment opportunities, and if there are no health and safety or specific conservation issues, there should be a presumption in favour of sustainable residential development, where sustainability is qualified mainly be ensuring that people have somewhere decent and affordable to live. It should also be the case that, to enable this, any receipt to the government should be ploughed back into the scheme to ensure that the affordability targets are met and that there is proper infrastructural provision in social, economic and environmental terms.

The tenor of this argument, which will be pressed home in Chapter 6 on development, is that planning should be the servant of meeting housing requirement, not the other way about, and that this should be a primary purpose, given the level of unmet need in many areas which is nothing short of a disgrace and an indictment of our so-called civilised society.

References

Barker, K./ODPM (Office of the Deputy Prime Minister), (2004) *Delivering Stability: Securing our Future Housing Needs*. Final Report. London: ODPM.

Chadwick, E., (1842) *The Sanitary Condition of the Labouring Population, London*. Available at: www.victorianweb.org/history/chadwick2.html, viewed 28 January 2012.

DCLG (Department of Communities and Local Government), (2007) Strategic Housing Market Assessments: Practice Guidance. London: DCLG.

DCLG, (2010) *Estimating Housing Need*. London: DCLG.

De Friend, R., (1978) The Housing (Homeless Persons) Act 1977, *The Modern Law Review*, 41 (2): 173–83.

Griffiths, (1988). *Community Care: Agenda for Action*, London: HMSO.

Joseph Rowntree Trust (no date). *Housing and Neighbourhoods Monitor: Demographic Trends*. Available at: www.hnm.org.uk/charts/demographic-trends.html, viewed 24 January 2012.

Lansley, S., (1979) *Housing and Public Policy*, London: Croom Helm.

Malthus, T., (1798) *An Essay in on the Principle of Population*. London: J. Johnson.

Maslow, A. H., (1943) A Theory of Human Motivation, *Psychological Review* 50 (4): 370–96.

ODPM (Office of the Deputy Prime Minister, (2004) *Housing Research Summary. The Impact of Overcrowding on Health and Education: A Review of the Evidence and Literature*. London: ODPM.

ODPM, (2006) *Housing Health and Safety Rating System Operating Guidance*. London: ODPM.

ONS (Office for National Statistics), (2007) *Key Population and Vital Statistics*, No. 34. Newport: ONS.

ONS, (2011) *Divorces in England and Wales, 2009: Statistical Bulletin*. Newport: ONS.

Sanderson W. C. and Scherbov S., (2010) Remeasuring Aging, *Science Policy Forum* 329: 1287–8.

Shelter, (2004) *Toying with their Future*. London: Shelter.

Smith, A., (1776) *An Inquiry into the Nature and Causes of the Wealth of Nations*. London: Printed for W. Strahan; and T. Cadell.

Thomas, P., (2002) Legislative responses to terrorism. *The Guardian*, 11 September. Available at: www.guardian.co.uk/world/2002/sep/11/september11.usa11, viewed 29 January 2012.

TSA/CLG (Tenants' Services Authority/ Communities and Local Government), (2009) *Overcrowding and under-occupation: Self-assessment for social landlords*. London: TSA/DCLG.

Tucker, I., (2011) *Economics Today*, 7th edition. Mason, OH: South-Western Cengage Learning.

UK government (no date). The 1948 National Assistance Act. Available at: www.legislation. gov.uk/ukpga/Geo6/11-12/29/section/21, viewed 28 January 2012.

UK parliament (no date). The ageing population. Available at: www.parliament.uk/ business/publications/research/key-issues-for-the-new-parliament/value-for-money-in-public-services/the-ageing-population/, viewed 29 January 2012.

United Nations, (1948) Universal Declaration of Human Rights. Assembly res. 217A (III), 10 December 1948. Available at: http://atschool.eduweb.co.uk/redschl/historydocs/Poverty %201830-1939%20A%20Level/The%20Poor%20Law%20Amendment%20Act% 201834.doc, viewed 28 January 2012.

2 Customer involvement and empowerment

Keywords: *development of consumer and customer cultures generally; political, social and economic drivers to customer empowerment; the rise of the customer in housing – Citizens' Charter to co-regulation; empowerment and the law; regulatory standards and local offers – theory and practice; models of involvement and empowerment; resident compacts; self-management options – the rise of the tenant management organisation; localism and its possible impact on customer empowerment.*

Introduction

'The customer is always right'. This is a saying associated with the retail entrepreneur Marshall Field, who established a department store in Chicago in the late nineteenth century. It is also said to be a favourite maxim of Harry Gordon Selfridge who founded Selfridges in London in 1909; and the phrase '*Le client n'a jamais tort*' (the customer is never wrong) is attributed to Cesar Ritz, a French hotel entrepreneur who established the hotel and restaurant of the same name in London's Mayfair. In retail this is a reasonable proposition. If you try to sell a thing that nobody likes, or that everyone finds fault with even though the product or service may have some use-value, unless it is an absolute necessity and you are a monopoly supplier, you will probably go out of business because someone else will make something or supply a service which people like more (or detest less) than your offering. The same is true of political parties vying for office. The voter is always right. If you alienate voters, you won't get in, which is why politics in the UK and indeed in most Western democracies tends to be middle of the road, as, by offending as few people as possible, you are likely to stay in power.

However, is this unconditionally true? We can all think of cases where a customer might demand a good in a shop in the belief that it will meet their needs or indeed their aspirations, and when they get it home, it turns out not to be the case, like an ill-fitting suit which looked good in the shop mirror, or the appliance of science which turns out to be less effective that the old-fashioned machine it was bought to replace. In these cases we might fairly say that the customer turned out not to be right, although they thought they were at the time. Similarly, we might also argue that a customer who buys a product which is the result of slave labour, or that of small children exploited in some unregulated sweat shop half way across the world, is not making the correct ethical decision and is therefore wrong to buy the good.

In conclusion, we might fairly say that in terms of commerce, if the desire is to sell something and make a profit, then it is reasonable to assume that the customer is always right, find out what they actually want, make it, market it, sell it and make as much profit as possible, and keep on finding out what people really really want and even try to tell them that this is actually what they want even if they do not. However, in other words, we can also hold that the customer is not always right, but almost never always wrong, due to some fact about the product or service at the presentation end or in its mode of production or origin. Another reason, and one which leads us into this chapter, is that is if they need it, they must have it whether or not they want it or have any opinion about it. The matter of whether they consider that they are right or not is irrelevant. If they thought that it was wrong, they would be mad. We all need air, and our opinion about whether this is right or not is neither here nor there. If someone asserts that they do not need air or do not want air, they are either non-human or insane. Another reason why the opinion of a customer may be irrelevant at best or marginal at least is where they do not know what is good for them. For example, a child may say that they do not want a certain medicine because it tastes unpleasant. That medicine may be absolutely necessary for the ongoing health of the child – the administering doctor knows that – and there may not be an alternative; the addition of sweeteners may in fact dent the efficacy of the drug. In this case, the child is wrong, or their opinion is at best irrelevant, although it would perhaps be nice if someone invented an equivalent medicine which tasted nice.

Turning to housing matters: everyone needs somewhere to live. Those with money can afford to choose where and how to live, within limits, but let us leave these folk to one side for the moment. The size of your household determines the size of the dwelling you require, and the nature of your ability or disability determines the detail of its design. The development costs and method of financing plus regulation determines the amount you shall pay for living there, and the law determines exactly your rights and responsibilities, with latter enforced by officials who are there to ensure that peace reigns on account of all the residents exercising their responsibilities as laid down and getting what is due to them. There is absolutely no room for debate on any of these points. It doesn't matter whether residents consider these points right or not, or even like them, that's the way it is. And if that's the way it is, why should those who live in housing provided to meet housing need and regulated absolutely by the law of the land have any say in the form of housing they get, or how the services are delivered, since essentially things are as they are, and no amount of debate will or should make them any different? The experts in the matter are the officials who understand the law, who know how to effect repairs, who know how many people should fit into a dwelling of a given size, and who have an overview of housing policy and strategy which is bigger than the aspirations and fears of the individuals who happen at any one time to live in the dwellings over which the local state or housing charity exercises stewardship. One might as well entrust the flying of an airliner to the sentiments of the passengers, and dictate the use of the controls by a majority vote.

There is – we can feel it – something very suspect about this line of reasoning. Hardly anyone would ever argue this way about social or affordable housing these days. The mantra and self evidency of resident involvement and consultation in virtually every aspect of housing policy and practice is everywhere, and it is a universal working assumption that it is a good thing in itself, and unquestionably the way forward. Go to virtually any housing association website or annual report and you will find some statement to the effect that the organisation is committed to customer/resident/tenant empowerment and involvement, with no further justification. So what is wrong with the line of reasoning which says that because housing is something that you need, that the need is dictated by the size and requirements of your household, that the way you live in it is determined by your rights and obligations at law, and that the rent you pay is dictated by regulation and finance policy, your opinions about whether you need it and what you need are irrelevant and you should just put up with it as those who delivered and manage it are experts and know more than you do about it, even if you live in it?

What is wrong is that the product and service associated with social and affordable housing is not delivered in a uniform manner in terms of quality: landlords do not always get it right, and residents are best placed to tell them when they get it wrong. Second, the provision made relates to the needs of individuals, and individuals being aware of the nature and extent of their needs are best placed to say whether their needs are being met adequately or satisfactorily. Third, they are paying customers: they part with their money in return for a service, and are therefore entitled to complain if the level of service is lower than what the landlord has promised in return for that payment, or to make suggestions as to how the landlord can improve their game to meet the service levels to which they are signatory. At root, here is nothing particularly specialist about the delivery of housing services; most people live somewhere, and therefore have an awareness of what they might expect to enjoy in a dwelling and what is not acceptable. A house is not like a medicine where one is only concerned with the effect (an unknown requirement to produce a known or desired consequence); it is or should be the known/understood consequence of known requirements. Therefore the opinion of the occupant is in most important respects as valid as that of the provider or manager. This justifies resident involvement in the provision and management of social and affordable housing.

The development of customer and consumer cultures

One of the first recognised housing managers in the modern sense was Octavia Hill (1838–1912). She came from a relatively privileged background (her family were corn merchants in Peterborough) and applied the values inculcated by her mother, Caroline Hill, to her approach to housing management. Her mother was active in encouraging her daughter to take part in domestic responsibilities and to work with her in administering and enthusing the Ladies' Co-operative Guild when they moved to London, which encouraged dignity through work, especially among poorer people. She was befriended by the artist John Ruskin, who encouraged her in developing a scheme to house poorer people which she had begun to devise, which was bolstered by a bequest left her by John Ruskin's father in 1864. Octavia bought some properties in Paradise Place near London's Marylebone High Street, refurbished them, and let them to 'respectable' lower paid working people at rents guaranteeing a 5 per cent return on her investment, with a sinking fund built in which could be used by tenants on common-use projects such as playgrounds which would benefit them. By 1874, due to reinvestment and her skill in obtaining financial backers' interest, she had 15 housing schemes with around 3,000 tenants – the size of a medium-sized housing association. In 1884, the Ecclesiastical Commissioners invited her to take over the management of their significant tenanted property holding in London.

This is impressive by any measure: so what was her management method which attracted investors and the church alike? She was enamoured of the principle that the best form of help is assisted self-help, not an uncommon sentiment in Victorian England, and a concept popularised by the writer and social theorist Samuel Smiles in his book, *Self-help* (Smiles, 1859). Interestingly, and in a way resonant with today's holistic approach to housing need including employment and educational advice often delivered as a part of an Enhanced Housing Options Service, she was also concerned to influence pathways into work, education and constructive leisure pursuits, although the last of these is not usually at the top of this list in today's social engineering approaches to craft 'the decent citizen'.

She preferred to refurbish and improve existing properties rather than build new ones. This arose from several concerns, including the wish to minimise the impact of development on rural areas abutting towns, which has an echo of the much later Green Belt policy, and shared the concerns of many Victorian philanthropists in relieving the appalling slum conditions in many inner cities of the day.

She is, however, most remembered for her distinctive approach to housing management, and her approach influenced generations of social housing managers. When we come to examine housing management in greater detail in Chapter 3, we will notice districts similarities between Octavia Hill's and contemporary approaches, as well as some significant departures. In the present chapter, I focus on her view of her tenants to contrast it with more contemporary viewpoints. She thought that an important aim of social reform should be to create or enable 'the useful worker' (see Hill, 1877). By this she meant a working person who would contribute not just to the national economy but be a good neighbour, a respecter of property and others. The implication is clearly that such cases were few and far between, and the task of the enlightened liberal was to ensure that these values were inculcated in errant members of society to make the world a better place. However, it is important not to caricature Octavia Hill as a do-gooder with a fixed generalised image of 'the poor' and equally rigid ideas about how they should be 'improved'. She devoted much time to studying the life of poorer people, including her tenants, in a quest to understand their needs and aspirations as a foundation for devising improvement plans. In order to endeavour to reach out to 'the poor', she engaged volunteers to visit them and give budgeting advice, and even pointers to getting a better job. She was strict on rent collection (and anti-social behaviour): arrears were not tolerated and met with eviction, as she wished to honour her guarantee of a 5 per cent return to investors.

The central point to take away is that she did not see tenants as customers, but as recipients of services and advice and as a source of rent, to be encouraged into good ways. Rather, society was the prime customer, and tenants would be beneficiaries of such improvement projects. It is doubtful whether she conducted any surveys to establish exactly what people wanted in terms of accommodation and services, as she already knew the answers. Interestingly, some of 'the poor' begged to differ. Octavia also established playgrounds in London which were supervised by paid workers. The motivation was not only to provide safe playing areas but also education, as the playgrounds also had a teaching facility. A charge was made for access. Some of these playgrounds were vandalised during the construction stage, which may be a reflection of the resentment some felt towards her improving tactics. Again, the main customer was society, and benefits to individuals were purely collateral.

The view of tenants as recipients of services rather than customers with rights, aspirations and obligations persisted until the early 1980s in very many organisations, and does raise the very interesting question of what social housing is actually for, as posed earlier in this work. On one level, it is clearly to ensure that people who cannot compete in the market place have somewhere decent to live which they can afford. There is no necessity to import any notion of customer choice into this definition – it could be done on an objective definition of need and resources without any reference to aspiration whatever, and without giving distinct rights to such individuals. On another level, it is there to ensure that society coheres, on the assumption that mass homelessness of large numbers of people housed in appalling conditions might give rise to social unrest. Again, there is nothing here which implies anything about (or that there should be an ascription of) customers.

There is no clearer expression of the objective view of tenants as recipients of services and people who need to be controlled for their own good than the statement that if you provide tenants with bathrooms, they will only keep coal in the bath. Looking at the Guinness Partnership website, there is an extract from a 'typical tenancy agreement' from 1949, which states that 'The bath was to be used for bathing only and not for any other purpose (it was common for people to keep coal in the baths!)' (Guinness Partnership, no date). Quite why it would be expected that tenants would generally keep coal in the bath is a mystery. It would be clearly inappropriate to do so, and not the sort of thing that one might expect of a rational human being and certainly not an action of someone which could fairly be termed a customer with aspirations and opinions worth noting. It can only be assumed, therefore, that tenants were not regarded as customers and that others knew what was in their best interests and that this 'objective' view would guide delivery.

It is not known when this attitude changed, and it would be wrong to think that it was at any time a general or exclusive view. However, it is worth reflecting that it was only in 1980 that the raft of arbitrary and landlord-centric contractual tenancies held by local authority and many housing association tenants were replaced by a the statutory secure tenancy form which clearly set out tenants' rights and responsibilities. It is likely that the emergence of the view of tenant as customer was influenced by factors and trends outside the housing world.

Political, social and economic drivers to customer empowerment

Enfranchisement (or the lack of it) is an excellent indicator of the way in which the state sees citizens. Today, in the UK, we take voting for granted as the way in which governments are legitimised through the parliamentary majority system, and most people of 18 and over are enfranchised. This is the case in most countries, although in some democracies is seen more in the breach than observance, despite the pretence of democratic elections and representatives allied to a number of parties. However, before 1832, enfranchisement was very limited, and votes for women (aged over 30!) were only granted in the UK in 1918, although some form of suffrage existed in Sweden from 1718. The path to enfranchisement has been a long one, and tenancy reform and the emergence of a customer culture in that area has lagged far behind it.

Other changes which have helped inculcate a customer culture include the increase in social mobility and breakdown of the old rather rigid class system in the UK and other parts of Europe. Deference was the hallmark of the class society. This is not the place for an in-depth discussion and appraisal of various theories of class, such as those propounded by Marx, Weber and Dahrendorf, but the ascription of upper, middle and working class/lower class are still to be heard today, and the proof that people still believe that there are class divisions is in the pudding of popular humour. Accent, dress style, locality and to a certain extent manners are often held to characterise and to an extent be characterised by class. Whatever one's view of the dynamics of class, one of the features of being middle class is that you defer to the upper class, and a major feature of being working or lower class is that you defer to both the middle and upper classes. Social status is still very important in the UK, although it has declined somewhat.

If deference is assumed to be a key feature of the class system, it can be understood why, in a class-ridden society, social tenants might be regarded as mere consumers rather than active customers with rights and obligations whose views should be taken into account. Those setting the rules are (or were) people of high status (often coinciding with economic power, to try to reconcile the Marxian and Weberian approaches to class theory), and therefore those of a lower class would be expected to defer to their judgement on what is right and wrong. There would be no reason to take account of the views of the deferee under these circumstances; and indeed this was the case regarding landlord and tenant law before the 1980s.

As the class system has weakened, so has deference. It is hard to say when the system started to decline in significance: we all have a concept of the grand age of class – some think of the Victorian and Edwardian era of servants and *Upstairs–Downstairs*; others of the cloth-capped multitudes marching to London in the Great Strike of 1926; and we all believe that this system has now all but crumbled. It may have done so as a result of a number of attritional factors – the wasted millions of mainly working-class lives during the First World War at the behest of aristocratically driven bids for conquest; the Bolshevik revolution in Russia of 1917, the real-term increase in wealth of working people in the 1960s enabling them to afford luxuries previously the preserve of the middle and upper classes, and the cross-class appeal of popular music and fashion, driven by the new mass media from the late 1950s. It is instructive to consider a number of texts on the subject which examine the breakdown of the class system and analyse it in terms of economic change, media influence, globalisation, and any number of other factors (for example Lipset and Bendix, 1959; Goldthorpe et al., 1969). What is certain is that 'class' as a fundamental concept and social regulator has all but disappeared in the UK and Western Europe, and was never a fundamental factor in US society. It has taken deference with it.

Yet another factor is the rise of consumerism. There is so much product choice these days, so much advertising and marketing even of basic commodities such as bread and toilet rolls, that people think that being able to choose between brands is a basic human right, which is why the old Ford dictum that you can have any car as long as it is black is found to be amusing. Ford produced black cars from 1914 until the 1930s because it is much more cost-effective for the producer to produce standard models including finishes and there was far less competitive pressure on car manufacturers than there is today. Consumerism was added by the rise of the mass media and especially the television, which could expose variants of products to the masses and extol their relative virtues. Legislation to regulate the rights and obligations of consumers followed this expansion (for example the Consumer Protection Act of 1967), as did magazines such as *Which?*, devoted to assisting consumers make informed choices and avoid scams. Consumerism as a concept has a relatively well-established pedigree, with the first recorded use of the term in 1915 in the Oxford English Dictionary, which defined it as advocacy of the rights and interests of consumers, but nonetheless it only found its mark in the 1960s. The rise of consumerism dovetails with the increase in real wages in the 1960s in the industrial world and virtually full employment – more money to spend, more things to buy, more commercial income, more things that can be produced, more things to buy, more jobs created and so on.

Choice is a feature of consumerism, and with choice comes critique. Buying one brand of the same thing rather than another is a choice not necessarily dictated by price or even quality, but often by slick advertising and peer pressure, but there will always be a reason to buy x rather than y. The idea of redress follows consumerism closely. If the product is not up to expectation, it is common to seek redress, and producers often welcome complaints and negative critique as it may help them improve their products and increase sales. This is why many firms producing consumer durables, as well as those offering services, use focus groups of consumers to establish their aspirations and dislikes before launching products on the market-place; and all serous retailers use questionnaire surveys and to try to up their game to steal a march on their competitors. The concept of choice and the utility of consumer evaluation were well established by the end of the 1960s and it is therefore no surprise that they influenced the landlord–tenant relationship two decades later. It is surprising that it did not do so before then.

All of the influences mentioned contributed towards a sea change in the way in which tenants were viewed from the 1980s, compared to earlier decades. Housing, even social houses, was starting to be seen as a consumerist commodity like any other, even if foundational, where choice was a factor as well as redress. Housing consumers were seen as paying customers, with rents that could perhaps equally be used (just in theory though in many cases) to pay for a mortgage or private rent, as levels of affluence rose. One of the proofs of this is the development of the Right to Buy – the fundamental choice as to whether to rent or buy the dwelling initially supplied on the basis of housing need by a local authority. In the UK, councils have been selling off dwellings to sitting tenants for decades, and many did so on a voluntary basis well before the 1980 Housing Act conferred the right. Examples include the voluntary sales scheme of Wandsworth Council from 1978. There is no doubt that dwellings built by councils were originally intended for rent, and that selling them seems to subvert this purpose, although it does beg the question as to whether they should always be seen as the preserve of those who cannot afford to exercise their choice in the market place – although that's where we seem to be going back to currently with the 'conditional tenure' option within the Localism Act.

Before we leave our brief look at influences, it is worth mentioning the impact of the housing cooperative movement on the development of active (or should it be termed, reactive) consumerism on social housing delivery and management. It is not a UK concept: there were many housing cooperatives in the sense of resident-owned and managed blocks in nineteenth-century Germany, and the earliest coops in the UK were developed in Victorian times, but they grew significantly in number from the early 1970s, and were positively encouraged by funding and advice by the Housing Corporation in that decade. There are several varieties of coop ranging from mutual ownership institutions to housing management organisations, some on a statutory footing, but the fundamental common factor is that those who live in the properties make decisions as to the style of management and development of new properties (if any) and that policies and procedures are decided in the main by democratic vote. The producer is also the consumer, with no fundamental conflict of interest between the functions as they are embodied together. The Co-operative Development Society (CDS) website contains a reasonable history of the movement (CDS, no date).

Further evidence of the impact of the consumerist ethic on social and affordable housing is to be found in the emergence of tenant participation and involvement in not only the management of estates but in helping to determine development and management policy. This is something that Octavia Hill would neither have welcomed nor tolerated, and some organisations still appear to look at the concept askance or obey the regulatory letter rather than the spirit.

Citizens' Charter to co-regulation

Given the development of consumerist society, it was only a matter of time before the law enshrined the rights and obligations of council and housing association tenants in the form of the secure tenancy, and the Right to Buy as a beacon of tenure choice. It should be remembered that in the early 1980s council tenure was in many areas an expression of choice in itself, and not the reserve of the needy. This is reflected in pre-points or banding allocation systems of the day. For example, when the author was a housing advisory officer working for Cambridge City Council in 1982, anyone aged over 18 could join the council waiting list who was living or working in the district and who was not an owner-occupier, and keys would be virtually guaranteed after a two-and-a-half year wait. Many joined the waiting list in anticipation of being able to buy a house at a discount of around 33 per cent after a qualifying period: council housing was seen by these people as a route into relatively low-cost home ownership, and much of the stock was in good condition and in pleasant areas with no stigma whatever.

Arguably, choice is one of the hallmarks of consumerism. If so, choice became firmly embedded in the social housing firmament, having been given impetus by the Right to Buy and the right to exchange, and from the mid-1980s onwards in the form of the Tenants' Choice and large-scale voluntary transfer initiatives. The idea behind Tenants' Choice was that tenants could elect to choose a new landlord by majority vote if they wished to switch collectively from their council. In fact this was sparingly used, with just two such transfers before the policy was scrapped. A far more pervasive choice which was taken up en masse was large-scale voluntary transfer, enabled initially by the Housing and Building Control Act 1984 and refined by the Housing Act 1988, which saw 1.16 million council homes transferred to housing association landlords by 2008 on the basis of majority tenant votes informed by offer documents setting out the pros and cons of so doing. The first of these was the transfer of the stock of Chiltern Hundreds District Council to the newly formed Chiltern Hundreds Housing Association in December 1988 of 4,650 properties. The extent to which this is a reflection of consumerist pressure is, however, debatable, as the proposals were initiated by councils themselves and not at the behest of tenants, often for financial reasons and in many cases to ensure the continuation of an adequate repairs and maintenance, and getting homes modernised and improved. The policy was sold on this basis, explicitly following the 2002 Housing Green Paper, *Quality and Choice – a Decent Home for All* (DETR, 2002) as one of the options for getting council stock up to Decent Homes standard.

The big push towards regarding tenants as customers with choice, rights and obligations as opposed to mere recipients of a social good who needed to be kept in line by their betters came after John Major's Citizen's Charter. The Citizen's Charter was promulgated in 1991 as a series of bills of rights for all users of public services, emphasising the rights of public users, their obligations and access to complaint mechanisms. John Major, the prime minister of the day, said:

> It will work for quality across the whole range of public services. It will give support to those who use services in seeking better standards. People who depend on public services – patients, passengers, parents, pupils, benefit claimants – all must know where they stand and what service they have a right to expect.
>
> (Major, 1991)

There was considerable publicity at the launch of this initiative, and leaflets about the charter contents were to be found in every library, council office, Citizens' Advice Bureau, doctor's surgery and social security office, up and down the land. As far as housing was concerned, the rights and obligations were clearly laid out, and included an improved local authority Tenants' Charter, further opportunities to transfer away from local authority control, a stronger tenants' guarantee for housing associations, and the extension of compulsory competitive tendering into the field of housing management.

The floodgates for consumerism in housing had been opened, and the flow continued. In 1993, the Leasehold Reform, Housing and Urban Development Act provided for council tenants with the ability to exercise the right to manage, following on from successful experiments by the Priority Estates Project in the mid-1980s into tenant control of housing management. The regulations were launched in 1994, along with a model modular management agreement which enabled tenants to take on as many or as few functions as they wished, subject to a majority vote of secure tenants on the 'property' (the patch subject to the management agreement proposal) with leaseholder and in some cases freeholder sentiment taken into account. Significantly, this was (and still is) accompanied by a test of competency, with tenants on the provisional board having to demonstrate that they are capable of effective governance including the control of housing management, maintenance and repairs functions, along with budgeting and client-contractor liaison. Tenant Management Organisations (TMOs) can be anything upward of 25 secure tenancies in size, and evidence suggests that satisfaction levels are higher in all respects than for council landlords who manage the stock themselves, although there are variations. Consumerism is also represented in the fact that TMOs are subject to a five-year confidence ballot, and their boards are dominated by resident-elected members, although some have manifestly failed to include leaseholders and freeholders on boards, even though they enjoy services from the TMO and pay for them through service charges levied by such bodies. This is discussed further in Chapter 7 on localism, but at their best TMOs represent one of the better forms of resident involvement.

Further expressions of tenant involvement in the local authority sector came after the right to manage in the form of the Tenant Participation Compact initiative of 1999 and its replication in the housing association world, albeit on a voluntary basis, followed through by the formation of the TSA (since abolished) in 2009 and its six consumer-centric regulatory standards launched on 1 April 2010, covering all 'registered providers', chiefly housing associations and stock-owning councils, based on tenants' survey and outreach research in 2008 and 2009. Currently, under co-regulation, residents and landlords interact to produce policy and strategy and service standards, and tenant scrutiny bodies act as sounding boards for new initiatives and a critical friend (at best) in examining performance.

The Tenant Participation Compact initiative was launched by the housing minister of the day, under the so-called duty of Best Value, which came into force on 1 April 2000, and which enjoined councils to demonstrate that their services had been influenced by residents' views, as well as providing the best possible value compared to other providers in the social housing sector (see ODPM, 2005). The compact was essentially conceived as an agreement between councils and their tenants, setting out how tenants could get involved collectively in local decisions on housing matters which affected them; what councils and tenants wanted to achieve locally through compacts, for example, better ways of working together, improving local services or a better quality of life; and how the compact would be put into action and monitored for efficiency and effectiveness. Evidence had to be given that such compacts were negotiated with tenants rather than drafted in some back office and launched on the council's web. Thus tenants as consumers were considered to be vital as a driving force for policy, strategic and operational improvements. At their best, such compacts were living documents, subject to annual review and updated in the light of best practice, experience and new primary and secondary legislation, and the philosophy of drafting such living agreements was adopted wholesale by the housing association movement, encouraged by their regulator and grant funder of the day, the Housing Corporation. They acted as a stimulus to tenant involvement and helped to revivify many moribund or ailing tenants and residents' associations, and borough-wide tenants' federations and forums which had hitherto in many cases been tokenistic moaning shops with no power, albeit having a social function and providing an effectless opportunity to let off steam and provide status to active citizens and the self-important and loud alike. Some councils engaged independent advice agencies such as the Tenant Participation Advisory Service and Priority Estates Project to assist them in brokering deals, as in many cases there was some distrust between landlords and tenants and dialogue became difficult, drawn away from common purpose by hidden agendas and the indignation of not a few councillors at seemingly being usurped of their democratic standing and purpose by a bunch of tenant representatives consorting directly with officers who had a direct responsibility to members.

The emergence of tenant scrutiny committees and co-regulation following the initiation of the TSA from 2010 are logical extensions of tenant participation compact philosophy. The basis for tenant scrutiny is that tenants are paying customers and therefore have a right to redress if the product or service falls below that contractually guaranteed, or in any case below their legitimate expectations defined locally and in terms of national regulations or standards. There is nothing new about tenant scrutiny: this was often performed by tenant federations (at an estate level) by tenants and residents' associations, but arrangements were often rather ad-hoc and unaccountable. It seems a reasonable business proposition: many companies employ focus groups to scrutinise product proposals and to give reactions to piloted brands before general release to reduce the risk of market failure, and this methodology has been part of the commercial kitbag for at least 40 years – so why not in the public sector, which also delivers products and services albeit mainly on a needs basis and with less competitive pressure?

The current position is that the Coalition government, while it supports the principle of tenant scrutiny in the sense of tenants being able to hold their landlords accountable for poor performance and that they should working a partnership context with their landlord to co-regulate delivery, it will not prescribe the form in which this is done, as long as the function is performed. Just as well perhaps, as it is unlikely that there will be particularly effective surview of these matters by an over-stretched housing ombudsman service and a multi-functional Homes and Communities Agency which has taken over the bulk of the regulatory functions of the TSA which have not been disbanded altogether.

Empowerment and the law

The only legislation which gives landlords a duty to empower tenants is the right to manage provisions of the 1993 Leasehold Reform, Housing and Urban Development Act which enable secure tenants of local authorities to establish a TMO. All other legislation refers to consultation and a bar on large-scale stock transfer without a majority vote. This is not really empowerment, by which I mean genuine moves to give tenants some sort of power over the day-to-day running of their homes and possibly the development of new social and affordable housing. However, I will concede that if consultation is undertaken properly and considered seriously, it can make a measurable difference to policy and practice, and in this instance a degree of empowerment may have been demonstrated in that there is a direct causal relationship between opinions expressed and what actually happened.

Consultation

Section 105 of the 1985 Housing Act requires councils in England and Wales to consult tenants on proposed changes in housing management arrangements. However, looking at the text of the section, there is a great deal of discretion as to how councils can do this, and case law proves this beyond reasonable doubt. The text of the section is as follows:

105   Consultation on matters of housing management

(1)   A landlord authority shall maintain such arrangements *as it considers appropriate* to enable those of its secure tenants who are likely to be *substantially affected* by a matter of housing management to which this section applies,

    (a)   to be informed of the authority's proposals in respect of the matter, and

    (b)   to make their views known to the authority within a specified period;

    (c)   and the authority shall, before making any decision on the matter, *consider any representations made to it in accordance with those arrangements.*

It is clear from the above that councils have to let tenants know what they propose to do. This is surely reasonable, as tenants are paying customers who finance the services they receive, and may have a view on the value for money such proposed changes represent.

There is no set format for consultation, or any guarantee whatever that the result of such consultation will be taken on board in the development of housing management policy or practice. To illustrate how these provisions have been used, many councils who wished to establish ALMOs to garner central government grants to ensure their stock met Decent Homes Standard by 2010 wrote to their tenants asking for their opinion of this proposal. No doubt many tenants replied on the basis of the often scant information on options supplied, and I am convinced that councils took these comments seriously, but since there was no requirement for a ballot on the matter, most councils who wanted to steamed ahead anyway and established ALMOs. One or two ran ballots, which showed good form, but this was by no means the majority policy. Many councils set up focus or discussion groups and invited comments from their tenants and residents' associations or tenants' forums in the lead up to the decision, and I am sure that this input was thought through by the decision makers, but since councils did not have to put this to the vote, the result may have been as it was in any case.

Thus, the subject matter to which consultation relates is circumscribed. For the purpose of the section, housing management covers '(a) the management, maintenance, improvement or demolition of dwelling-houses let by the authority under secure tenancies, or (b) the provision of services or amenities in connection with such dwelling-houses', but not rent or service charge provision, although councils at one time had to consult tenants on the annual proposed rent rise. The reason for the exclusion is that the rent restructuring formula is the way in which secure tenancy rents are now set; this is the government's expectation, so there is really no room for debate about the matter. However, there is a case for consultation on the level of affordable rents, which are supposed to be set at up to 80 per cent of market rental levels. Councils have the power to develop such accommodation and re-let on this basis if they wish. Since the legislation says that rents should be up to 80 per cent of market rent rather than at that figure, surely this allows some window of consultation before setting the actual rent, perhaps on the basis of comparative expenditure models linked to service levels – a menu-type approach.

There was extensive consultation by councils of tenants before CCT was introduced in 1991, even though the government insisted that councils go along this path, and one wonders what the point of such a consultation was if it would have happened anyway. In the author's view, there is only a point in consulting people if their views could make a difference to the decision, otherwise you might as well just get on with it.

Yet effective consultation which will have some effect is absolutely vital to the interests of tenants and leaseholders, in fact anyone who lives in property managed by social landlords, since any changes, even those of a comparatively minor nature, will have an effect on their lives, for example, a proposal to move to a basic approach to repairs and maintenance on a health and safety basis on the grounds of affordability in relation to rent income. The rights embodied in tenancy agreements do offer some protection to the interests of tenants, and if they are not performed to these standards tenants may have some redress in law, but should tenants be forced to have recourse to legal remedies if landlords choose to offer minimal services which lower service standards, particularly where their rent is paying for them? Another example is where a council or other landlord proposes to redevelop or regenerate an area: is it enough to simply consult with those affected and then go ahead without being compelled to take on board the comments and fears of those who stand to lose their homes or be seriously inconvenienced by such proposals and take account of representations when they embark on such schemes? There is a parallel duty to consult on planning strategies which has been somewhat strengthened by the Localism Act 2011, but there are many instances where such projects have gone ahead in any case in the teeth of fierce local opposition with token consultation and involvement, as will be discussed and exemplified in Chapter 6 on regeneration. There is at least a moral case for effective consultation in such cases.

The argument against strengthening consultation duties is that local authorities are the democratic representative of the people in their designated areas, and that allowing a group of residents in one area to veto such plans would effectively be a subversion of local democracy. If local voters do not like the plans of the council, they can always vote their representatives out at the next possible opportunity; but the efficacy of this rather depends on the frequency of local elections and the volume of local opposition as opposed to the sentiment of all voters in the area, who will not all be directly affected by such developments and who will in any cases have divergent interests in its outcome.

Ballots

A ballot is a voting arrangement, and has been deployed in a number of housing and related issues over the past decades. It is required where there will be a change of identity of landlord, as in the case of large-scale voluntary transfers, of which there have (as of January 2012) been 299 in England and Wales (HCA, 2012) and, as has been mentioned, where tenants propose to take over the management of their homes. Large scale voluntary transfer entails not only a change in the owner of the stock, but also significant changes in the terms and conditions of tenancies and in some cases leasehold arrangements. One of the key features in the lead up to such ballots is the use of independent resident advice services to impartially advise tenants and other residents of the pros and cons of large-scale voluntary transfers. Their services are invariably paid for by the sponsoring councils, which is the case for 90 per cent of other cases where independent advisers are utilised. The reader might consider this to be odd, since clearly the council wants to achieve transfer and is therefore hardly impartial in this matter: and yet they are funding a service which might advise on balance that large-scale voluntary transfer is not in the interests of tenants and frustrate their aim. This is also the case where councils wish to progress regeneration initiatives where they wish to consult with residents: again, it seems odd that counter-advice should be funded by the body who has an interest in such projects coming to fruition. A much more satisfactory route would be for central government, or an agency such as the Homes and Communities Agency (HCA), to fund such advice so that no undue pressure can be put on independent advisory services to deliver their paymasters' messages.

In the case of large-scale voluntary transfers, if a majority of tenants do not wish the transfer to proceed, it cannot. The offer document is required to be as full as possible, spelling out implications for rents, management and maintenance conditions and tenure changes – and the likely gains, in terms of more resources for property improvement – as a basis for their decisions. In other words, consultation has to be fit for purpose in enabling rational decision-making, and not just information giving for the sake of it, which is what much so-called consultation amounts to.

Economic and social empowerment

Incoming tenants of local authorities and housing associations, whether they take up tenancies on a secure, assured or 'flexible tenure' basis, are more likely to be unemployed or less employment-ready than either long-term tenants who obtained their home before the total dominance of needs-based allocations or households in general. Approximately 60 per cent of social housing tenants claim housing benefit and this statistic has been stable for some time, although it grew during the 1980s when needs-based allocation systems started to dominate. DCLG statistics for 2009–2010 showed that 9 per cent of social renters were unemployed and 58 per cent were economically inactive, compared to 1 per cent and 36 per cent respectively of owner-occupiers and 7 per cent and 24 per cent of private renters (DCLG, 2011), and it is likely that this will grow with the increasing economic marginalisation of the stock. This is a waste of human resources, and many landlords have for some years endeavoured to empower unemployed and underemployed tenants to enable them to find work, through a variety of in-house schemes and those connected with the Ways Into Work initiatives promoted by local authorities in partnership with state agencies. This makes sense from the point of view of personal dignity, income management and collection maximisation in the absence of state subsidy, and reductions in anti-social behaviour. Housing associations started to develop work and training initiatives as part of their offer in the 1980s under the Housing Plus Scheme, which is now part of the National Housing Federation-sponsored In Business For Neighbourhoods programme. The programme, which was initiated in 2003, aims to supplement housing management and property offers with community-strengthening deals such as providing apprenticeship schemes, promoting residents' services organisations to provide a range of services such as grounds maintenance and day-to-day repairs, community wardens, school holiday clubs, healthy eating classes and low-cost loans. It is instructive to look at the National Housing Federation's InBiz website (NHF, 2012) to find examples of how housing associations have taken such initiatives forward, and the difference they have made through community investment. There is self-interest for housing organisations here as well: anti-social behaviour and worklessness are linked, and it costs money in terms of increased housing management and maintenance costs, so it makes sense to tackle the root causes of financial waste to help guarantee a healthy income surplus which can be reinvested in new and existing properties to meet housing need.

Models of involvement and empowerment

Involvement and empowerment models can be classified into three groups: passive, semi-active and active and effective. Examples of passive models include reliance on surveys, focus groups and newsletter responses to find out what tenants and other residents think about the service offered, without offering any significant input into the decision-making or scrutiny process. This is where most housing organisations were in the 1980s. Semi-active models are where residents groups or forums are set up by the landlord on a permanent, semi-permanent or task-oriented basis, and consulted with whenever the organisation wishes to implement a new policy or practice, or to undertake a development or regeneration programme, and asked for their opinion on how the landlord is doing, which could involve the scrutiny of a function or programme output (for example changes in arrears management). They are semi-active as they do not involve residents doing anything more than making suggestions. Active and effective models are where tenants and other residents are enabled to take part in the governance and management of the organisation, or even to take over that function, as is the case for TMOs and other forms of resident-led housing management organisations. We will now examine these broad classifications in more detail, with examples.

Passive models

These are well exemplified by the annual tenants' survey which most social and affordable housing organisations undertake. These started to become common following the requirement imposed on local authorities to provide annual reports to tenants on key aspects of their performance from 1990 onwards, which was abolished as a requirement and then revivified as a result of the TSA's 2010 housing standards which had regulatory force for all registered providers. Such surveys were often used as 'can-openers' to find out which aspects of the service needed attention through looking at comparative satisfaction rates between operations within organisations, and between 'peer group' members of similar bodies. The only activity that such surveys require, and this applies to focus groups too, is that tenants return them or discuss issues within the hearing of the landlord. Arguably, many tenants and residents' associations would also fit within the passive model if they are used mainly as sounding boards by landlords when proposing new policy or evaluating existing practices, as is tenant board membership of housing associations, unless they propose policy and practice reforms and campaign for change.

Semi-active models

A good example of of a semi-active model is a tenant scrutiny committee, set up by a landlord to monitor the effectiveness of its operations from a customer viewpoint, suggest changes and even in some cases suggest new initiatives. Such committees have been running for some time in the UK, and were stimulated by the national Tenant Participation Compact policy commenced in 1999, which gave rise to many resident-led deliberative forums. Some organisations have embedded such committees into their governance structure to the extent that no new policies can be passed by the board or existing policies modified unless the scrutiny committee has had a chance to examine and comment on them, regardless of whether there are tenant/leaseholder representatives on the governance body, even though legally the board is the housing association. It is common practice for such committees to be asked to examine a policy area in detail as it affects tenants (for example anti-social behaviour), to conduct a survey among users of its effectiveness and drawbacks, and to report back to the governance body on its findings to assist in service improvement. This may be supplemented by focus group activity, meetings, conferences and outreach events.

Such arrangements are categorised as semi-active in this chapter not for any pejorative reason, but because they do not imply tenant control over an organisation's activities, nor any sanctioning power. They are at best a very useful way of involving tenants in discussions about priorities and practices from the user viewpoint, and a method of breaking down barriers between the managers and those managed, as well as in some cases a precursor to more direct influence. They cannot be more than this, since such committees are not governance bodies provided for within the constitution of registered providers and there would be legal problems in devolving governance to them, including the expenditure of significant budgets, although this is more so in relation to local authorities than housing associations. Another example of semi-active involvement and empowerment is encouraging tenants to become board members of the association. This can only ever be semi-active in most formulations since the law prohibits a majority of tenants on any registered provider board, and therefore their views could never carry the day through their own democratic mandate unless assisted by other constituencies.

Active and effective models

For empowerment to be active and effective, those involved must produce some effect through direct control over a process. An example of this is where residents run a management board of a housing organisation, for example a TMO or cooperative, but it could be something on a different scale, for example, working in or managing a resident service organisation (RSO). The Joseph Rowntree Trust has defined RSOs as 'community-led enterprises, based in neighbourhoods, employing local residents to deliver local services' (Joseph Rowntree Foundation, 2002). A RSO is any group of residents who perform an economic function in their locality for monetary reward, and typically where they and their neighbours (those living in the patch within which they operate) benefit from this operation individually (for example they get their repairs done to a given quality at a set time, they learn new skills or enhance existing ones, and improve performance through practice and training) and collectively (for example the estate is tidier, the natural environment looks better through planting, there is a collective sense of wellbeing and ownership, etc.). The Joseph Rowntree Foundation publication gives examples of pilot RSOs studied between 1998 and 2002, including one run by Amicus Horizon housing association in the Ore Valley, Hastings, an area of high unemployment, and based on three estates of around 1,400 homes. The RSO undertakes caretaking and grounds maintenance, but at time of the report, was bidding for other contracts. Another example is in Stepney, where the RSO was developed by a specialist employment regeneration agency, SHADA, with close links to the Bangladeshi community and Tower Hamlets council. In addition to caretaking and estates maintenance, the RSO has also delivered pre-recruitment training courses to decrease worklessness in its area of operation. RSOs have a number of desirable features and outputs, including having a neighbourhood focus, being community led, delivering local services, earning revenue, employing local residents, targeting jobs and offering transitional employment leading to jobs in other organisations. They compare favourably to TMOs, community development trusts and local labour construction initiatives in all these respects. A cashless example which exemplifies the active/effective model is the Local Exchange Trading Scheme (LETS) 'bartering' arrangement, where local residents do jobs for others according to their skills, 'bank' points when they do so, and cash in their points by calling on the services of someone in the pool when needed. This scheme has the advantage of avoiding any benefits reductions, while up-skilling individuals and helping them towards employment. A number of housing organisations have encouraged residents to set these schemes up as part of their community investment function. Some LETS schemes were set up in response to demand from specific demographic sectors – for example the Quines LETS group in West Glasgow, where membership is only open to women. The coordinator is reported to have said:

> It's not a group against men, it's one that's for women. We set it up because some women were not very keen to have a strange man come in to the house. We also wanted to encourage women to learn things like plumbing and other skills usually monopolised by men.
>
> (Croall, 1997, p. 57)

LETS schemes can assist people with learning budgeting skills, making friends, engaging with the wider community, and certainly resonate with the 'choice and responsibility' and localism agendas. Most LETS schemes have their own non-cash currency which is associated with points earned, and some even have shops in which such currency can be redeemed along with cash. It is by no means difficult to see how a local LETS scheme could be set up which would at once utilise building and maintenance skills of unemployed or retired skilled workers and reduce the maintenance outlay of a housing association or other registered provider as well as empowering those working within it. RSOs could be set up on a cashless basis as well.

There is no ladder of involvement or empowerment; some may find passive forms quite acceptable, others may wish to comment on and scrutinise housing activities, and yet others may wish to take hold of the reigns of self-management, but housing organisations who wish to assist residents to realise their full potential and move them out of worklessness should have opportunities at all three levels available as part of their community investment offer.

Regulatory standards and local offers – theory and practice

Why, and to what extent should housing organisations be forced to embrace resident involvement and empowerment? On the face of it, if a housing body is performing well – doing repairs on time to good quality, controlling anti-social behaviour, collecting rent with a low arrears level, turning property over effectively and efficiently when it become vacant, and dealing with customers promptly, accessibly and courteously, surely these are marks of a quality outfit. So why should some official body regulate to ensure that residents are able to be involved in the running of housing deliverers? Why would a tenant or leaseholder wish to get involved in running or scrutinising housing services if everything is running well? And why should they feel the need to get involved even if things are not so good; after all, isn't that what staff are paid for, and what board members should oversee as governors?

To a certain extent, it is a question of economy. Co-regulation was a concept introduced by the TSA in 2010, and landlords were promised a lighter touch on regulation and inspection if they involved tenants in setting local performance standards and in scrutinising processes and outputs to some effect. The transfer of the regulatory function in England to the HCA is (at the time of writing) expected to entail a reduced emphasis on consumer protection and more on value for money, efficiency and effectiveness. By and large, registered providers have complied with the regulatory regime (TSA, 2010b) and have made and adhered to local offers. The regulatory standards include those laid out in Table 2.1.

Table 2.1 TSA regulatory standards

Standard	Containing requirements relating to the following areas
1. Tenant Involvement and Empowerment	• Customer service, choice and complaints • Involvement and empowerment • Understanding and responding to the diverse needs of tenants
2. Home	• Quality of accommodation • Repairs and maintenance
3. Tenancy	• Allocations • Rent • Tenure
4. Neighbourhood and Community	• Neighbourhood management • Local area cooperation • Anti-social behaviour
5. Value for Money	• Value for money
6. Governance and Financial Viability	• Governance • Financial viability

Source: TSA, 2010. Figure 1, p. 11

Compulsory 'local offers' were applied to the Tenant Involvement and Empowerment Standard, the Home Standard, and the Neighbourhood and Community Standard. There was outline guidance issued subsequently on how providers should go about negotiating local offers, or what their shape should be, and there was ambiguity about what 'local' meant: whether it should refer to a local service standard which would apply to a specific geographical area (for example a regional division of an housing association or even a specific part of a borough), or 'local' to an entire housing organisation. There was no extensive guidance on how providers should engage with tenants to broker such deals – for example, how such negotiation groups should be constituted. The TSA chose leave the detail and some of the definition substantially up to providers, evidence of the 'light touch' it applied generally throughout its brief existence.

The regulatory guidance issued in April 2010 said that providers, in offering opportunities for their tenants to agree local offers, should take account of (1) standards of performance offered to tenants, (2) how performance would be monitored, reported to and scrutinised by tenants, (3) what happens if local offers, having been agreed with tenants, are not met, which may include redress for tenants, and (4) the arrangements for reviewing local offers on a periodic basis. There was also a requirement in the Tenant Involvement and Empowerment Standard for providers to say how they would provide support to build tenants' capacity so they are effectively engaged and involved.

On the definition of 'local', the regulations stated that:

> It is not for the TSA to define this, but we expect providers to consider their obligations under the Neighbourhood and Community Standard in relation to local area co-operation, which requires meaningful co-operation with Local Strategic Partnerships and the strategic housing function of local authorities. Providers should therefore consider whether services to the tenants could be improved by participating in an area-based offer. In these cases it may be reasonable for a provider to define 'local' as the local authority area or a subset of it, such as a neighbourhood or estate. Providers are not under a regulatory obligation to agree local offers with local authorities. We recognise that some providers may want to tailor their services by factors other than geography such as in relation to demographics (for example older tenants).
>
> (TSA, 2010a)

This allowed local authorities and their managing agents to go down to quite small defined areas where they and tenants believed that specific actions are needed to address particular issues which are more prominent in those areas than in others (for example rent arrears, disrepair, lack of engagement, anti-social behaviour) which would otherwise have compromised the ability of the provider to meet the relevant standard.

It is too early to say how the HCA will adapt the regulatory code to focus on efficiency and effectiveness, nor how quality will be independently assessed by the Audit Commission or its successor, but in some ways the shift in emphasis shows that the transition from old-style housing management by landlord diktat to a type of partnership between service providers and consumers has now been embedded widely, or more probably that it has been embedded sufficiently to convince legislators that it is no longer necessary to inspect landlords in this area with a fine tooth comb.

Resident compacts

Chronologically, the development of agreements or 'compacts' between landlords and tenants as to how they should be involved in housing policy and management predates the regulatory regime already discussed, but in terms of influence, it is arguably more significant than regulation, and perhaps more pervasive. It has already been suggested that the impetus for such agreements arose out of the growth of the consumerist ethos in the public services in the UK, and that ethos is still current in the UK and elsewhere. It is therefore likely that these agreements will remain a semi-permanent feature of the social and affordable housing landscape for some time. It is also consistent with the current government's predilection with localism, citizen power and the Big Society which emphasises the role of local volunteers and organisations alike in running services and improving their communities, as a form of devolution of state power. If this notion is to be taken seriously, it implies that there should be a virtuous partnership between local governors and the governed, and that the balance of power should be tilted more to the latter than traditionally has been the case. If a social provider exists on the income of those for whom it provides, and if its existence is largely justified by the needs and aspirations of those it serves, it surely makes sense for it to take account of what its consumers are saying to enable it to more nearly focus its services and products to meet them. It also makes good sense in terms of sustaining and raising satisfaction levels, which has often been used as a key indicator of organisational health by regulators and scrutineers along with measures of financial viability and robust, rational and legal governance.

In the public sector, the policy that landlords should negotiate compacts between themselves and residents managed, principally tenants, was initiated in the local authority sphere in England and Wales in 2000 by the New Labour government, with similar arrangements for Scotland, following pilot projects to test their viability. A report on the initiative's progress (DETR, 2000), suggested that the main early output was the formation of resident panels, steering groups and forums set up to examine the performance of local authority housing providers, but that further work was needed to link these into decision-making structures. This work is, at the time of writing, still ongoing. The policy was spread to housing associations through guidance published by its then regulator, the Housing Corporation, including practical advice on how to involve residents in policy and practice discussions in 2007, updated by the TSA (TSA, 2010b), and has proved effective in fostering engagement. At their best, such agreements are living documents, updated as a result of changes in legislation and best practice in the sector and as a result of resident pressure for further involvement in policy-making and scrutiny. Many of the earlier compacts involved devolving budgets (subject to ratification by the governance body) to residents' representative groups to spend on estate environmental improvements, community-building activities such as employment clubs, and in some cases local management initiatives.

An interesting case study which shows that resident compacts primarily oriented towards involvement in housing management can be widened out to cover more general community matters is showcased in the TSA report (TSA, 2010b). In the case of CityWest Homes, Westminster Council's ALMO in London, services are delivered to 18 areas designated as 'villages' roughly corresponding to pre-existing areas recognised as 'home' areas by residents. Each 'village' has its own local service improvement compact (LSIC) negotiated between the managing agent and residents on a cross-tenure basis, with performance targets reviewed twice yearly. Initially, the compact concerned just housing management issues, but was widened to include community issues such as examining the impact of planning and development proposals in 2009, when the LSICs were renamed as residents' community compacts to address the change in scope. This development is particularly pertinent in the light of government policy to promote localist approaches to community governance and town and country planning in particular, crystallised in the provisions of the Localism Act 2011, and such compacts could easily form the basis for the development of neighbourhood forums with real influence over planning proposals and even community acquisition and management of surplus or under-used publically owned buildings envisaged in that act, as well as providing a significant support to other features of the Big Society such as volunteering and the development of local enterprise, through the use of transferable skills developed in taking part in compact negotiations and monitoring. Time will tell.

Self-management options – the rise of the TMO

Arguably, the pinnacle of resident involvement is self-management, where the locus of power is transferred from the custodian of rent and service-charge money to the rent and service-charge payers themselves. Philosophically this sits well with the notion of localism (as will be discussed) as well as providing a neat and (in best cases) balanced approach to power sharing between the owners of public or social resources and those who use and pay for them. The logic and justification of self-management flows from the proposition that those who live in premises and are of sound mind know best about their requirements, and that their opinions are therefore of paramount importance in deciding how their homes should be managed and what is an acceptable standard of quality for what they pay. Self-management enables the consumer to determine the nature and quality of the product that they are paying for, even if they do not own the properties themselves, which is a high form of empowerment compared to the experience of the consumer in the marketplace. For all the focus groups and interactive market research which companies selling things and services may indulge in, there is often little significant consumer determination of the end product or service; that is usually determined by the judgement of the producer mediated by uptake and feedback, and in competition with others. This is largely due to the relative imbalance of power between the manufacturer – the large company – and the consumer (the individual unit) and perhaps the power of advertising and marketing. In the case of self-management, the consumer is at once the producer and the quality standards associated with (in this case) the service are in the consumer's ownership.

Perhaps because of the suggested nexus between the service delivered and ownership of delivery, several respectable sources report that self-management organisations deliver services better than 'external' managers. One reports that TMOs in England 'are doing better than their host local authorities and compare favourably with the top 25 per cent of local authorities in England in terms of repairs, relets, rent collection and tenant satisfaction' (ODPM 2002). The same source cites reasons why tenants decided to set up TMOs, and mirrors the areas where they compare favourably. This indicates that such organisations often succeed in their objectives, if measured in terms of addressing areas of dissatisfaction. There is a very good history of the evolution of tenant management initiatives in the UK to be found in Power (1993), especially in Part 3 which focuses on the British experience, although there are some excellent studies of the development of the concept in Europe elsewhere in the work.

TMOs can take on as many or as few functions as they feel comfortable with, and can contract to take on further ones if they wish, and have the capacity to do so. They currently operate under one of two main agreements, either the original right to Manage modular management agreement arising out of the right to manage regulations published in 1994, or a revised and updated agreement launched in 2005 (DCLG, 2005). They are specific to local authorities in their statutory form– only their secure tenants have the right to manage – although some housing associations have adopted similar models. They come about after up to two years' hard negotiation and capacity-building, and then only if a majority of secure tenants vote for the proposition. They are also subject to five-year ballots of confidence, and have to report regularly to their client on performance indicators relating to all the areas they manage under contract. In some cases, TMOs have become housing ownership organisations, but this has been rare. These are truly resident-led organisations, as the boards consist of tenants, leaseholders and in some cases freeholders living on the estate or street properties managed, which in most cases employ and direct professional paid staff. Most local authority estates are multi-tenure, and it is essential that there is good representation of all tenures on boards to ensure that all residents genuinely feel that their interests are represented in governance. This is despite the source of the allowances, which are generally paid from the Housing Revenue Account, since many the management functions which are delivered have an impact on everybody. For example, the effectiveness and efficiency of grounds maintenance affects the quality of everyone's life, regardless of tenure, as does the way in which anti-social behaviour is handled. There may be issues about how the expenditure should be apportioned between income primarily derived from tenants, but most services are rechargeable, and there is nothing to stop councils paying TMOs from their general funds to undertake activities which benefit the community as a whole, for example employment advice and sustainment projects and training activities aimed at younger people. Additionally, TMOs are often used under the terms of their contract as the estate consultation agent, for example in the case of major regeneration projects, and it is hard to see how the TMO can effectively do so without governance representation from all tenures to avoid the charge of partiality.

It has already been mentioned that other registered providers, such as housing associations, can foster local management initiatives on a voluntary basis, even though they are not currently required to by the law. The author has had experience of trying to encourage housing associations to consider self-management having been approached by tenants and leaseholders mainly in blocks and estates who wish to pursue this option among others, or at least enter into discussions with their landlord on ways forward. The response has been variable, which leads to the question as to what the route might be to persuade such organisations to consider localist alternatives.

At the time of writing (February 2012), the HCA, which is primarily a funder of housing association development through disbursement of grant money from the National Affordable Housing Programme, is preparing to take over the regulatory functions of the TSA in England. It is clear from their published views that they will focus on economy and efficiency when regulating the sector rather than consumer protection, which will presumably be dealt with by the ombudsman if tenants and other residents are unable to get satisfaction through the organisations' complaint processes. Economy and efficiency at ground level translates into value for money in respect of the service-charge element of the weekly payment ('rent' in common usage), and driving down unit costs across housing organisations generally while maintaining service levels expected by the law, regulation and the organisation's own performance regime, as well as helping to meet tenant expectations individually and collectively, signalled through surveys and the resident scrutiny process. This being so, any initiative likely to (a) reduce the service charge element of the weekly payment and (b) the unit costs of housing providers would presumably go down well not only with tenants and its board, but also with the regulator, given the new value-for-money focus.

If landlords are unwilling or feel unable to initiate the options investigation process, tenants, leaseholders and other residents operating as a tenants' and residents' association or another form of collective body might consider making a researched proposal to deliver a limited range of services through contracts with local maintenance firms and the like, which may prove to be cheaper than those already provided, but at the same or even better quality than those currently provided. If landlords express nervousness about a long-term commitment, which is entirely understandable, the services could be delivered on a pilot basis for, say, six months, after a reasonable and audited work-up period. That way, and if the contracts succeeded in delivering against the organisation's own performance indicators, and if economies and efficiencies were demonstrated during the trial period, it is likely that they may agree to talk to the residents' body about further services it could take on in the future, which may eventually result in a greater degree of self-management and tenancy management, subject to negotiations and the assistance of an independent adviser.

Clearly, to assist the residents' body to put together such a proposal, they would need a detailed breakdown of the costs of the functions they would like to provide via their own contracts from their landlord. This would enable them to contrast and compare the prices offered by local contractors with the cost of the existing service elements, and make their case.

It would also be necessary for the residents' body to demonstrate that it has the financial and management acumen to manage such contracts to the standard required by the landlord, and capacity training may be needed as well as verification. There is very little reason for landlords to refuse such approaches, unless they hold the dated belief that they know best how to manage the stock, and that rent-paying customers' views are of interest only in assessing the quality of the service through surveys and the like to present a positive picture of their business to those who need to see it. Another approach would be to persuade the regulator to unilaterally fund housing association tenant-initiated self-management proposals, or the government to extend the right to manage to housing association tenants in line with its localism and Big Society aspirations.

Perspectives on local management from elsewhere – the Swedish experience

Sweden is in many ways a good exemplar for the development of tenant management organisations in the form of cooperative ventures. The course of its development dates from 1923, when tenants' organisations set up an umbrella organisation, HSB Riksförbund organised as discrete regional bodies, to make representations to the government and political parties to garner support. Their agenda was relatively simple: everyone, regardless of means or tenure, should have the chance to manage their own housing communities, although they also lobbied for increased funding to develop affordable housing. The result has been the so-called 'mother and daughter' approach to development, where larger 'mother' secondary coops develop and then sell homes to smaller 'daughter' organisations, who then manage the homes. The majority of the smaller coops buy administrative repairs services from their regional HSB, which helps achieves economies of scale and to maintain consistency of delivery quality. There have been significant changes in the development funding of such coops over the last 30 years, in that there is no longer any state subsidy for this, and new developments are financed through a combination of share capital and member resources raised by the individual coops and commercial development loans. Members are responsible for maintaining their own homes, while the coop is responsible for maintaining common areas and facilities. The coops are governed by a board selected from their own membership, and staff are hired locally or through HSBs. Transferability of this model to the UK would involve examining the structure of existing self-financing coops, of which there are good examples, and assessing the degree to which existing social tenants were able to raise finds to part-finance major repairs and improvement works collectively in the absence of significant state support through the National Affordable Housing Programme – but it is a model which bears investigation, and it would give tenants a financial as well as a management stake in their homes and communities.

The future?

The concept of tenants managing their own estate using funds which would otherwise have been used for this purpose by their landlord is not in principle a complex one and nor is that of co-ownership, subject to means. There has recently been little innovation in this area, but the austere second decade of the twenty-first century is surely as good a time as any to consider how to get greater buy-in from those living in social or affordable housing, through extended community management agreements which go beyond the housing function, subject to the competence of those who wish to take up such opportunities and the political will at local and national levels to promote this. We will turn again to this theme at the end of the chapter.

Localism and its impact on customer empowerment

Localism, as espoused by the UK's Coalition government and embodied in the measures of the Localism Act 2011 is a tremendous stimulus to resident involvement and empowerment, and could deliver some of the outcomes mentioned in the previous paragraph. The concept of localism is that democratic power should be devolved to the lowest geographical level possible, subject to the competence of local communities to manage their affairs and with the need to retain some public functions for management at less-local (for example local state, national) levels. So far, legislation has been concerned mainly with extending planning powers – plan-making and development control functions – to local communities at parish or neighbourhood forum level, subject to demand and the democratic status of such bodies, and with significant overview on the part of local authorities who still retain primacy in the hierarchy of local decision-making. In housing terms, localism has so far been confined to giving councils more say in the way they allocate housing and the form of tenure granted, including the option of a time-limited flexible tenancy and a reduction in the regulatory influence of central government and its agents, combined with financial freedoms in respect of the expenditure of rental income in exchange for the abolition of national revenue subsidy arrangements in April 2012.

It is too early to say what the impact of 'statutory localism' – the powers embodied in the Localism Act 2012 – will be, but it is possible to speculate. Another concept which dovetails with localism is that of the Big Society, which emphasises the importance of voluntarism in delivering services which were once delivered by local authorities or other funded bodies, partly driven by the austerity measures which have been thought necessary in the light of macroeconomic challenges.

It is entirely conceivable that, if and when local planning bodies which are controlled by community representatives take off and have an influence on the nature and location of developments of all classes (although not necessarily on the quantum – see Chapter 6), the government may decide to enable them to adopt housing management powers as well. This would truly devolve housing management and maintenance to the local neighbourhood level, albeit as an option which needs to be brought about by ballot, as with neighbourhood planning bodies. There is no reason why such bodies should be tenure specific: they could be based on the neighbourhood as a geographical entity and cut across ownership boundaries, with stock owners contributing what they would have spent themselves into a general pot to be disbursed by the local management agency. Because the stock owners have a financial interest, they could be members of a joint financial and performance scrutiny board, which makes legal as well financially prudent sense as the arrangements would probably be in the form of a contract between the local forum and each owner.

Volunteering, as has been said, is a key component of the Big Society concept, and could form a significant element of housing devolution to local groups. When Prime Minister David Cameron launched the concept in July 2010 in Liverpool, shortly after the formation of the Coalition government, he emphasised the role of voluntary groups in running public services such as libraries, post offices and transport services, as well as housing services. One of the most memorable things he said on this occasion, which is indicative of his general philosophy in this respect, is that Big Society schemes would represent 'the biggest, most dramatic redistribution of power from elites in Whitehall to the man and woman on the street' (BBC News, 2010). He indicated that some of the resources could come from dormant bank accounts, but there was some scepticism from the voluntary sector as to how the projects would be adequately funded. Since then, various pilots have been launched to test the concept, notably community-run schools and libraries, with variable degrees of take-up and success. In July the following year, the Big Society Bank was launched with £600 million, managed by a former head of research for JP Morgan, an international bank. £400 million of this was resourced from dormant bank accounts, and the remainder from four national UK banks which benefited from government bail-outs following the 2007 credit crisis, under the terms of the Merlin Agreement brokered at the time. At the time of writing, there are mixed messages on progress, with some on the parliamentary cross-party Public Administration Committee urging more focus on engaging new providers and small charities not hitherto involved, and greater clarity on its objectives. Tax breaks for Big Society providers have been suggested to incentivise action, along with a Big Society minister to focus efforts which are spread across departments. Much reliance is being placed on the provisions of the Localism Act which lays out the legal foundations for democratically constituted community groups to take over public assets and a limited number of public functions, and it is not yet clear whether there is a sufficient head of steam or reserve of volunteers to take up the opportunities available.

Perhaps part of the answer could be to set up a national initiative to take proposals from communities interested in managing housing 'patches' which may include a variety of owner organisations and tenures, vet them for legality, consistency, lack of duplication and financial coherence, and then issue an instruction to local authorities to recognise the group and provide it with the resources it would have used for the equivalent function. It would be harder to legislate to require non-public bodies to devote equivalent funds to assist such groups to run, and unrealistic to expect that the Big Society Bank could possibly meet these costs – it would be best to reserve this for start-up funding, publicity and guidance, as well as perhaps funding a training academy for volunteers to equip them with the necessary business, management and operational skills which they might need to acquire to run local enterprises if they do not already have them.

There is also, perhaps, something to be said about encouraging enterprises which rely on local communities for their profits (for example, large supermarket chains) to help fund such initiatives at a local and national level, through directing some of the funds from the Community Infrastructure Levy development betterment tax given teeth by the Localism Act, both to the Big Society Bank and to the accounts of community organisations, in addition to 'in kind' benefits such as office space, equipment and staff assistance. Part of the rationale for this is that by sustaining such initiatives, which will probably involve developing the skills of workless or underemployed members of the community who are seeking full-time work or training to facilitate this, they will be contributing to the growth of the local economy as volunteers of this sort gain paid work. It may also be possible to divert some of the considerable revenue that the government receives from such organisations through corporation tax yields to funding local initiatives through grants to local authorities as enablers, or directly subject to proofs of competence, financial prudence, and achievement of objectives.

In conclusion, there is plenty of scope to develop resident involvement and empowerment to a greater extent than now, and a very good social and economic case for so doing which dovetails nicely with cross-party political aspirations to devolve power to those who benefit from local services.

References

BBC News, (2010) David Cameron launches Tories' 'big society' plan. 19 July, London: BBC. Available at: www.bbc.co.uk/news/uk-10680062, viewed 9 February 2012

CDS (Co-operative Development Society), (no date) A brief history of the co-operative movement, available at: www.cds.coop/coop_movement/new-to-co-ops, viewed 2 February 2012.

J. Croal, (1997) LETS Act Locally. London: Calouste Gulbenkian Foundation.

DCLG (Department of Communities and Local Goverment), 2005. *Volume 2: Right to Manage: Modular Guidance Management Agreement for Tenant Management Organisations – Guidance on the schedules*. London: DCLG.

DCLG, (2010) *Review of Social Housing Regulation*. London: DCLG.

DCLG, (2011) Housing and planning key facts. Available at: www.communities.gov.uk/publications/corporate/statistics/keyfactsmay2011, viewed 4 February 2012.

DETR (Department of Environment, Transport and the Regions), (2000) *Tenant Participation in Transition: Issues and trends in the development of tenant participation in the local authority sector in England*. London: Housing Support Unit.

DETR, (2002) *Quality and Choice – a Decent Home for All*. London: DETR.

Goldthorpe, J., Lockwood, D., Bechhoffer, F. and Platt, J., 1969. *The Affluent Worker in the Class Structure*. Cambridge: Cambridge University Press.

Guinness Partnership, (no date) Down memory lane, available at: www.guinnesspartnership.com/about-us/about-the-partnership/our-history.aspx, viewed 2 February 2012.

HCA (Homes and Communities Agency, 2012. LSVT statistics table, available at: www.homesandcommunities.co.uk/ourwork/existing-stock##lsvt, viewed 4 February 2012.

Hill, O., (1877) *Our Common Land*. London: MacMillan.

Joseph Rowntree Foundation, (2002) *Findings, 472: Resident Services Organisations: Lessons from the pilot projects*. York: JRF.

Lipset, S. and Bendix, R., (1959) *Social Mobility in Industrial Society*. Berkeley, CA: University of California Press.

Major, J. (1991) Speech by Rt Hon John Major MP to Conservative Central Council annual meeting, 23 March. Available at: www.publications.parliament.uk/pa/cm200708/cmselect/cmpubadm/411/41105.htm, viewed 4 February 2012.

ODPM (Office of the Deputy Prime Minister), (2002) *Tenants Managing: An Evaluation of Tenant Management Organisations in England.* London Office of the Deputy Prime Minister.

ODPM, (2005) *Tenant Participation Compacts – a Guide for Tenants.* Wetherby: ODPM publications.

National Housing Federation, (2012) In Business for Neighbourhoods site. Available at: www.housing.org.uk/get-involved/in-business-for-neighbourhoods, viewed 4 February 2012.

Power, A, (1993) *Hovels to High Rise: State Housing in Europe since 1850.* London: Routledge

Smiles, S., (1859) *Self-Help: With Illustrations of Character, Conduct, and Perseverance.* Oxford: Oxford World Classics.

TSA (Tenants' Services Authority), (2010a) *The Regulatory Framework for Social Housing in England from April 2010.* Manchester: TSA.

TSA, (2010b) *Making Voices Count.* Manchester: TSA.

3　Housing management and maintenance

Keywords: *what is housing management; social engineering versus rights and respon-sibilities; general needs housing management; alternative management strategies – in-house and arms' length; managing the patch; there goes the neighbourhood; special needs housing management; special consideration groups; households who suffer economic and social discrimination and disadvantage through racial, ethnic or cultural status; unfavourable medical or related conditions; possession of other characteristics meeting with social disapproval and marginalisation; street sleepers; other victims of societal prejudice – gypsies and travellers; students; victims of domestic violence; refugees and asylum seekers; the management of temporary accommodation; Decent Homes and asset management; repairs and maintenance; systems thinking approaches to repairs and maintenance planning and provision; securing value for money; a repairs service for the future; some organisational management issues; recruitment, job design and business planning; staff retention; the future of housing management.*

Introduction

Housing management is more than about managing housing. As has been said in the introductory chapter, the core functions involve ensuring that the landlord's obligations are performed according to the tenancy or leasehold agreement, and that the tenant or leaseholder likewise performs their obligations. This encompasses a wide range of activities, including collecting rent and service charges, performing reactive and planned maintenance, ensuring that the stock remains in good condition and is improved to reasonable standards depending on the statutory or regulatory requirements of the day, and ensuring that friction between residents is at a minimum, according to the expectations of the tenancy agreement. There is, though, a lot more to housing management than this, much of which arises from the way in which social and affordable housing has been allocated in the past and currently, and this is likely to be increasingly the case as a result of the primacy of the reasonable preference 'need' categories in informing allocations policies, even though there is some scope for local variation, and also in relation to the flexible tenancy option for local authorities following the Localism Act 2011 which may residualise estates even further. These conditions require a considerable focus on activities which relate to community sustainment, including work and training initiatives, welfare benefits and budgeting advice, signposting into alternative forms of tenure on or off-patch. It also means that housing management will be increasingly concerned with dealing with customers requiring specific management on account of needs related to disability, health or other factors which make them less able to manage independently than others. There is also a high degree of customer segmentation in terms of client groups, which poses its own challenges and explains why there are so many niche housing management organisations and housing functions performed by bodies which have something else as their primary objective. For example, the management of student accommodation by universities which are primarily educational providers; that of tied accommodation, where it still exists, by public and private sector employers which may include the procurement and supervision of privately owned properties; and that of luxury housing for highly paid international executives who need to be close to their corporate head quarters to do effective business, although the latter category hardly falls within the ambit of social or affordable housing! It will be necessary to examine the most appropriate way of managing customer segmented housing along with 'general needs' approaches, and we will not be dealing here with high-end markets.

The task of ensuring that housing management approaches respect the diversity of communities and deliver a service which will not be worse for one equalities strand than another is essential, and not just because the law requires it. The populations of housing management patches are often highly diverse in terms of race and ethnicity, age, sex, sexual orientation, religion/faith, disability and other relevant characteristics which people value, and approaches to individuals and even the nature of management-related issues (for example anti-social behaviour) may vary per group, and it behoves organisations which have the responsibility of managing community homes to address and respect their diversity in their management offer.

A notable feature of the past 20 years in the UK has been the outsourcing of housing management on the basis of testing alternative providers to establish which ones are more efficient and effective, often justified by reducing public purse costs, or as a matter of convenience for the owning organisation or a combination of these. Sometimes this has resulted in innovatory and improved services to residents of all tenures – TMOs have already been discussed in this context – and at other times service standards have declined as a result. Outsourcing seems to be a constant of UK housing policy, and also something which has happened across the developed world, and it is important to examine whether and to what extent this affects the customer experience as well as the structure and function of housing businesses themselves.

Housing management can be divided into people and property themes. The former is what may be called tenancy management, the latter asset management, but they are interactive and interrelated. If people live in warm, dry, well-provisioned homes which are reasonably up to date and enjoy a repairs and maintenance service which is timely and effective, it is likely that they will be more satisfied with their accommodation than otherwise; and if there is a problem with the asset management side of the equation it is likely that discontent may manifest itself in complaints and possibly less care than might otherwise be taken in abiding by tenancy agreements, although there is no automatic causal relationship implied.

Asset management is of abiding importance to providers of social and affordable housing. At root, it is about maintaining the property in a good condition consistent with its function for as long as possible, and that it performs its function efficiently and effectively in relation to existing and future customer requirements. Another aspect to asset management is to ensure that the asset retains its value for a given period of time, especially where loan finance has been raised against stock, and in anticipation to sales to sitting tenants where the organisation will seek to maximise its receipt subject to any discount rules applying at the time. It may also wish to sell its housing assets either in part or wholly to another organisation at some stage, in which case it has a fiduciary interest in ensuring that the stock is kept in best condition. Finally, there are legal imperatives which penalise stock owners for allowing property to fall below a given standard in relation to the needs of occupiers. There have been many approaches to maximising asset values and returns over the past few years, coinciding with (but not wholly attributable to) the move to a mixed funding financial environment for housing association development from the late 1980s, and policies encouraging the disposal of local authority stock to other providers. Significant changes in the way that local authority housing revenue costs are financed, principally the move towards HRA self-financing, provide the sort of incentives to councils to concentrate their minds on asset management that others have had for some years. It is not just about financial resources: there are various methods of conducting reactive and planned maintenance and improvement programmes which vary in cost-effectiveness and which can impact on other areas of the business such as work creation and training initiatives. Housing management is, then, a diverse and extensive area with significant challenges from internal and external environments and it is important to understand its limitations and possibilities when considering its impact on those who matter most – those who live in the housing which is its subject.

What is housing management? Is it social engineering?

The functional question has already been answered ostensively by identifying its two divisions and content falling within them, but there is the more philosophical question of what housing management is for. Bluntly, is it a social engineering function devolved from the national to the local state or non-state providers and managers, is it property protection, or a reasoned response to the legitimate demands of rent and service charge payers, or does it involve all of these to a greater or lesser extent? By social engineering, I mean the practice of trying to achieve an overriding social objective by manipulating people to act in a certain way and/or hold given views so that they are compliant with the ends desired and the means to be used. This philosophy was espoused in a very obvious but ultimately unsuccessful way by state communist regimes in the early to mid-twentieth century, and by Hitler's Nazi state in the 1930s and has been the subject of many fine fictional works, for example George Orwell's *1984*. Social engineering relies on a social scientific approach to discovering what the key levers which regulate society are (assuming that there is such a thing as society, and if so what sort of entity it is), and then considering the best way to manipulate them to effect the desired solution. There is no consensus on the correct theory, and testing of such propositions will always be controversial and morally questionable, but best guesses have been made over the years. The reader may wish to pursue the definition and scope of social engineering further: one starting point is the philosopher Karl Popper's influential book *The Open Society and its Enemies* (Popper, 1971) or any half-decent sociology textbook (for example Haralambous et al., 2008). I will take it as read in this chapter that readers are familiar with at least some of the theoretical approaches, if not their consent to their propositions and reasoning.

In terms of social engineering, housing management could be seen as a way of ensuring that those who find it hard or simply cannot compete in the market place for suitable housing on account of lack of resources or some other disadvantage can play a part in the functioning of society by providing a secure affordable home. This, as has been argued, is foundational for any positive interaction in society, including obtaining and sustaining education, training and employment. Therefore, a failure to provide or to manage such a foundational resource for the benefit of these people would risk eroding the worth of the social capital they represent. In this term, I include their actual or potential contribution to society through work, neighbour-liness, raising children who may also be of use in meeting societal ends, but not as ends in themselves. In more straightforward terms, not to provide a housing management service to provide for the needs of and to an extent to regulate the behaviour of those who live in it would compromise the supply of lower-paid functions which are necessary for society's health. There is also the view that unless some form of robust housing management service were provided, those living in such housing might become discontented, with implications for the security of society as a whole or at least those who do not have to resort to it. This is rather an unsympathetic view of society, as an organism which is straining at the seams due to incompatible or at least different objectives of players, and that there needs to be some functional way of ensuring that things do not get out of hand for the benefit of all, or at least to the benefit of those who hold the upper hand and have the most to lose from societal dysfunction.

Under this view of society, the most drastic and controlling measures in relation to housing management are justified. There can be no risk to the common good through failing to ensure that tenancy agreements are enforced, that estates are peaceful and not the font of mayhem there or otherwise, that rent is paid to sustain the management function, and that those living in the dwellings managed have a healthy respect both for the condition of their homes and for the organisation and its staff. If people are viewed as a means to an end rather than an end in themselves, many things can be justified, for example, demolishing the homes of well-established communities and relocating them elsewhere en masse or in a dispersed fashion to enable some objective of the local or national state – for example to develop the area to attract a different sort of client group who may contribute more cash to the local system and private enterprise and see the area primarily as a dormitory from which to access the workplace. The ends of social engineering also justify the regulation of behaviour by introductory or probationary tenancies to ensure that the 'right' sort of person is living in an area, and flexible tenure where households will lose their entitlement to their home once they are able to move to another form, such as home ownership to make way for households standing in need of that property. It depends on how you look at it – and theories of social organisation are just that. However such theories, even if and probably especially where they are informally held and not reflected upon, can and do influence social policy and practice on the ground, of which housing management is an established part.

Is it about rights and responsibilities?

An alternative view is that housing management in its widest sense is there to serve the aspirations and other requirements of those who choose to or otherwise find themselves there, in return for their contractual payment. This could be called the 'rights and responsibilities' model which is based on the English law approach to the relationship between people and people, and between citizens and the state. This is probably as wide of the mark as the social engineering model, but some aspects of the way in which housing management is justified and conducted approximate more to this underlying theory than to the other.

Under this approach, there is no underlying or wider control mechanism; individuals living in homes managed by social and affordable housing providers are regarded as citizens with a series of rights granted by the law and responsibilities also sourced from legislation. It is assumed that at their best, residents will act as rational people in full knowledge of their rights and responsibilities, and that, also at their best, landlords will supply the range of services that they are contracted to do so under their agreements (notably and most straightforwardly, the tenancy agreement). Intervention is only necessary where one side or the other fail to deliver against their obligations, and where rights of the individual, those in the vicinity of an individual, or of the organisation, are compromised.

The rights and responsibilities model is the one which most social and affordable landlords would probably claim to follow, embellished somewhat by the desire to develop social capital – for example through providing training, involvement and in some cases economic betterment and tenure choice options.

The rights and responsibilities agenda has heavily influenced government welfare provision in the UK since at least 1997, so it is not surprising that it has also influenced the management of housing directed towards relieving need where approximately 60 per cent of tenants are at any time in receipt of some form of state housing support. An example of the evolution of the agenda is in the New Deal approach to job-seeker benefits promoted from the late 1990s and continued in spirit currently, where the 'option' of deciding to remain on benefit without actively seeking work, where there is a capability to work, has been removed. The underlying principle is that the individual has a contract with the state which demands that they endeavour to contribute something to it, and only if this is the case can they expect any support from the state when required. In housing management terms, it could be said that this translates into the thought that people have the right to social housing only if they act responsibly, and in the absence of this, that right can justifiably be removed through enforcement of the tenancy agreement.

The rights and responsibilities agenda is bound up with the concept of the 'active citizen': the citizen who takes responsibility for his or her wellbeing and who is unwilling simply to be the passive recipient of public or semi-public services. Examples of active citizenship in the form of resident involvement and self-management have already been given earlier: in terms of housing management short of self-management, active citizenship translates into a willingness to do the things which are required in the tenancy agreement to maintain standards in the home and environment – for example doing tenants' repairs, promptly reporting main-tenance issues, reporting anti-social behaviour rather than assuming someone else will do so, and alerting the housing management organisation (or another appropriate agency) when an isolated neighbour appears to be in need of social care or medical intervention rather than turning the other way. None of this requires heavy-handed intervention on the part of the housing management organisation; rather an encouragement to act in a certain way by exemplification, incentivisation and definitely not through coercion. Incentivisation to move out of an under-occupied dwelling to a smaller home to free up living space for a larger household living in cramped conditions elsewhere in the stock could be seen as an exemplifi-cation of the rights and responsibilities approach in that in taking up the incentive (rather an being coerced into it), the tenants recognise that they have a responsi-bility to consider the needs of others in relation their own, where an alternative is offered which would suit their needs, even though they could continue to exercise their right to live in the under-occupied home. This is being modified through the introduction of flexible tenure in the UK, where under-occupancy could be the spur to non-renewal; here, the responsibility element is being given somewhat greater weight than the rights element.

In practice, however, modern housing management is actually a mix of the social engineering and the more liberalistic rights and responsibility models, although it is in practice difficult to assign each function into the respective camp. Allocation systems, which give rise to management challenges, are certainly a form of social engineering, as the likelihood of being housed (and often where a household is housed) depends on the weight of needs assessed in relation to others, modified by the organisation's community-building aspirations (for example to increase the proportion of employed people on an estate) or in an area justified by the economic sustainability model advanced by Hills (2007) in *Ends and Means*. This inevitably gives rise to neighbourhoods which are characterised by un or under-employment, a lack of employment role-models, and in some cases dysfunctionality giving rise to higher than average level of anti-social behaviour. However, having allocated in such a matter, the housing management response is to endeavour to enforce tenancy conditions while all the time recognising that tenants should be left alone (in the main to exercise their responsibilities, otherwise the management task would be very labour intensive and costly which would fly in the face of endeavours to create leaner organisations and probably be unfundable in any case). Within the management task itself, taken broadly, some aspects lean more towards social engineering, for example, steering tenants into work and training, and ensuring that gardens are properly maintained (which could be seen as trying to ensure that all residents' actions are influenced in a certain direction by peer pressure), while others lean more towards rights and responsibility, for example, guidance to tenants on how to effect minor repairs and indeed allowing them to enter into contracts with maintenance suppliers to effect even the landlord's repairs on occasions, and clear information at the start of each tenancy on its terms and conditions, updated when the law or policy changes.

General needs housing management

The term 'general needs' is supposed to distinguish the housing and management services provided for households without any specific needs, apart from somewhere decent to live, from other groups who, through vulnerability as a result of illness, abuse, youth, disability or age, are less able to secure accommodation for themselves than others and who require a more tailored housing management approach. Housing for non-general needs customers used to be referred to as special needs accommodation although this term is now thought to be too pejorative, although supported housing is a phrase which is often used in the industry in this context. What, then, are the key features of general needs housing management?

First, it is about balancing the interests of landlords and tenants, to ensure that rights and obligations are observed. This is fundamental in helping to ensure that the property is in a fit condition to be re-let (or in some cases sold on) and does not represent a disproportionate drain on financial resources preventing expenditure on other properties or services within the landlord's remit, and that those living in the dwellings are able to do so in a manner consistent with modern living, income, freedoms and household requirements.

Second, it is about endeavouring to guarantee that communities live harmoniously together. Lack of this can threaten both the assets themselves, in terms of damage or even destruction in extreme cases and the welfare of those who live in them; and there are costs associated with disharmony and some of the behaviour which can arise from it, for example, those of repairing the fabric of homes and the opportunity costs of officers' time spent on resolving anti-social behaviour cases and related complaints. The nature of the housing management task in this respect is often related to the way in properties have been allocated: corralling people with multiple needs together or creating high child densities might present their own challenges as regards patch management. Likewise, the built form may well influence behaviour – for example, tower blocks which are relatively dense in occupation terms and where there is little play space within the blocks may be associated with a higher number of anti-social behaviour complaints relating to noise compared with lower-density estates characterised by traditional house types. However, it is very difficult to establish a causal link between built form and behaviour, although several academics have tried to show the nature of the connection, for example Alice Coleman (1985), in *Utopia on Trail*, who tried to associate crime with specific physical aspects of dwelling and estate design. Several housing providers (for example Westminster City Council, on the Mozart Estate) have taken on board her remodelling ideas and have removed features which are supposed to provide opportunities for escape for burglars and muggers, including raised walkways connecting blocks. We will return to this theme in the Chapter 6.

Third, it is about ensuring that revenue is realised from the dwellings to ensure that the service is financed. This is very vulnerable to changes in social security policies and operational arrangements, as will be further explored in Chapter 4. For example, the impending move away from housing benefit being paid direct to landlords which has already affected the private rented sector in England in the social and affordable rented sector except in the case of financial vulnerability as a result of welfare reforms to be rolled out from October 2013 has given cause for concern to many landlords who have hitherto relied on tenants to sign over their housing benefit to them as a way of preventing arrears. At the time of writing, it is not clear whether the reforms will be amended to enable social and affordable landlords the comfort of direct payments by tenants' consent in some albeit limited way, nor whether councils who have previously rebated (reduced) the rent will be partially or completely exempt from this regime. In addition to giving welfare benefits advice to maximise income, general needs housing management may also seek ways of encouraging tenants to take up sustainable employment where they do not have this as a way of building their capacity to pay the rent and spend on other items without getting into debt or budgetary problems, as well as a way of reducing the dominance of underemployed or unemployed households in some neighbourhoods. This is in many ways a positive reaction to Hills' (2007, p. 1) three key questions:

- What can social housing do in helping create genuinely mixed communities?
- Can the way we run it encourage social mobility and opportunities, including in the labour market, for people to get on in their lives?
- Can social housing and other support be more responsive to changing needs and enable greater geographical mobility?

There is some controversy over these aims and objectives, but they seem to have been taken on board in housing strategies and practices.

One of the consequences of housing management as a way of endeavouring to control behaviour and promote harmonious communities has been the proliferation of introductory tenancies or probationary tenancies in social housing, following the 1996 Housing Act, a sort of 'try before you buy' tactic to establish the social credentials of tenants before granting lifetime tenancies, and latterly the creation of flexible tenancies following the Localism Act 2011, which are partly conditional on tenants acting in a way consistent with the idea of community harmony, as well as encouraging tenure diversity through a form of means test towards the end of the arrangement to establish whether tenants have the ability to move to other forms of housing arrangements such as home ownership. Another has been the increasing emphasis on the control of anti-social behaviour through housing and related legislation.

There has also been a growth in the expectation that tenants will have a greater degree of self-sufficiency than previously. This is manifest not only in the promotion of resident-led housing management organisations, which has already been discussed but through self-help policies such as the right to repair and schemes encouraging tenants to contract directly with contractors to undertake repairs which landlords would previously have effected. In 2011, the UK Coalition government launched a scheme whereby social tenants would receive up to £1,000 – roughly what social landlords spend on average on repairs and maintenance per property per year – if they chose to do repairs themselves or through a contractor. The idea was that the £4 billion repair bill picked up annually by social landlords could be significantly reduced if tenants claimed money from their landlord to do a range of repairs themselves, and would be incentivised to do so by being able to keep the difference between what they received and their actual expenditure. The primary motive for this may have been to save money for landlords to deploy elsewhere, or simply reduce their outgoings, but the other agenda is the promotion of self-reliance. There is very little consensus on this scheme; some landlords have welcomed it and others have expressed concerns that it might in some cases compromise quality and health and safety, and the extent of its applicability, but many home occupiers do DIY and there is no reason to think that tenants would be any worse at this than others. Obviously, some form of quality check would be necessary, even if on a random basis, which would incur administrative costs, and it will clearly be necessary to conduct a cost–benefit analysis to see if the scheme really results in savings, but it is worthwhile piloting it to see if benefits arise. There is also the link between enabling tenants to commission their own work and capacity skills building, and it could also stimulate LETS schemes as discussed and other forms of local resident-run enterprise as added value. A useful summary briefing on the scheme was produced by the National Housing Federation (NHF) in June 2011, which explores its possibilities and challenges (NHF, 2011).

Before we leave this general discussion, it is worth considering whether it makes sense to separate housing management functions into 'core' or 'non-core' as has often been the case. The division became important when the UK government considered replacing the CCT regime with best value, and an important consultation paper released in 1999 on the subject endeavoured to list the core functions as: repairs and maintenance; rent setting and collection; tenancy management; tenant consultation and involvement; allocations/re-lets; and asset management, differentiating these from investment activity and other action in the area, through private sector renovation and related-area renewal activity; fitness enforcement activity; empty homes strategies; and energy efficiency strategies (DETR, 1999). It further separated out functions which did not involve delivery to tenants, and which were often funded through other sources than rental income and associated subsidies to councils' HRAs, such as homelessness assessment and action; so-called strategic and enabling roles such as commissioning housing needs surveys and writing overarching strategies to guide development and management of the stock over typically five years and delivering homes through other bodies respectively; and work conducted by housing departments which assisted other local authority divisions to meet their aims and objectives – for example in supporting social services departments to develop community care initiatives, and corporate efforts to address anti-social behaviour. The 'core functions' were those initially expected to be subjected to the test of best value, although in practice many councils extended its ambit to non-core elements as well.

The definition was in essence rolled forward when the policy of encouraging the establishment of ALMOs was proposed as a result of the Green Paper *Quality and Choice: A Decent Home for All* (DETR, 2000), as a vehicle for the disbursement of Decent Homes cash where councils could not afford to resource these improvements themselves.

It is wholly understandable why such distinctions might be made – especially if the object is to isolate precisely those functions which tenants pay for directly through their rent and improve these to provide value for money to this group, and tackle economy and efficiency in relation to other functions in another way, but there are obvious interlinkages and the reality is that core and non-core functions must interact and take account of each other for housing management to make coherent sense. For example, does it make any sense to view the homelessness function apart from the allocations function, as a failure to see the bigger picture might add to the risk of residualising housing areas? Similarly, it makes sense for the development enabling role to work jointly with the allocations function in ensuring that all social and affordable landlords and developers in the area can contribute to sustainable communities which are usually not landlord or tenure specific. Arguably, the division of housing functions into core and non-core functions may make such an integrative view more difficult to achieve.

Alternative management strategies – in-house and arms' length

The question as to whether organisations should provide general needs and other forms of housing management themselves or engage others to do so has long been an item on the UK housing policy agenda. Sometimes this has been driven by financial considerations – for example, trying to drive down the cost of housing subsidy – and at other times, to test the efficiency and effectiveness of alternative arrangements in quality as well as cost terms. Before the 1980s it was rare for housing organisations in the UK to contract their management function out; the case for contrasting and comparing different ways of doing so had not been raised as a priority. It was only with the rise of the political philosophy of challenging national or local state monopoly provision in the Thatcher years that this approach was examined in the field. It was first expressed on any scale through the policy of CCT, which forced local authorities to submit many of their delivery functions to market testing by pitting their in-house organisation against private sector bidders. This is sometimes referred to as part of the new public management agenda, when public authorities were encouraged to adopt some of the business practices of the private sector in the interests of efficiency and effectiveness. It never really took off in the public housing sector, with relatively few external management contracts being let, and with not a few companies set up to take advantage of the policy initiative going to the wall, or going back to their core functions. Unsurprisingly, there is very little official criticism of the CCT regime: the Office of the Deputy Prime Minister's publication *Evaluation of English Housing Policy 1975–2000: Theme 5 Management Effectiveness* simply states that:

> There has never been a specific official evaluation of housing management CCT. However, there is some evidence that CCT was a significant catalyst for change in the housing service and that few of these gains would have been secured in the absence of compulsion. Some of the most significant changes were to management structures, processes and attitudes.
>
> (ODPM, 2005, p. 6)

These were translated into the best value regime which was introduced fully in 2000, which included the possibility of tendering out services but did not compel councils to do so. Under this regime, many councils followed housing associations in contracting out some if not all housing management functions to a range of bodies, some of these housing associations, others bespoke companies set up to take advantage of the regime, and yet others which were established property management organisations. Best value moved away from the stark price and quality test of CCT, and instead put forward a 'four C's' test, that is, that the exercised involved *challenging* whether the particular service was required, as well as how it was delivered; *comparing* existing performance with that which could be delivered by others; *consulting* with those actually using the service, and others in the district on what standards should be applied to services and how they could be improved; and finally considering *competition* to evaluate its potential to deliver improved performance as well as economies. It can be seen that this is a much more holistic approach to market testing, and the philosophy lives on even though the programme as such has long since been replaced by other initiatives. Notably, and unlike CCT, it also applied to strategic as well as tenancy management services, and did not entail contracting out, rather testing the existing service against others, even if for a short time, to see if efficiency and effectiveness would increase as a result. The spirit of best value lingered on, and influenced the performance indicators set used by the Audit Commission, the public sector body commissioned by the government and the Housing Corporation and its successor the TSA to evaluate the quality of tenancy management and strategic services. Currently, competitive forces have become very important in driving efficiencies in the face of the brave new world of self-financing for local authorities and the continuous quest for economies on the part of all providers in the face of welfare reforms which may lead to income management issues and reduced resources to manage and maintain properties, as will be explored later.

Managing the patch

There has long been debate as to how to manage social and affordable housing in terms of centralisation or dispersal to neighbourhoods. There are pros and cons to either approach, although intuitively one might expect that localised housing management might lead to greater resident participation and involvement with the organisation due to proximity. However, a more centralist approach may be more economical in staff and premises terms, albeit less convenient for customers if they wish to call in for face-to-face discussion and problem resolution.

Local housing management sits well with the localism ethos: that services should be responsive to local sentiment and requirement characteristics rather than devised to suit bureaucratic convenience, which arguably centralist approaches are. At its best, local housing management will be overseen by a scrutiny panel of residents who will be able to gauge the quality of service delivery at first hand and feed back on generic issues from neighbours and other associates as they arise. There are several good examples of local panel scrutiny of neighbourhood housing management. Arguably, localism in housing management is about ensuring that communities are able to improve their own homes, safeguard their health and develop their environment without some central diktat which tends towards uniformity. Some housing associations in the UK have got together under the Place Shapers umbrella, and have directly espoused localist approaches for some time. Place Shapers was founded in 2008 and comprises 70 housing associations. The ethos is that by 'getting local' and engaging with partners who have a neighbourhood role in direct contact with proximate patches (for example neighbourhood police), housing management can tackle some of the issues which need to be dealt with to ensure social cohesion, such as crime/anti-social behaviour, educational underachievement, worklessness and health in a joined-up manner. The associations who are part of this movement believe that some housing associations which have gone national or regional via mergers have lost touch with their grassroots in the process of seeking economies of scale, perhaps even where they have adopted or retained some form of local board which has governance overview of a specific geographical area. The Place Shapers group released a report entitled *Localism that Works* (Place Shapers, 2011) which details a variety of local management and community development schemes which appear to have made a big difference to people's lives, such as the Berinsfield Community Business initiative in Oxfordshire which provides cleaning and maintenance services to around 1,000 homes in the village, and which provides local employment which both enhances the environment and demonstrates trust in communities on the part of the provider. There are several other examples of local community sustainment initiatives – for example apprenticeship schemes – which ensure that local residents are included in developing their own futures and have a direct interest in the prosperity of their areas.

What is so special about a local management approach?

The key reason for the success of local management initiatives is accessibility and the engendering of a feeling of shared aims and values which is just not possible on a larger scale. The concept of *gemeinschaft* is an old one, dating back to 1887 and espoused by the German philosopher Ferdinand Tonnies, who defined it as a culture with shared mores and attitudes, where there is a sense of kinship and belonging. A fundamental aspect of *gemeinschaft* is the concept of shared space (although Tonnies considered that global religions could also fit into such a concept). Local housing management can assist in developing such a culture, by promoting local community growth initiatives such as local co-regulation where residents scrutinise and suggest, and organisations adapt their practices in accordance with local sentiment. One of the key attributes of societies which espouse *gemeinschaft* is a sense of loyalty to that community; responsive local housing management, in delivering a good and responsive service subject to local surview can engender such trust, with results which may include lower rent arrears, less anti-social behaviour and less tokenistic involvement in shaping policies and procedures.

Housing management acting locally will be able to pick up on issues far more readily than a under a more centralised approach. One reason is that of visibility – housing managers can literally see what is going on in terms of youth activities, people making their way across estates and patches to get to work or to avail themselves of recreation, shopping or other day-to-day activities, which personalises the process of management to the extent that the manager feels part of the community themselves, and therefore wishes to contribute to its performance in a meaningful manner. Residents are no longer units but human beings in day-to-day contact with officialdom. This feeling of community embeddedness can be reinforced by engaging with residents on estate walkabouts to check on the quality of communal repairs, or where they might be needed, or where environmental enhancements might be sited. It can also be bolstered by community events, for example estate open days where residents come together to exchange views and interact with management, often for a specific purpose, for example to get dogs 'chipped' while discussing anti-social behaviour, a tool used by the author in encouraging younger people to come forward to describe their experiences of being a victim and (in some cases) the purveyor of anti-social behaviour in East London. The local housing management approach should also be cost effective: staff travel ranges should be shorter, thus consuming less fuel and time which could better be spent on other activities.

Centralism

More centralist models are founded on the concept of economies of scale. Such economies are generated in industry by mass production, where the production of the nth + 1 unit may be less than that of the nth because the cost of starting the machinery has already been absorbed by the production cost of earlier units. It is fairly obvious that if a machine costs (say) £1,000 to buy and £200 to fuel for the process for which it is intended, and the cost of each unit to the consumer is £10 (ignoring profits), the 121st unit will be effectively free of production costs if the purchase price of the machine and the cost of fuel are the only relevant variables. The more units produced after the 121st unit, the cheaper each will be, taking into account wear and tear on the machine and the higher possibility of breakdown the longer it runs, and the cheaper every unit will be if the costs are divided among the final product. The same logic can be applied to housing management: the on-costs of office procurement and staff can be divided among all residents, rather than a few, therefore leading to lower unit costs and the possibility of greater investment in things that matter to the governance structure, such as financing development from operational surpluses. The down side to this is that such operations are rather remote and often inaccessible – many housing associations have chosen to locate their offices in industrial parks which are at distance from any customer base and not designed for customer interaction on any meaningful scale. It is important to determine how customers wish to be contacted, and build management systems around this, otherwise there is bound to be disappointment and low customer satisfaction ratings.

There goes the neighbourhood

Neighbourhood housing management is in many ways the essence of localism. The idea of neighbourhood management dates back to Octavia Hill's endeavours in the nineteenth century, and has developed since then into a holistic product, which combines traditional housing management with social sustainment. We have already discussed tenant management initiatives which are essentially localistic, and it could be argued that this is a prime example of local power and influence. The reason why many organisations continue to undertake neighbourhood management is to keep in touch with their customers, to be available when required and to maintain a local presence.

Today's neighbourhoods are often mixed tenure in nature, requiring a range of skills and knowledge, including leasehold management as well as (frequently) an attempt to reconcile the interests of owner-occupiers and tenants, who may have very different perceptions of their requirements and of those close to them. Today's neighbourhoods are also mixed income in nature, which also requires skills in giving welfare advice as well as social sustainment initiatives. The Joseph Rowntree Foundation (2006) produced an interesting paper in 2006 discussing the way to achieve success in this area. Key issues, which may seem counterintuitive to some readers, include the finding that mixed-income communities are often very successful, and not characterised by the stereotypes of problems which are often supposed to exist there, such as anti-social behaviour and other dysfunctional issues. Another interesting finding is that people of mixed tenure regard each other as 'ordinary people' – relationships are civil and polite, and the idea often espoused of 'role modelling' does not seem to be exemplified. Another misconception is that mixed-tenure communities make it more difficult to market owner-occupied products. The Joseph Rowntree Foundation research indicates that factors such as design, location and quality are more important in determining success in attracting people to market products.

This is against a background of trying to assuage the problem of severe inequalities at a variety of geographical levels, and significant divisions between mixed communities created through changes in older housing areas where mixed income and mixed tenure have evolved over a number of years, as a by-product of mass housing schemes such as new towns, where the right to buy and subsequent market developments have created a mixed-tenure and mixed-income environment, through 'master planning' where such mixes have been created by design as a consequence of regeneration, and where existing council and housing estates have become mixed tenure through demolition and infill. Admittedly, there are cases where such developments do not work; a case cited in the Joseph Rowntree Foundation paper (2006) illustrates this point, where a development consisted mainly of large properties was dominated by large families which seemed to exacerbate complaints of anti-social behaviour. Ill-judged allocations and lettings policies have given rise to clusters of residents dependent on benefits raising problems mainly in relation to the perceptions of those outside the area of 'sink-estates', and problems of self-labelling. On the whole, the conclusions are positive, indicating that developers are willing to support mixed-tenure and mixed-income communities in their plans, gaining comfort from evidence that this does not depress demand for the market element.

One significant neighbourhood housing issue is residualisation. This is where typically allocations policies have given rise to concentrations of poorer people selected through a points or banding system on the basis of the presence of one or more need factors, following the reasonable preference guidance reinforced by the Localism Act. In essence, Section 147 of the act requires that local authorities give preference in allocating their property to people who are homeless, or owed some related duty, and those occupying insanitary or overcrowded housing or otherwise living in unsatisfactory housing conditions; people who need to move on medical or welfare grounds (including any grounds relating to a disability); and those needing to move to a particular locality in the district of the authority, where failure to meet that need would cause hardship to themselves or others. There is also some discretion to give additional preference to particular descriptions of people within this subsection, largely those with urgent housing needs, along with an ability to consider previous tenant behaviour, local connection and financial circumstances. Taken as a whole, this prioritisation system might be expected to lead to residual estates dominated by relatively needy people, which may give rise to relatively concentrated needs-based housing management which may be held to be relatively uneconomical, and certainly does not accord with the philosophy espoused in the Hills report (2007), as already discussed. The idea of estate residualisation has been attacked by several recent commentators (for example Greenhalgh and Moss, 2009), as a sign of allocations failure attributed largely to the Housing (Homeless Persons) Act 1977, which allegedly gave rise to a 'culture of entitlement to welfare housing, epitomised by teenage girls getting pregnant in order to secure a home from the Council' (p. 27). This is something of an exaggeration, but is a popular conception. The authors claim early in their monograph that social housing has become a form of welfare housing, characterised by a welfare culture and dependency, citing the statistic that 50 per cent of social housing is located in the most deprived 20 per cent wards of the UK, and that it has in a sense failed those who it intended to help. A number of strategies are suggested to rectify this, including the philosophy of a hand up rather than a hand out to social tenants who wish to better themselves, chiefly into some form of owner-occupation, be it on a shared or full-ownership basis. The consequence of this is believed by the authors to include the rescuing of a 'broken society' and a degree of community integration, with consequent falls in crime, although little hard evidence is given for these assertions. Some of the proposals of this interesting paper have been taken forward by the UK Coalition government, one of which is the duty to fix broken neighbourhoods through councils having to work closely with others to evolve a tenancy strategy which takes account of tenure mix as well as social sustainability, although its deregulationalist proposals have been transformed into the flexible fixed-term tenure models now adopted by many councils, which enable them to move tenants out of affordable or social tenure when they can afford to do so. Another rather prescient comment was that there should be duties to help and to house, making a neat distinction between those who could afford near-market rents and others who need recourse to state assistance through infirmity or some other factor (Greenhalgh and Moss, 2009). If both sets were located in the same area, the implication the authors seem to be drawing later in the monograph is that role modelling might encourage those on benefits to better themselves, although the Joseph Rowntree Foundation paper (2006) seems to be at variance with this. This is reinforced by praise for councils who have sought to increase the number of working people on the patch through selective allocation policies, albeit those who do not dominate the system. Arguably, such areas might be easier to manage.

Anti-social behaviour is a theme which arises time and time again as a bugbear of neighbourhood management. Anti-social behaviour ranges from noise nuisance to drug dealing and racism, and most housing organisations have a strategy to endeavour to control its levels and to support victims. There has been comparatively recent movement in the UK in terms of stronger legislation to control this form of activity, and will be further discussed in Chapter 5, and professional representative institutes such as the Chartered Institute of Housing (CIH) have worked together with other agencies to endeavour to mitigate its effects. In November 2009, the TSA commissioned the CIH to work closely with around 130 local authority landlords to endeavour to share existing best practice and share good practice across the piece with all social landlords, and one of the key outputs has been a series of publications and toolkits to embed good practice, drawing on legislation and guidance published by a variety of sources, including the Safer Neighbourhoods Group. In April 2010, the CIH launched a national action squad to give advice to landlords on how to prevent and tackle anti-social behaviour, on the basis that tenants surveyed had informed the TSA that anti-social behaviour control was one of their premier issues of discontent. Arguably, effective neighbourhood management could make a real difference in terms of knowledge of the patch and those who live on it, and through presence to facilitate monitoring and control. The most recent output of concern over anti-social behaviour is the 2011 Respect Standard, deriving from the 2006 model which included the notion of community leadership as key to controlling this phenomenon, as well as promoting respect between residents as a key antidote, and many housing organisations have since signed up to this new incarnation. Some forms of anti-social behaviour are arguably the result of poor design, for example, where flats have been built without adequate soundproofing and where dwellings are located too close to each other. Child density also has its part to play, as well as criminal activity from outside using estates and neighbourhoods as rat-runs or targets for their endeavours. However, it should perhaps be wrong to over-stress the crime by design argument arising from Alice Coleman's *Utopia on Trail* (Coleman, 1985) which attempts to prove a link between certain aspect of estate design and bad behaviour, including criminality, which has been used as a model for estate regeneration or block modification by some local authorities, notably by Westminster City Council in respect of the Mozart Estate, famed for the removal of walkways between flats to prevent access and exit by burglars and other like criminals with some success. Much depends on social environment, as well as built form.

It would be easy to stereotype certain groups in society as major purveyors of anti-social behaviour, such as young people, who tend to be disproportionately victims and offenders. Mention anti-social behaviour orders and the image of a younger person behaving badly may come to mind; although these remedies are available for anyone, there has been a focus on youth justice in recent years, and a predilection for assuming that any young person not in education, employment or training is a likely candidate for anti-social behaviour. Neighbourhood initiatives such as youth venues, graffiti walls and kick-about areas have gone some way to refocusing activity into more acceptable forms, although surely rebellion and misbehaviour is of the essence of growing up, and it would be wrong to regard something quite ordinary as abnormal.

Special needs housing management

The term 'special needs' has not had an easy ride, and in a previous work, I received no particular opprobrium in relation to the term, although it can be used in a pejorative way. The term encompasses any households who require specific care and support, such as those suffering from some debilitating illness who require medical care or respite; those who have a disabling condition and who require support on or offsite; people who are being rehabilitated from prison, vulnerable young adults and homeless people requiring life skills and welfare advice in a residential setting. A more appropriate term these days is supported housing, which does away with the ascription of special need, as 'special' has been used in a demeaning manner over the years and has entered the ergot as a byword for unacceptably different in some contexts. There are a number of ways of dividing the class: there are those who for some physical or mental reason cannot live independently and who require on-site or offsite assistance; those who are capable of living a full and independent life after some form of rehabilitation (for example people coming off drugs, and many in homeless hostels who have ended up there through miscircumstance) and others who are vulnerable through youth or age. There are other examples of special/supported needs candidates, probably too numerous to mention, but the reader will already be able to populate the matrix.

All of these groups require some form of support, be it housing related (for example assistance with welfare advice, navigating the dwelling, etc), medical support (someone to administer drugs and therapy) or social support (younger people who are worklessness being trained in the context of a foyer, perhaps), and the form of assistance may vary considerably, and may or may not be delivered in the setting of a specific housing scheme. Sheltered housing for elderly people is an excellent example of where a nexus of support is available, ranging over social, occupational therapy and medical in a contained environment, although since the mid-1980s and the Care in the Community initiative, the tendency has been to provide peripatetic support where at all possible and feasible as opposed to the 'warehousing' approach of 'Part Three' accommodation and many sheltered schemes.

It is undeniable that Care in the Community has made a significant difference to attitudes towards and the treatment or assistance of some 'special needs' groups, such as the elderly. In the 1970s it was common in the UK to allocate elderly and infirm individuals to geriatric wards in hospitals on the grounds of economy and on the assumption that they were better off and safer in a controlled environment than outside. The pre-Care in the Community approach is often and rightly referred to as institutionalisation, and was challenged by the Audit Commission's report, *Making a Reality of Community Care* (Audit Commission, 1986) which challenged the assumption that warehousing was any cheaper than delivering support in the community – to people at home or in housing adapted for their especial needs. One of the issues it raised is that there were already thousands of households requiring care in the community, and that support networks could cope quite well with their requirements, so what was the point in allocating them to special supervised buildings away from their friends and family? It also found that institutional care was in many cases more expensive per unit than its community counterpart, and administratively top heavy, with relatively high staff to resident ratios.

Care in the Community blossomed in the Thatcherite mid-1980s, and saw the demolition of many a mental institution, many of which have been converted into apartments or the land sold for housing development. The roots of Care in the Community are to be found in the 1956 Guillebaud Committee's deliberations on the most appropriate mode of care for older people. It arrived at the firm conclusion that it would in many cases be more humane and economical to provide care on a domiciliary basis rather than by dumping in an institution. It can also be seen in the distinction between social and medical care arising from the division of labour between social services departments and medical institutions arising partly from the deliberations of the Griffiths report (1988). The 1989 White Paper, *Caring for People, Community Care in the Next Decade and Beyond* (Department of Health, 1989), which followed was hugely influential. Its main tenets were that the state should enable rather than provide care, through local government and other bodies, with an emphasis on purchasing care from other organisations, often in the private sector. One important aspect was that the roles of purchaser and provider should be clearly separated, as in CCT, and that budgets should be devolved from the state to local public bodies. Its provisions were enacted in the National Health Service and Community Care Act 1990, which was a landmark piece of legislation, and came into effect in 1993; and the voluntary sector has been the main beneficiary of such changes, as the main bodies which deliver care and support services to this day.

There has therefore been a shift in philosophy from the 'medical' or pathological to the social model of disability. The former regards people with some disabling condition as in some way abnormal, focusing on the disability rather than the person, and assuming that it is best dealt with in a confined context. An example of this pathological approach which still exists is the so-called secure wings of hospitals in which those who have been 'sectioned' are incarcerated while being assessed to establish whether they are indeed a threat to themselves or others' safety. Many such institutions rely upon a cocktail of drugs and a strict regime to manage the inmates, who in many cases are quite capable of living in the community while being assessed, although this is admittedly an option. The social model regards disability as an attribute of a person rather than the defining characteristic, and argues that reasonable adaptations to the exiting home environment or surrounding environs may be all that is necessary to help people with disabilities live as full a life as anyone else. The concept of lifetime homes which will be discussed in Chapter 6 arose out of the thought that dwellings can be disabling, and that homes should be built to accommodate every stage of the household lifecycle from youth, maturity to old age without necessitating moving out.

That is not to say that there are not some individuals or households who require the intensive and sheltered care – and protection from or to society that institutions offer. The redoubtably insane, the bedridden sick (in many cases), dangerous criminals, and the very frail elderly are probably candidates for some form of institutional care, but they are few and far between. In the case of housing, they are few indeed.

The funding of housing care was challenged in 2009 with the deringfencing of the Supporting People grant which had hitherto been earmarked for social services authorities to fund this form of care. The consequences of this have in many cases been that Supporting People funding has leaked into other areas of local authority general fund expenditure, to the detriment of the services that it was supposed to support, which makes a nonsense of the needs-based formula distribution which was supposed to inform its targeting.

Special consideration groups

Special needs groups are generally those with a specific requirement which marks them out for specific care or housing solutions, but there is a wider group who are housed by local authorities and housing associations not because of any special physical or mental attribute but because they are otherwise disadvantaged by the market. These include households who suffer economic and social discrimination and disadvantage through racial, ethnic or cultural status; unfavourable medical or related conditions; possession of other characteristics meeting with social disapproval and marginalisation for example street sleepers; other victims of societal prejudice for example gypsies and travellers; students; victims of domestic violence; refugees and asylum seekers. This is probably not an exclusive list, but it will do as a start.

It is fair to say that the common factor shared by these groups is social and/or economic marginalisation. Sub-categories of some of the above might include:

- **Unfavourable medical or related conditions**
  - AIDS and HIV victims
  - Drug abusers and their dependents
  - Alcohol abusers

- **Possession of other characteristics meeting with social disapproval and**

marginalisation

- Young and lone-parent households
- Young offenders
- Time-served criminals
- Street sleepers
- Beggars

- **Victims of societal prejudice and indifference not itemised above**
  - Asylum seekers and refugees
  - Gypsies and travellers
  - Those discharged from the armed forces
  - Anyone who does not conform with the prevalent societal view of 'normality'

- **Others who are hard to fit into the above categories, but who find it hard to secure mainstream market or social housing**
  - students
  - victims of domestic violence

This is a relatively long list. It is notable that many who do not fit neatly into the above categories are able to find housing in the market, or through the traditional allocations systems of social and affordable housing, but they may find greater barriers in so doing than other groups, and several housing providers have come into existence to meet their needs. It is worth considering in detail why some such groups are marginalised, and the type of accommodation provided for them, as well as their routes into it.

Households suffering economic and social discrimination and disadvantage through racial, ethnic or cultural status

Legislation outlaws differential and disadvantageous treatment of individuals on the grounds of race, ethnic origin, sex, gender, faith, age, disability and sexual orientation. The Equalities Act 2010 brings together legislation passed to outlaw discrimination since the 1975 Sex Discrimination Act and adds a new take on discrimination, promoting a public sector duty to promote equality. For all that, discrimination and prejudice still exist, which in many cases entail a less favourable position in the market for such groups than others with equivalent requirements, although this is less the case now than it was 20 years ago. However, it is very difficult to dissuade prejudice, which is an orientation towards someone else on the grounds of unjustified belief and received opinion, and it may be the case that many a private landlord still harbours these views when selecting potential tenants. Best practice in this may be guaranteed by a robust strategy which endeavours to underpin this, and it should contain reference to the guidance contained in the Equalities Act, along with a statistical analysis of the presence of ethnic groups within the area and a method of ensuring that they cohere. For example, Merton Council's (2004) *Ethnic Minority Housing Strategy* 2004–2006 aims to identify the to identify the housing needs and aspirations of ethnic minority communities in Merton through research and improvement of their information base; to develop an ethnic minority housing policy which recognises and responds to diverse needs of different ethnic minority groups; and to develop and implement an action plan to improve housing provision and services for ethnic minority groups. They have identified that people from ethnic minority groups are disproportionately affected by deprivation, and are more likely than others to live in deprived areas in more unpopular housing, and to be unemployed, regardless of their age, sex qualifications and where they live. They also identified that Pakistani and Bangladeshi men are significantly more likely to be unemployed than their white counterparts, and also more likely to be in ill-health. They were also more likely to be concentrated in overcrowded housing. Additionally, they are likely to be the victims of racist crimes. The report acknowledges that they had comparatively little information about the needs of ethnic minority groups, and that comparatively little was known about their problems nationally on which to draw, although they were able to go into some detail regarding key housing and social exclusion issues that local groups face. Their database is fairly full in this regard: for example, they have identified that the proportion of ethnic minority groups in the borough had reached one quarter of the population compared to 16.2 per cent in 1991, and that the Asian community would make up 17 per cent of the total population by 2011. It also identified a relative rise in the Chinese community, growing faster than other sectors, from 1,220 in 1991 to 5,069 in 2001. In terms of housing need it identified that 42 per cent of housing register applicants in the borough were from black and ethnic minority (BME) groups compared to just 25 per cent in the general population, indicating that housing need was far greater for them than other groups. They were also far more represented in seeking housing aid and advice than other groups, in line with the national situation. Social exclusion of BME groups was also identified as a significant issue. In terms of promoting racial equality, Merton also went to great lengths to provide an inclusive policy in working with housing associations and other providers to ensure that there was a borough-wide and seamless approach to inclusion and fair treatment, with BME housing associations represented on its forum to encourage diversity (Merton Council, 2004). Indeed, the Equalities Act 2010 enjoins local authorities and others to promote racial equality and enable diversity, so there is a firm statutory base for such an orientation.

Unfavourable medical or related conditions

It is often the case that society regards medical or related conditions in one light and others in another light, depending on the moral climate of the day. Standards vary radically over time: one thinks of opium consumption – in Victorian times, this was quite acceptable, but hardly so today, and laudanum taken in small quantities was thought to be quite beneficial to health. There is considerable housing provision for the victims of drug abuse, with some housing associations such as Look Ahead Housing Association (London) specialising in supportive care and outreach work. Look Ahead supports around 6,000 customers, many of whom are recovering from drug dependency and require a personalised service to do so, and offers personal budgeting advice under the personalisation agenda to ensure that they can make the most of benefits and other income in sustaining themselves, which is also a key part of their therapy. They are focused on providing supportive help to people whose lives may seem highly chaotic, and see their role as working with individuals to devise a plan of action to lift them out of dependency and to help them get employment.

Other housing associations and associated companies – for example Inward House Products – have become key in providing an in-house supported drug recovery environment, and commission health and social care providers to make this a reality. The personalisation agenda is an example of an approach which endeavours to provide more vulnerable people, for example those in this category, to devise personal budgets and spend limited amounts delivered through the supporting people regime, cognisant of the terms of the National Drug Strategy, to facilitate their care, a very different approach to that of the institutional mode. See Inward House (2011) for further useful detail on this organisation and its approach.

Others included in this group are victims of HIV and AIDS, and several groups have been formed to try to ensure that they receive a high level of support in an outreach or residential managed environment. An example of such an organisation is the Terrence Higgins Trust, in business since the 1950s, and which provides a supportive and therapeutic environment to such clients, and aims to combat discrimination. Most of the clients end up at Terrence Higgins through homelessness caused by discrimination in being unable to access market housing, and a range of care is provided including medical and social to support victims in a safe environment. One of the things that Terrence Higgins tries to prevent is the homelessness 'revolving door', where ill individuals are given temporary housing for just a few months before often ending back on the streets having not received the support they need. It is essential that such victims are given a space to rebuild their lives in a supportive environment which may even be managed by those who were at some time also dependent on the services of the Trust. The director of the Trust, Tom Howarth, was quoted in the *Independent* (1994) as saying that the needs of such sufferers should be included in assessments of housing needs in local authorities and other providers, and that there should be a stronger operational link between housing and care services. This has in fact occurred over the years, through joint housing and health boards, and combined services, for example the primary care trust at Hammersmith and Fulham was directed by the community services director, who was also responsible for housing services, which helped the joint appreciation greatly, and made for a seamless housing and care environment, albeit funded through very different streams.

The management of temporary accommodation

Temporary accommodation is provided to meet the needs of those judged to be intentionally homeless under Part 6 of the Housing Act 1996, as modified by the Homelessness Act 2002, as well as those awaiting the outcome of investigations. There are several routes to such management; housing associations have been doing so for some years, often under contract to local authorities with regard to the private leasing scheme whereby private sector housing is leased by either a housing association for a term of years ranging from around one to ten years, and sub-let to a local authority referral under non-secure tenancy arrangement if the local authority itself is the procurer and secondary landlord, or as assured shorthold tenancy arrangement where the housing association itself has taken on the lease. This provides a relatively acceptable form of housing, which is cost-effective as much of the outlay is provided from recycled benefits payments and subsidy from councils' general funds. Other arrangements include bed and breakfast usually for single people since the prohibition of the use of this form of housing for families except in the case of emergency from 2007, although arguably this is often a very reasonable method of providing support for single younger people who may not have the skills to manage their own accommodation well, or older single people for which such accommodation is an adequate respite.

This form of housing is funded from councils' general funds on the basis that it is a service to the community rather than to tenants of the council, although in practice in many cases the councils housing department will pay initially for the service through the HRA and then recharge the general fund accordingly.

Other forms of temporary accommodation include hostels, where there is often ambiguity as regards tenancy arrangements. If the occupant has a key to his/her room, and exclusive occupation, he or she may well have the status of tenancy regardless of how the occupation arrangement is labelled, as we shall see in Chapter 5. Hostels are a relatively old-fashioned way of housing homeless people as a stop-gap measure, and have in many areas been abandoned as a practice. They offer relatively little security, although some organisations (for example, Centrepoint) do offer support services in relation to training and job seeking to enable individuals to move on into more settled accommodation.

Decent Homes and asset management

The achievement of Decent Homes status was one of the planks of the 2000 Green Paper, *Quality and Choice – A Decent Home For All* (DETR, 2000). It must be remembered that when the paper was written, it was estimated that in 2000, 3 million households lived in homes in all tenures which failed the then fitness standard, were in poor repair, or needed modernisation, and that by 1996, a £10 billion backlog of renewal work in local authority housing in the UK had built up, often concentrated in estates (DETR, 2000). The government of the day decided that local authorities in England should be given four options to improve their stock, all of which had management implications, namely large-scale voluntary stock transfer, the formation of ALMOs, the Private Finance Initiative (PFI) which deals usually in relation to part of the stock, or, if the councils had sufficient finds to achieve decent homes standards through their own resources, stock retention. Whichever route was chosen, councils found it necessary to refocus their efforts on producing an asset management plan which would assist in meeting the target, which was set for 2010.

An asset management plan essentially seeks to fit resources over a given period of time to projects which will realise the goal of ensuring that stock is renovated to and maintained at a given standard. Typically, it will identify the deficiencies by stock and type, and seek to prioritise actions over that period to ensure that the programme is completed to target and within the resources envelope. This is made difficult in practice by the fact that it is hard to predict beyond a few years what resources will be available to carry out the tasks, and in some cases by goalposts moving. For example, the Decent Homes standard was changed in 2006 as a result of the introduction of the HHSRS brought in by the 2004 Housing Act, replacing the old fitness system incorporated into the 1985 Housing Act, to the extent that councils had to ensure that properties were free from 29 'category 1' hazards identified in the legislation which in most cases linked the nature of the occupant (for example frail elderly person) to the condition of the dwelling (for example steepness of stairs, broken banister) and (in the case above) a hazard would be produced due to the interaction of personal and property characteristics. Some hazards are less related to the occupant, as shall be seen in Chapter 5, but this is an example of where an unpredictable change can alter the best-laid plans to improve assets to a given standard.

The definition of a Decent Home is one which, according to DCLG (2006):

- meets the statutory minimum standard for housing having regard to the HHSRS introduced in June 2006 through the 2004 Housing Act;
- is in a reasonable state of repair, which is failed if one or more major building components (for example a roof) needs replacement or major repairs, or where two or more other components are old, and should be replaced or subject to major repairs;
- has reasonably modern facilities, failed if the property lacks three or more of the following: 20-year old kitchen or less which is reasonably modern; and with adequate space and layout; a reasonably modern bathroom (30-years old or less); an appropriately located bathroom and toilet; adequate insulation against noise where this could be a problem (for example beside a busy road, in a block of flats, etc); adequate layout of common parts (for flats);
- provides a reasonable degree of thermal comfort.

It can be seen from this list that a dwelling that is deficient only in that it does not have a reasonably modern kitchen could still be assessed as decent, which was the source of much criticism of the adequacy of the standard during the mid-2000s as councils and housing associations shouldered the challenges of meeting these standards within the timeframe available.

The management challenges of meeting the standard were several: in some cases works could be performed with tenants in situ, but in other cases, it was necessary to decant (move out) tenants to other dwellings to enable the necessary modernisation, especially where several of the criteria were failed, or where it was necessary to do works to the entire block to meet the relevant standards. Decanting is always a sensitive matter, especially where the tenant had lived in the dwelling or area for a considerable time, and where moving could mean dislocation from friends, family and facilities that have been used for some time (for example schools, medical centres, shops), and so care is needed to ensure that tenants are given a degree of choice over their dwelling for occupation on either a temporary or permanent basis.

Good social landlords publish guides for tenants to ready them for the process; there should be a full explanation of the circumstances under which decanting will take place, reference to the section(s) of the relevant legislation which in the case of Secure Tenants is the 1985 Housing Act as modified by the Localism Act 2011. In this case, the relevant clause is Ground 8, where tenants have to relinquish the property into which they are decanted which they accepted on a secure tenancy basis when their original home is ready for reoccupation. In some cases, the scale of the work may be such that the property in which the tenant lives needs extensive redevelopment or indeed demolition, as it is too far gone to meet the Decent Homes standard and is otherwise no longer suitable for occupation, in which case Grounds 10 or 11 can be used to possess the property. Both of these are mandatory, but will be granted only if there is suitable alternative accommodation available, whereas Ground 8 is discretionary. For flexible tenancies, it is much easier to determine these in order to undertake essential works (see Localism Act, section 154). More will be said about decanting and the rights and responsibilities of landlords in Chapter 5.

The role of the housing manager in this context is essential in giving information about the nature of tenure arrangements in the patch, which will affect the ability of the landlord to gain possession, the needs of individual households so that they can be matched to suitable properties or encouraged to find alternative accommodation through a choice-based letting system, and giving guidance to tenants on the facilities available in new areas tenants may choose to live in, as well as liaison arrangements with other registered providers which may be cooperating in facilitating move-in property. Such a move may entail swopping one form of tenancy for another – for example secure to assured, or even assured shorthold, with a very different suite of rights and possibly rent levels, which will require significant information giving at an early stage.

To return to asset management, it is essential that there is both a strategy and a plan, and that residents are involved in the formulation of both. If the plan is a costed map of a process of moving stock from one condition to another over a finite period, a strategy is more like a business plan which informs the plan. A good strategy will explore the aims and objectives of the organisation as a housing provider, which will include stock improvement aspirations and chart a way forward in terms of business environment awareness, invariably containing a SWOT (strengths, weaknesses, opportunities and threats) analysis, a PEST (political, economic, social and technological) evaluation, a variety of costed alternative scenarios for achieving the desired result, and a decision matrix to assist in making the correct choices. Arguably, as key stakeholders through rent and service charge payment, tenants and leaseholders should be involved from the first in discussions on how to move from the current state of affairs to that required, for example, in the specification of new kitchens and bathrooms, decant arrangements, and quality checking throughout the works in liaison with the provider and contractor. Enlightened registered providers also involve residents in contractor selection panels for major works, especially in regard to how effectively resident–contractor information and other liaison will be performed.

Repairs and maintenance

The repairs and maintenance function is perhaps the most fundamental service provided to residents; surveys show that this is regarded as the most significant element determining overall satisfaction with landlords, and it is therefore no wonder why it was picked out for consideration under the TSA's Home Standard, effective from 1 April 2010. In essence, the standard requires registered providers to provide a cost-effective repairs and maintenance service to the homes and communal areas they manage, which takes account of the expressed needs and choices of tenants, and most importantly has the effect of ensuring that repairs and improvements are completed on a 'right first time' basis, in addition to ensuring that all health and safety requirements prescribed by the law are met.

What this means in details is that repairs and maintenance services should be prudently planned and that there should be a reasonable balance in programme panning between responsive (day to day) and planned maintenance (for example boiler servicing or replacement), including not only occupied but empty dwellings. There is considerable scope for resident involvement in the order in which works take place on an estate in line with their priorities as residents – for example, work to secure property against crime may well be a priority for them, along with the installation of more cost-effective heating systems at a time of national austerity and changes to the welfare benefits regime which may adversely affect the ability of tenants to pay for such essentials.

One approach to repairs and maintenance rethinking which has been used to try to reduce the back-office component of repairs and maintenance services and achieve a better allocation of resources to provide value for money through cost minimisation for the same or better result has been that of systems thinking. Popularised by John Seddon in various publications including *Systems Thinking in the Public Sector* (Seddon, 2008), the central philosophy is to reduce end-to-end times by reducing duplication and waste in systems, and to try to ensure that as many processes as possible are dealt with by front-office operatives, so that when a customer requests a repair, they can be given a diagnosis and expected time of delivery there and then instead of having to go through a complex reporting system which may elongate the process unnecessarily. Seddon's (2005) book, *Freedom from Command and Control* specifically discussed the inadequacies of performance indicator target-driven repairs systems which often ignore quality and tenant feedback and argues for a leaner approach where repairs systems are designed around customer needs rather than to suit the nature of the existing bureaucracy. An example of bureaucracy-led repairs systems are those where part of a job is closed if it is not completed within a given time, to give the impression that a whole job has been completed to target, and then reopened so that the series of 'jobs' appears to have been completed on target, whereas if this segmentation did not occur, it would be plain to see that the job took longer than it should have. The secret to better repairs and maintenance according to Seddon is to enable operatives to be involved in re-specifying systems to eliminate duplication and waste, to ensure that systems are not clogged by what he terms 'failure demand' – that is calls from tenants complaining about the standard of repairs or the time taken to effect them, or chasing up on when the repair would be done, to leave more space for 'value demand' – that is the initial request. This makes sense in the context of call centres where systems can be easily clogged by failure demand, slowing the process of ordering repairs.

What then is the role of housing management in securing an efficient and effective repairs service? One answer is to get as close to the customer as possible, so that the repair can be diagnosed efficiently and effectively. This could mean the greater use of hand-held devices into which conditions data can be readily entered, transmitted to the contractor, and the order sent straight to the contractor, who would prioritise the repair against the schedule given by the organisation, and rapidly let the customer know when it could be effected. Another is to provide customers with a diagnostic tool to help them specify the repair themselves and to communicate directly with the contractor, who will call and verify what needs to be done without involving housing management staff at all. Naturally, this would entail quality checks from time to time, and may not be appropriate for all, but it could form a basis for empowerment.

In April 2011, the then Minister for Housing, Grant Shapps, announced a scheme which would enable tenants of housing associations and local authorities to undertake their own repairs, with the landlord paying the tenant directly. The scheme was piloted in Summer 2011 by a number of local authorities and housing associations, to check uptake and feasibility, specifically its scope, scale, costs of implementing such a scheme, including set-up costs for organisations, as well as its likely benefits for landlords and tenants, and contractual issues (between tenants and the repairs contractor they might decide to use), and was subject to further consultation by the TSA, which incorporated the scheme into a revised direction to landlords. This generated some controversy; some feared that it would lead to poorly performed work of an amateur DIY nature, although much depends on the training and skills of those attempting to do so, and it seems entirely reasonable to let tenants undertake their own repairs provided they can prove that they have the necessary skills and experience, and observe basic health and safety measures. The collateral risk of injury to tenants and the need for inspection are, of course, part and parcel of this approach which needs to be factored into the business plans and policies of landlords. They is also the need to ensure that repairs jobs are properly receipted and full verifiable details given as proof that they have actually been done in the manner specified and to the cost presented. This scheme was introduced in mid-2012, but it is not yet possible to say whether it will succeed in ensuring that repairs are done to a timeframe desired by tenants, or to the quality required by themselves or landlords, but it is surely worth trying.

Securing value for money

Value for money has become something of a byword in the social and affordable housing world. It is hard to give an exact definition of what this might mean in terms of repairs and maintenance, although a good start is to consider the cost of performing a repair against a benchmark standard, for example the schedule of rates used by many housing associations and local authorities. In the 1990s, it was thought that it could be secured through competition through CCT, and then through Best Value. The introduction of ALMOs for local authorities in England in the mid-2000s, organisations focusing on the housing management function and its specific costs, was thought by many to be a vehicle to drive down repairs and maintenance costs and achieve value for money by prudent contracting. It is likely that value for money can be secured by comparing and contrasting the output of various maintenance providers in relation to similar jobs, and choosing the most cost-effective contractor in line with quality standards, and this is the line taken by most housing organisations. It is of course essential to involve tenants in giving feedback to assess the quality of repairs, along with routine inspections and contract reviews. To assist public and voluntary sector organisations in their quest for value for money in this area, Housemark (a subsidiary of the CIH, specialising in quality inspections) produced a useful toolkit, available on a subscription basis, and housing organisations have benefited from applying its lessons. The toolkit incorporates benchmark data on an annual basis from well-performing organisations against which repairs costs can be compared in a meaningful manner, as well as incorporating scores against 60 relevant performance indicators. One strength of this approach is the inclusivity of the data, although it may also be a weakness in that it may be hard to disaggregate each of the factors to find which those that are critical in producing the desired result.

A repairs service for the future

What would a good repairs service look like? It is possible to list some features which all repairs services should have:

1.   Repairs should be completed within the correct time as specified by the landlord.
2.   Repair categorisations (for example emergency, urgent, routine) should be open to review in relation to legislative change and consultation with users.
3.   There should be regular reviews of service efficiency, benchmarked against other peer organisations. Inspections by an impartial body (for example the HCA) will undoubtedly help to drive up quality through comparative analysis.
4.   The service should be customer responsive – lessons must be learned from complaints and compliments.
5.   Innovation should not be shied away from, provided that new systems are tested for fitness of purpose.

Organisational management issues

The is no one ideal form of housing organisational structure, although it is likely that there will always be a team alignment in relation to function – so organisations will contain repairs and maintenance teams, tenancy management teams, revenue management teams and so forth, as the scope of the tasks have become highly complex partly as a result of burgeoning legislative demands. It is probably unrealistic to suppose that a generic housing management officer could operate competently in all of these areas, or could prioritise the tasks effectively unless the organisation is small (for example a cooperative with a handful of dwellings), or unless the law were to be changed to reduce the quantity of landlord duties which follow from the forms of tenancy created since the early 1980s.

Specialism in housing management is probably here to stay, although at its upper layers, one might expect to find senior managers who have at some stage performed a variety of functions within organisations, although the personnel management role is itself a specialism, often bolstered by appropriate qualifications. It is an open question as to whether it is strictly necessary for chief executives and very senior management staff to have had a specific housing background, as housing organisations possess the characteristics of other businesses, for example, quality control, measuring output against input, and ensuring that good practice from elsewhere is utilised. Adverts for senior housing personnel often specify generic business experience rather than any particular branch of housing knowledge, on the assumption that such personnel will be supported by specialists in the field.

There are several candidates for organisational structure which build on the above, but the common factor is the corporate business plan which determines the mission and aims of the organisation. It is surely reasonable to build a staff contingent around what needs to be done. This is what good business planning entails. In practice, however, it is likely that the business plan will inherit a predefined organisational structure, and that organisational adaptation will have to take place through an incremental process which may or may not result in an effective and efficient outcome.

Recruitment and job design

It is not possible to effectively recruit or design the jobs to be filled through the recruitment and selection process without some form of business plan which indicates the priorities of the organisation. It may also be that some flexibility is required so that new jobs can be created to meet newly arising challenges – for example a major change in tenancy law or additional functions (for example development or closer partnership working with private sector housing providers) which may entail a new skill set. Therefore the job design and recruitment function is fundamental to achieving present and future aims. At the heart of effective recruitment lies the ability to formulate a description of the role which will reflect the present and future needs of the organisation. Take the area of tenancy support, this is a fundamental function, and covers a variety of areas such as ensuring that tenants understand and adhere to their statutory and contractual terms and conditions, and are empowered to seek advice regarding paying their rent in what may be a difficult economic environment for them, against the background of welfare benefits reform and changes in local economies. The officer would therefore need a good grounding not only in landlord–tenant law, but also in ways into work and training enablement, and the ability to update their knowledge and skills to fulfil the requirements of the post, however it is designated.

It is best to start by mapping the objectives of the organisation, for example to provide affordable homes, to provide a quality housing management service, and so forth, and then to design job roles around these. This is often a luxury afforded only to new companies, but even those which have been going for some time can endeavour to stand back and take a fresh look at what they intend to do, and then remodel existing jobs around the roles which emerge. If jobs have to change in response to new challenges, this may well be beneficial to those doing them, as it may provide for job enrichment which has been shown to be a positive factor in staff retention, as long as appropriate lead-in training is given.

Staff retention

It is often said that housing organisations are, if anything, people organisations. Their products are affordable homes for rent and for sale, and services to those who inhabit the properties they have created or acquired. They would not be able to run efficiently or effectively without well-trained and motivated staff who subscribe to the business plan and who therefore judge their progress against its aims and objectives. There is a famous theory which still has some currency in organisational management theory – that of McGregor's (1960) Theory X and Y, which is pertinent in guiding managers in respect of retaining enthused staff. Theory X is basically that workers turn up for wages and do the minimum required to remain employed. Theory Y is that employees are motivated to perform well for the sake of achievement and to further the objectives of the body they work for. These are opposite ends of a very long and complex spectrum, and it is far from likely that any such employees conform to either stereotype. It doesn't matter whether they do or not, because this theory is directed towards management attitude. If a manager holds Theory X views, he or she will endeavour to command and control via orders and demand obedience on pain of disciplinary action and other sanctions. Coercion will be the name of the game. This is likely to be counterproductive in a business environment where (or if) there are many similar organisations which the employee could move to, since it would lead to relatively high turnover. It is highly time intensive, as such a manager would spend most of his or her time observing the work processes of employees rather than doing other aspects of their job, to their own detriment, and may well reinforce the belief in his or her manager that he or she is indeed a Theory X type. It can be surmised that Theory X is iterative and could infect an entire company with negativity, leading to mutual resentment and low productivity. This is undesirable in the extreme, given the cost of recruitment and training associated with incoming staff. By contrast, a Theory Y approach majors on motivational management, leading from the front, mentoring and taking care of the employees requests and welfare, and excusing the occasional transgression on the basis of medium to long-term good or excellent performance through nurturing. The Theory Y approach to management plays well to Maslow's (1954) hierarchy of needs principle, where social needs are placed above basic physiological and health and safety requirements which are in any case guaranteed by law, and which Theory Y can address, and the next level in the hierarchy emphasises the need for esteem which is completely incompatible with Theory X but wholly compatible with Theory Y, and which leads naturally to self-actualisation, where employees perform tasks which they consider they 'own' and which characterise them as meaningful human beings. For Maslow, this is equivalent to self-motivation, which at best means that workers do the job well and do not need the same intensive level of supervision implied by the Theory X approach. Another theory relevant to staff retention is that of Herzberg et al. (1959), who studied a cohort of 600 accountants, and who found that motivation to a do a job well could only be achieved once 'hygiene' factors had been satisfied, including appropriate supervision and interpersonal relations. If a manager holds a Theory X view of employees, it is unlikely that they will emerge from the hygiene state to the next level which, for Herzberg, is the motivational state, with contributory factors which play well with Theory Y, such as status, opportunities for advancement, responsibility and willingness to accept challenges. Accepting for the moment the logic of applying a Theory Y approach to workers, we can then bolt on to this the recommendations of Herzberg et al. that there should be job enlargement, job rotation and job enrichment built into personnel development.

What does this mean for housing organisations? First, jobs should be designed to contain a number of functions which are varied enough to stimulate mental activity to achieve as variety of tasks. This is very important in inducting new staff into an organisation, so that they fully understand the context within which they are working and can participate in a variety of activities across the piece, including development, finance, management and strategy, whatever their entry level. This helps them see the big picture and routes within an organisation for advancement, although there is the collateral risk that having seen the picture, they may opt for another organisation having learned sufficiently to make that leap, although this will naturally depend upon the opportunities within the organisation to progress – clearly this will be more so in a larger body like a regional housing association or a large local or central government department. Second, secondments to other roles should be available to enable employees to find out whether their skill sets are better fitted to another role than the substantive one. This could be quite cost-effective, as the role relinquished could be backfilled by a more junior employee, where the cost of recruitment may be less than for the more senior move-on personnel. Agency workers could also be brought in at short notice to fill the secondee's substantive position and let go when or if the secondee returns to their post. Third, job enrichment entails ensuring that the work itself is varied enough to make it interesting and challenging – therefore setting up projects for workers to fulfil may be a way forward here, for example intensive involvement in devising a communications strategy.

The future of housing management

It is hard to predict what the future of housing management will be. Much depends upon the social and economic challenges which we shall see played out in the years beyond. We have already seen a sea-change shift from the personal interventional style of Octavia Hill to the case-oriented approach and on to the functional low-interventionist style adopted by many organisations, often taking their lead from tenants and other residents via scrutiny panel deliberations which are often reflected in executive decisions. As the list of possible tenancy types burgeons, it is very likely that there will be an increase in the number of tenancy sustainment posts within housing bodies, along with a greater emphasis on assisting tenants into work and out of social and affordable tenure altogether and into home ownership, a hand up rather than a hand out, perhaps on the basis of the limited availability of social or affordable new lets or re-lets, and continued low turnover in the stock. There is also likely to be an increasing distinction between officers who manage stock and those who manage people, due to the ongoing imperative to ensure that homes remain decent and the scale of the challenge given the age of stock, and as has already been identified, the complexity of the tenure management task itself.

References

Audit Commission, (1986) *Making a Reality of Community Care*. London: HMSO.

Coleman, A.M., (1985) *Utopia on Trial: Vision and reality in planned housing*. London: Hilary Shipman.

DCLG (Department of Communities and Local Government), (2006) *A Decent Home: Definition and guidance for implementation June 2006 – Update*. London: DCLG.

Department of Health, (1989) *Caring for People, Community Care in the Next Decade and Beyond*. London: HMSO.

DETR (Department of Environment, Transport and the Regions), (1999) *Best Value in Housing Framework: Consultation paper*. Norwich: HMSO.

DETR, (2000) *Quality and Choice: A Decent Home for All*. London: DETR.

Greenhalgh, S. and Moss, J. (2009) *Principles of Social Housing Reform*. London: Localis.

Griffiths, R., (1988) *Community Care: An Agenda for Action*. London: HMSO.

Hackney Homes, (no date) Decanting: Rehousing. Available at: www.hackneyhomes.org.uk/hhs-decanting.htm, viewed 1 April 2012.

Haralambos, M., Holborn, M. and Heald, M., (2008) *Sociology; Themes and Perspectives*. 7th edition. London: HarperCollins.

Herzberg, F., Mausner, B. and Snyderman, B. B., (1959) *The Motivation to Work*. New York: John Wiley.

Hills, J., (2007) *Ends and Means: The future role of social housing in England*. London: ESRC Research Centre for Analysis of Social Exclusion.

Independent, (1994) The HIV tenants nobody wants. Sunday 15 May. Available at: www.independent.co.uk/news/uk/home-news/the-hiv-tenants-nobody-wants-1436084.html, viewed 1 April 2012.

Inward House, (2011) About Inward House. Available at: www.inwardhouse.co.uk/about-us.html, viewed 1 April 2012.

Joseph Rowntree Foundation, (2006) *Mixed Communities*. York: JRF.

Maslow, A., (1954) *Motivation and Personality*. New York: HarperCollins.

McGregor, D., (1960) *The Human Side of Enterprise*. New York: McGraw-Hill.

Merton Council, (2004) *Ethnic Minority Housing Strategy for Merton*. London: Merton Council.

NHF (National Housing Federation), 2011. *Briefing – Tenant Cashback*. London: NHF.

ODPM (Office of the Deputy Prime Minister), (2005) *Evaluation of English Housing Policy 1975–2000: Theme 5, Management Effectiveness*. London: ODPM.

Place Shapers, (2011) *Localism that works – how housing associations make things happen*. London: Bridge Group.

Popper, K., (1971) *The Open Society and its Enemies*. New Jersey: Princeton.

Seddon, J., (2005) *Freedom from Command and Control*. New York: Productivity Press.

Seddon, J., (2008) *Systems Thinking in the Public Sector*. Axminster: Triarchy Press.

4   Housing finance

Keywords: *introduction to housing finance; housing finance in context; government macroeconomic controls; spending review and the budget; housing balances; integrative overview – capital and revenue finance; key elements of and differences between housing association and local authority housing finance; capital operations in the affordable and social housing sector; local authority housing capital finance; notional independence – the post-2012 approach to capital finance resourcing, spending allocation and control, borrowing and spending limits; capital receipts; prudential borrowing; scope for reform in capital finance; housing association capital finance; the impact of the post-2011 National Affordable Housing Programme; scope for reform in the housing association capital area; revenue operations in the affordable and social housing sector; council housing revenue operations; HRA self-financing – financial freedoms post-2012; the price of reforming the HRA subsidy regime; features of the residual HRA subsidy arrangements; general fund input; scope for further revenue reform; rent restructuring; which subsidy – capital grant or revenue?; income-generation options; housing association revenue finance; housing association accounts; rent influencing; affordable rents; the impact of adverse sales and affordable rents on development and management; self-financing and income-generation possibilities; subsidy alternatives in the housing association sector; housing benefit and local housing allowances; development, principles and the rules; the impact of affordable rents on housing benefit expenditure and households; impact of the unified benefits system on housing customers and providers; options for further reform.*

Introduction

Housing finance concerns the method of funding capital development and running housing businesses effectively and efficiently, and planning for the future in both respects. There is little more to it than that, but it is obviously necessary to understand the dimensions of housing finance in order to undertake any of this, and the subject itself is relatively complex. On a walk-though basis, local authorities and housing associations in England share some vital characteristics and opportunities which a decade ago would not have been the case. They both have to produce 30-year business plans to justify capital investment in new homes on the back of Affordable

Housing Programme allocations between 2011 and 2015, and are both able to receive capital grant to realise development ambitions to provide mainly affordable housing at up to 80 per cent of local market rents, on flexible or assured shorthold tenures depending on the nature of the provider. Both have to apply business reasoning to the management of stock, through a reformed housing revenue account which is now unsubsidised through government revenue grant, and through the semi-commercial income and expenditure account and cash flow accounting applied by housing associations, and both have to produce balance sheets showing how much they owe and own to internal and external stakeholders and regulators. And they are both highly dependent upon external welfare subsidy in the form of housing benefit transfers, and will likely still be in this position post-2013.

By way of introduction, local authority housing finance in England and Wales is driven by two major factors: first, capital investment (or rather the lack of it) to produce new homes and refurbish existing ones; and second, revenue finance to ensure that stock is managed efficiently and effectively in response to the expressed and other needs of those who live in the stock.

All organisations need to finance their operations. All rely upon income to spend on current services and capital works, if they do undertake these tasks. In the case of housing organisations, the principal income source is rent and service charges, and principal outgoings are loan repayments, interest and capital, and maintaining the stock.

Housing organisations which have the aim of providing for housing need or sub-market demand frequently enter into contracts with central government departments or statutory agencies to assist them with money to develop new homes and in some cases to run the stock they have without having to charge exorbitant rents. There is little point in forcing housing bodies whose clients are in the main those on lower incomes to charge high rents, since they would not be paid, and the cash flow situation of the organisation would soon be dire, and they would go under without state assistance. Therefore, to maintain rents at affordable levels, it is necessary to ensure that housing bodies providing for lower-income groups are appropriately subsidised, as a matter of national policy, since no state would wish to exhibit thousands of families on the streets. Having said that, the subsidy in question could come from the organisation itself through surplus-generating activities, or from the state from national taxation or from both of these sources. There is also the open question as to whether rents could actually take the strain of administering housing services without reliance on subsidy, or so much of it, and this debate has been played out in the introduction of affordable rents in the not-for-profit sector in England since 2011.

There is a choice to be had between subsidising property to keep rents low or subsidising the individual on the basis of the gap between the income they can comfortably commit to paying rent and the rent itself. The former usually involves an external body paying enough money to the provider to keep rents low, either through an initial capital subsidy granted at the time of development thus defraying costs which would otherwise have to be met through loan finance to be covered through charging an economic rent, or continuous subsidy to the individual to enable them to pay the economic rent. Here, by 'economic rent' I mean the amount equivalent to the ongoing expenditure incurred by an organisation in respect to the development, management and maintenance of a dwelling. Straightforwardly, if I build a three-bed house for £100,000, and apply £50,000 savings to the project, I will have to borrow £50,000 to complete the project, unless this sum is gifted from someone else. Let us suppose the loan is an interest-only arrangement, and the annual rate is 10 per cent. The annual loan charge would be in the region of £5,000 and the capital recharge would depend on the term of the loan. Now suppose that I set up a sinking fund of say 5 per cent per annum of the cost of the property to cover the deterioration of components which will need to be replaced over the term. That's £5,000. Now I engage a manager to manage the property and commission maintenance, which I estimate at £2,000 and £3,000 respectively, as I have other properties in my portfolio to apportion the costs to. I also need to insure the property, and will endeavour to roll up the acquisition fees into the cost to be met through income, and will be looking for a 10 per cent return per annum on my investment. I will assume that the property has a useful life of 60 years. Putting this all together, the rounded costs I need to cover are displayed in Table 4.1.

Table 4.1 Costs of developing, financing and managing a three-bed house

Item	Cost, per annum and rounded
Rolled-up acquisition cost at 5 per cent of development costs	£5,000 divided by 60 = £83
Loan cost (interest) at 10 per cent principal	£5,000
Capital recharge spread over 30 years	£3,333
M&M costs	£5,000
Sinking fund	£5,000
Profit on investment at 10 per cent invested over 30 years (year 1)	£5,000
Total income required per year	£23,416
Per month	£1,951
Per week	£450.31

This is a high rent by any standard. I could reduce it in a number of ways. First, by reducing M&M costs through competitive tender, although this might result in a diminution of service levels, but let's assume I could save 25 per cent on this basis. The new figure for M&M becomes £3,750 per year and reduces the rent to £19,666 divided by 52 to £378.19 per week. Now I decide to reassign my profit to a prudent surplus required against inflation and non-insurable disasters. This has no effect on the rent. I find that most people on lower quartile incomes looking to me for re-housing earn approximately £400 a week and can only afford one third of their income to pay towards housing costs exclusive of council tax and bills. I am a true philanthropist and want to do the best by my community.

The rent which lower quartile earners can afford is 1/3 x £400, which is £133.33. This is a lot lower than the economic rent of £378 (rounded down). If I am a sole supplier and will not reduce my rent to this level, or simply let the property to higher quartile earners, I could be persuaded to let the property to the low earner if someone else pays the difference in the form of housing benefit (something in the order of £245 week), or accept external grant help towards the building and acquisition costs (£100,000) which, if at the rate of 100 per cent (I am after all performing a necessary social function) leaves M&M costs at £3,750 and a sinking fund at £5,000, together with a prudent surplus at £5,000. The total to cover would now be £13,750 which works out at £264.42 per week, which means that I would expect the state to come up with £131 (rounded down) per week. To get the rent to £133.33, I would require the state to either commit to the housing benefit sum stated, or indeed to pay me to acquire the land and undertake construction as well as bearing the entire outlay! It quickly becomes apparent, through this tale, that at some stage, subsidy is needed to bring rents in line with what people can afford.

How to produce affordable housing which is affordable to the state and to the individual is a question which has beset policy-makers since the dawn of non-market housing. The crude alternatives are to produce housing at market rates, recharge the ongoing costs including development loans to the occupier and expect the state to pick up the tab to enable them to remain in occupation without defaulting immediately, or to subsidise the development and possibly the ongoing costs to the extent that the rent is affordable to the occupier. It will be seen that there has been a move in England at least from the latter approach to the former, witness the reduction of the Affordable Housing Programme for 2011–2015 to £4.5 billion from £8.4 billion for the previous affordable housing round, with very similar production targets, and the consequent decision to promote affordable rents at up to 80 per cent of local market values.

The other big question is, when the relationship between state subsidy – object and/or subject – has been settled, how are care costs associated with the occupant to be paid for? Many in social and affordable housing have support needs related to the accommodation in which they live, for example, mobility problems where a carer may be needed to help the person cope; the need for money and other advice to be delivered; and assistance with claiming benefits. Many of these functions are provided by social services departments and the charge is met from Supporting People-based budgets which are either directly or indirectly controlled by the customer, with advice as and where appropriate. These themes will be explored in depth in this chapter.

Housing finance in context

Housing is not a big player in the macroeconomic theatre. This is shown in an analysis of the 2010 Comprehensive Spending Review (CSR). The government's CSR, which fixes spending budgets for each government department up to 2014–2015, is comprehensive in that it covers all areas of government-assisted expenditure and starts from a zero base, and does not just adjust previous spending review figures by inflation. It came at a time when the state was spending significantly more money than it raised in tax, and had to plan to meet the gap – called the deficit – by borrowing at record levels. The Affordable Housing Programme 2011–2015 consisted of a pledge to grant £4.4 billion (down from £8.8 billion over the previous three-year period) to support the production of up to 150,000 new homes for rent and for sale, with some of this reserved for the completion of social housing programmes. The question is, how does the government decide to cut the expenditure-support cake?

The government perceived that the problems with public expenditure were essentially around record and unsustainable borrowing levels: in 2009–2010, £1 in every £4 spent was borrowed, and it was noted that interest payments on the nation's public debt each year were more than the government spent on schools in England, at £43 billion per year.

There was a particular focus on what the new government decided was wasteful expenditure and reducing welfare costs, along with an imperative to endeavour not to raise taxes, or to spend to foster economic growth in a Keynesian fashion. The only way to stabilise public expenditure therefore seemed to be to go for an austerity approach in terms of support for public services, which indeed transpired. This meant that departmental spending, other than on health and overseas aid, was cut by approximately 19 per cent over the four years of the CSR. In the case of housing capital support, the budget was halved. For the first time, the government decided to incorporate annually managed expenditure into the CSR – for example, welfare benefit payments, to try to impose a universal cap on even volatile areas. It is in principle difficult to achieve this, as it cannot know known in advance how many citizens will begin to rely on welfare support at any one time, although statistical records can be a reasonable guide, such as the observation that at any one time, 60 per cent of social housing tenants are reliant upon housing benefit.

In practice, the government has a limited number of macroeconomic controls at its disposal – many have been tried and have failed. In the early 1980s attempts were made in the UK to limit the amount of money in circulation by imposing draconian credit controls which created queues for borrowing; at other times the government has used interest rates as a means of controlling demand, as credit is a very common way of acquiring goods and even services, but this was hardly a vote winner. Each of these strategies was based on the belief that money behaves much like any other commodity: if its velocity in circulation increases, its value will diminish. For example, if the government releases £5 million pounds into the economy, it will of course circulate quickly, but without anything to back it (for example increased productivity) it will not represent any real growth in national wealth, and in fact will foster inflation, as the market reacts to increased money supply by raising prices: wage inflation will surely follow. The same cycle could be started the other way around: increasing wages increases buying power, and markets tend to react to this by raising prices. The net result is that commodities cost more, driven by increased money supply. This is at the heart of the monetarist theory popularised by Milton Friedman, and espoused by the Thatcher regime from 1979, and essentially followed by successive governments in an attempt to stabilise inflation without moving to stagflation, which is held to be just as disastrous.

The authors of the CSR certainly held to these maxims, although greater freedoms were given to local authorities to spend the grant they got from central government through deringfencing, so that currently very few grants are earmarked for specific projects or services.

The charity for the homeless and badly housed, Shelter, suggested in its CSR briefing (Shelter, 2010) that for every £1 cut in housing investment, the national economy will take a hit of £3.50. The reasoning was that this would arise through construction job losses, and reduced demand for homewares and components which would follow, with reduced tax income. This does not seem to be an unreasonable proposition if one considers what goes into building a house, and the expenditure needed to deck it out, added to the cost of temporary accommodation which is never recovered when housing people who would otherwise have bought a home or rented one.

The CSR informs the annual budget, which broadly sets out the revenue amounts which government intends to raise through taxation and gives an indication of spending plans. Budgets have to subsist within the three-year CSR envelope, and are in themselves highly political. The March 2012 budget was not particularly significant for housing in that it raised very little money for development and gave no guarantees that the increase in stamp duty for very expensive house purchases would be channelled into affordable housing development.

Capital and revenue finance

Capital finance has a revenue tail: whenever an organisation borrows to build, it must be mindful that the debt created has to be repaid. Much depends upon how the debt is repaid – what measures are used, the nature of loan finance and how costs can be deferred to later years. An obvious relationship is that between rent and loan repayments. In the current housing world, where 'affordable' rents can be charged at up to 80 per cent of local market value, the implication is that housing organisations can rebalance the relationship between grant and loans by taking advantage of higher rental income, in addition to cross-subsidisation from market or near-market activities. This may be a dangerous approach, as much depends upon the reality of rent collection rates, which may be expected to become more onerous with increased rent and the changes to be brought about to the welfare benefits system, principally paying universal credit straight to tenants and less stable for direct-to-landlord welfare payments. Revenue also has a capital tail in that the revenue costs of the scheme can be minimised or at least reduced by prudent investment in sustainable materials which will require perhaps less maintenance over the years, and on designs which are flexible enough to adapt to lifecycle changes without entailing moves to other dwellings – the so-called lifetime homes concept.

Key elements of and differences between housing association and local authority housing finance

It used to be said that the key difference between local authority and housing assoc-iation finance was that councils received revenue grant support and no capital grants to support developments and that housing associations received no revenue support but did get capital grant support to ensure that the homes they built for rent were affordable to those who inhabited them. Since 2012, the world has turned on its head in this respect, almost. Under the 2011–2015 Affordable Housing Programme, some councils have received capital grant resources to assist them in developing affordable homes for rent, alongside housing associations, which is a major sea change. The number of homes to be produced by councils is not insignificant – for example, Barking and Dagenham Council in East London received some £18.3 million to assist them to produce 762 homes, and Hillingdon signed up to produce 225 homes assisted by £3.4 million from the HCA. There is of course no reason in principle why councils should not develop affordable homes as well as housing associations – after all, they have done so since the late 1800s, and must have learned a thing or two over that period!

Capital operations in the affordable and social housing sector

We begin out examination of capital operations by considering what are valid members of that set. It has already been explained that capital is distinct from revenue insofar that capital expenditure is intended to produce something of value, which will last for more than one year. This certainly applies to the construction of houses and flats, and to major components therein such as roofs and plumbing, as well as to roads and other permanent infrastructure, including (arguably) trees and hard land-scaping. Capital are those activities which create capital items, such as development, planting and improvement works which may or may not enhance the value of the asset. There is sometimes a fine line to be drawn between capital and revenue operations. Replacing a roof is undoubtedly a capital activity, since the roof will last for more than one year and has value; but when does a roof repair, which may entail replacing one or many tiles, or a rafter or two, become a capital work, or, for that matter, shade down to revenue? Much depends on the intention behind the works. If it was to make good, to ensure that rain and snow do not enter the dwelling, and was not intended to add value to the property or to create something new, it feels like a revenue matter to be funded from the housing revenue account, but if the intention was to replace sufficiently many tiles so as to virtually create a new roof, then it feels like a capital operation, even though the outcomes may look identical to the bystander.

Capital operations generally involve a local authority contracting out to a developer rather than undertaking the work directly, although this was not always the case. The reason for this is that virtually no local authority has a continuous building programme, and the question is, what would the works unit do when no development programme is current? One answer may be, work for someone else. There is nothing to stop local authorities in the UK at least undertaking work for another body as a trading option. One way to retain a development arm might be to form a joint venture company with a number of other councils which will be a dedicated development organisation; it is almost certain, given the entry into HCA funding on the part of councils via the Affordable Housing Programme, that someone in the region will be developing at any one time, and considerable economies of scale could be generated through this approach. The case for joint venture companies will be considered later.

Ashford Council, in Kent, is a premier example of a local authority which has opted to build council housing once more, by employing an external contractor. It identified land within its ownership, and then contracted one or more developers to erect dwellings on the sites where feasible. On one site, modern methods of construction were used to deliver 44 homes within 21 weeks on site, top level 4 of the Code for Sustainable Homes. One feature of the materials used – block work – was that the raw material to make the materials was derived from Britain, thus helping to sustain the national economy. Additionally, much of the material used to make the blocks was recycled and therefore ecologically sustainable.

Housing associations divide between those who use their in-house contractor for capital operations and those which contract the function out. Some larger associations such as London and Quadrant Housing Trust (L&Q) have set up their own in-house development agency. In the case of L&Q, this is Quadrant Construction, which is a wholly owned subsidiary and was set up in January 2011 to deliver a significant part of its 10,000 home pipeline, funded by a loan from the parent company. Among its first output was a 146-home scheme in the London Borough of Lewisham. Among the reasons cited for developing the in-house development route was to minimise the risk of developments failing to materialise due to the collapse of the development partner, perhaps thinking back to the demise of Connaught construction. It was also decided to do so to diversify the business, which makes sense in a recessional context, and could lead to active development on behalf of other registered providers, thus providing valuable income to plough back into the core business (L&Q, 2011). There is absolutely no reason why this company could not develop on behalf of other associations, and it already works in partnership with councils to develop or refurbish homes.

In addition to setting up their own development companies, associations have also set up joint venture companies and limited liability partnerships to take advantage of economies of scale in capital development. This is not a particularly new approach: a notable example of joint venture development in the sector is given by the case of Iceni Homes, a joint venture company established by Cotman Housing, Colne and Suffolk Housing Societies who considered themselves too small to develop directly and who wished to take advantage of economies of scale and minimise developer risk, and established the non-charitable joint venture company in 2004. It went on to increase its client base, including local authorities in East Anglia, and is now a major player in East Anglia.

To return to the core area, capital activities can be funded through loans or financial instruments such as bonds and share issues, via grant, surpluses or a combination of the above. Many organisations seeking to provide affordable housing have business plans which do not rely upon grant finance to sustain their activities, usually those who believe that they can effectively cross-subsidise from (for example) land or house sales, but there is surely a moral point to be made here regarding central grant. Ultimately, the housing produced is destined for those who for one reason or another cannot satisfy their needs through the market, and if we accept for a moment that having some form of accommodation is primary to being able to conduct any other area of life, it could be argued that grant reflects a social necessity and embodies the idea that there should be some form of redistribution from those that have to those that have not through the tax system, and if this is the case, why should organisations producing affordable homes for sale and for rent at sub-market prices not be able to access grant as of right? This level of argument is rarely pursued by policy-makers, but should nonetheless be deployed from time to time to remind them what the core function of affordable housing provision is, and that it is in essence redistributional. It is also justified in terms of sustaining an economically active population who would not perform as well were they not to inhabit decent homes within reach of their modestly paid jobs, although developments in the housing and welfare benefit fields do not bode well for this.

Let us examine the role of grants and loans in producing affordable housing, and review it against various models of capital support which could have been brought into train or continued. This will illustrate some of the strengths and weaknesses of the various approaches:

1   Capital development with no grant whatever
    1.1   Development cost including land acquisition/unit £200,000
    1.2   Financed through £50,000 surplus + £150,000 loan
    1.3   Interest (year one) on loan at 6.67 per cent £10,000
    1.4   Allowance to take account of lost interest on surplus (year 1 divided by 5 per cent) £2,500
    1.5   Standard M&M costs per annum £5,000
    1.6   Sinking fund for major repairs at 1 per cent of development cost/30 years £2,000
    1.7   Total base income to raise to cover revenue outgoings associated £19,500
    1.8   Cost-rent per week 19,500 divided by 52 = £375
    1.9   Local area market rent for this type of unit per week £250
    1.10   Policy to charge 80 per cent of local market rent at rent cap £200
    1.11   Amount to subsidise internally: 1.8 -1.10 = £175
    1.12   Decision: use investments producing £9,100 per annum (£175 x 52) at 5 per cent yield to cross-subsidise, or derive from sales assets invested i.e. £182,000 capital
    1.13   Assume a scheme of 50 affordable rent dwellings with linear M&M costs
    1.14   Total amount to subsidise internally = 50 x £182,000 = £9,100,000
    1.15   Decision: develop the equivalent of 50 affordable units for rent and 50 units for outright sale retailing at £182,000 each net of capital addition: add capital sum required to the sales price, divided between each unit
    1.16   Capital addition per unit therefore is £200,000, added to sale price
    1.17   Unit price of for-sale dwellings = £200,000 + £182,000 = £382,000 per unit

This model might work quite well where there is demand for medium to up-market dwellings. It might also be possible to produce 100 dwellings for sale at 50 per cent first tranche shared ownership, or a mix of outright for-sale and shared ownership homes (not necessarily on the same site) to effect the cross-subsidy, and even sell some land which may have been land banked to top up the internal subsidy arrangement. The risk is that the for-sale properties might not sell readily, so the body may have to raise loan finance to cover this eventuality until sales can be completed.

- Strengths
  1. The proposal could produce a mixed tenure sustainable solution to provide for a variety of aspirations.
  2. The model plays well to product diversification.
  3. It plays well to the Coalition government's policy that organisations should consider mixed-tenure solutions (see Hills report, discussed in Chapter 3).

- Weaknesses
  1. There is a reliance on open market trends, although some of the market units could be let at prevailing market rents to generate revenue cross-subsidy or even a sizeable sinking fund.
  2. Much depends on the availability of bridging loans to finance this form of development, with the uncertainty of interest rates as a factor.
  3. Take-up of the for-rent units may be mediated by housing benefit/welfare benefit constraints in the area.

      2   Capital development with 25 per cent grant restricted to the for-rent units

      2.1   Development cost including land acquisition/unit £200,000
      2.2   Financed through £50,000 grant + £150,000 loan
      2.3   Interest (year one) on loan at 6.67 per cent £10,000
      2.4   Allowance to take account of lost interest on surplus (year 1 divided by 5 per cent) £0
      2.5   Standard M&M costs per annum £5,000
      2.6   Sinking fund for major repairs at 1 per cent of development cost/30 years £2,000
      2.7   Total base income to raise to cover revenue outgoings associated £17,000
      2.8   Cost-rent per week £17,000 divided by 52 = £327
      2.9   Local area market rent for this type of unit per week £250
      2.10 Policy to charge 80 per cent of local market rent at rent cap £200
      2.11 Amount to subsidise internally: 2.8 - 2.10 = £127
      2.12 Decision: use investments producing £6,604 per annum (£127 x 52) at 5 per cent yield to cross-subsidise, or *derive from sales assets invested i.e. £182,000 capital*
      2.13 Assume a scheme of 25 affordable rent dwellings with linear M&M costs
      2.14 Total amount to subsidise internally = 25 x £132,080 = £3,302,000
      2.15 Decision: develop the equivalent of 50 affordable units for rent and 25 units for outright sale retailing at £132,080 each net of capital addition: add capital sum required to the sales price, divided between each unit

2.16 Capital addition per unit therefore is £200,000, added to sale price

2.17 Unit price of for-sale dwellings = £200,000 + £132,080 = £332,080 per unit

It can be seen that this solution lowers the for-sale unit price, which makes the units more competitive; first tranche (set at 50 per cent) would be more affordable than under the first option. The rents could be set at a lower level, but then the internal subsidy would increase. The trouble is obtaining grant to back such a scheme. Again, as with the first option, such rents may not be compatible with housing benefit/welfare benefit caps, so care would have to be taken to align them so that they are truly affordable. Sticking strictly to 80 per cent of market rent would, of course, mean dependency on internal subsidy as per the first scheme.

This is the sort of reasoning which registered providers will have to wrestle with in the absence of higher grant rates, along with the obvious difficulties of guaranteeing market sales, even with shared ownership options. We will explore these themes again in the Chapter 6.

Local authority housing capital finance

Traditionally, local authorities have borrowed long from the Public Works Loan Board (PWLB) which is an arm of the Treasury. In the 1980s it was not uncommon to raise capital in this way over 60 years for new builds and over 30 years for conversion or renovation, based on the expected economic life of the unit. Interest rates charged by the PWLB have varied over time, and have often been uncompetitive compared to best market rates. The interest portion of the loan was generally recharged to the HRA from the general fund, which borrowed the money, and assumptions were made on repayment rates for the purposes of HRA subsidy in the government model. In the past, the quantum of borrowing receiving subsidy was known as supported borrowing, and anything else supported by local revenue was termed prudential borrowing, and authorised under part 1 of the Local Government Act 2003. The scope for HRA prudential borrowing is now reduced for many councils following the reforms implemented in March 2012 due to the debt adjustments concomitant on the self-financing regime, but some still undertake this form of borrowing on the basis of any borrowing 'headroom' they may have.

This is the right time to introduce the concept of debt, and the way in which is has been manipulated in relation to the HRA subsidy reform. Consider the sources of finance for council capital activity: they are broadly loan finance, capital receipts and surpluses/reserves. Loan finance has already been dealt with – borrow long, pay interest on the loan, and receive subsidy on the HRA portion was the way. In terms of capital receipts, during the 1980s right to buy boom, many councils in England and Wales became debt free as a result of applying receipts to pay off HRA debt. Reform is on the way at the time of writing in relation to capital receipts, but since 1990, with a few variations, councils were only able to use 25 per cent of receipts from house sales under the right to buy and 50 per cent of land receipts, with the rest going to the Treasury, although it was possible to use 100 per cent of right to buy receipts if they were earmarked for regeneration projects by resolution of the council, and it was always possible to use 100 per cent of receipts of vacant sales. As already mentioned, many councils used right to buy receipts to pay down debt, although the wisdom of doing so may be questioned following the self-financing reforms which will be outlined shortly. In doing so, the opportunity cost of using receipts to finance new builds or stock improvement is raised; and if a high proportion of interest on debt is subsidised, the motivation for driving down debt levels in this way may be less than otherwise. Nonetheless, the prudence of non-indebtedness seemed to be an attractive prospect for many in governance.

Essentially what has happened is that some councils have been relieved of some of their debt and others have had to take on debt from the PWLB as a way of abolishing the pre-2012 HRA subsidy regime. Logically, if subsidy is related in the main to debt charge levels, then the way to abolish subsidy is to play around with debt levels, as will be seen when the HRA subsidy regime is discussed, but for now consider this simple two-authority model (this is a subsidy calculation which never happened!):

- Authority A owns 200 homes with rents calculated by the government at £100 average per week (£1,040,000 yield per annum). It is deemed to spend £1,040,000 per annum on managing and maintaining the stock, and no other costs are taken into account under this head. It is deemed to have borrowed a sum equivalent to an interest charge of £500,000 per annum. Its deemed expenditure, taking nothing else into account, is therefore £500,000 higher than its deemed income. Under the old system it would have received circa £500,000 in subsidy to assist it to run its housing services.
- Authority B also owns 200 homes, with rent calculated by the government at £150 average per week (£1,560,000 yield per annum). It is deemed to spend £1,000,000 per annum on managing and maintaining the stock, and no other costs are taken into account under this head. It has no borrowing, having paid down debt through capital receipt use. Its deemed expenditure, taking nothing else into account, is therefore £560,000 lower than its deemed income. Under the old system it would have had to pay £560,000 in negative HRA subsidy to the government to recycle to other authorities of type A to help run their housing services.

It was decided to reform the system so that Authority A ceased to receive subsidy and Authority B ceased to pay anything into the pot (as it would no longer be necessary). On 31 March 2012 at the stroke of midnight, the government removed Authority A's entire HRA debt and put it in the PWLB pot, and then lent the sum to Authority B. It adjusted the interest rate so that Authority B would have to pay £500,000 per year to the Treasury, but would no longer have to pay any negative subsidy. It said to Authority B that the £60,000 left could be used for additional borrowing and would not be touched by the government. In doing so, it abolished the subsidy system at a stroke, and the two authorities were effectively self-financing, although Authority B had more scope for additional borrowing than A, assuming that the figures bore a 1:1 relationship to the actual figures. In fact, Authority A's M&M costs were only £800,000, so when the dust had settled, it actually had £240,000 per year which it decided to use to build two houses. As for Authority B, its M&M costs were actually £160,000 per year, and the other assumed figures were as the actuals, so in practice it did not have any surplus to borrow against, although it did have plenty of incentive to shave its M&M costs!

You couldn't make it up.

Scope for reform in capital finance

With the level of change in capital financing already seen in 2012, it is perhaps a step too far to imagine what further reform may be like, but there will always be a number of options along a spectrum. They are as follows:

1. Housing bodies can borrow what they like as long as they can afford to repay any associated loans and otherwise have sufficient capital.
2. Housing bodies can borrow what it is deemed they need by their regulator to fulfil a given development programme, as long as they can afford to repay any associated loans and otherwise have sufficient capital.
3. Housing bodies do not incur capital expenditure directly but take over schemes at the end of the development process and manage them.

Option One is the total freedom option in that judgements about what can be borrowed are made entirely by the provider on the basis of their assessment of need and demand. There is in practice no regulation here – except self-regulation. This is the logical extension of the so-called prudential borrowing route, where business plans dictate the level of borrowing against an assessment of market conditions. All the risk is taken on by the borrower, and it becomes very important to ensure that the assessment of market take-up of for-sale and market rent products is sound, as the value of these products will almost certainly be used as collateral for longer-term loans. Under this option, providers are very much on their own, operating under conditions of market uncertainty, and failure might look grim indeed. If the for-sale or market rent markets failed, or performed below expectations, it is highly likely that the risk increase would drive up interest rates for associated loans, and this would impact on affordable rent levels unless there were some sort of adjustment subsidy available to control such rents. However, if the provider judged the market soundly, or overestimated its volatility, it could be looking at a very favourable loan environment indeed, which might in itself help to stabilise affordable rents. It could be argued that the free-for-all scenario outlined here is not something which should apply to something as vital as housing for those unable to access the market, for which there is a clear and present – and growing – need.

Option Two is closer to the one which obtains at present (2012), where there is a degree of control over borrowing exerted by a regulator through the medium of grant limitation. Under this model, the higher the grant element, the less the need to borrow, and lenders have the comfort that borrowing is overseen by an independent body which may or may not underwrite such borrowing. The availability of capital within the organisation, plus the ability to borrow against assets subject to regulations means that such bodies can show a degree of strength when approaching the market for loans, and can deliver programmes with a high degree of certainty.

Option Three is interesting but unlikely. This is where all affordable housing for rent is delivered by a central agency which uses its tremendous buying power to drive down development and other associated costs, and then farms the product out to what are essentially managing agencies. It is a model which has no parallels anywhere at present, and smacks of extreme state-ism, but ideology aside, it may stack up financially. It is undeniably the case that large organisations do have tremendous buying power especially where they are the main consumer, and one can imagine a situation whereby individual housing organisations are consulted as to the number and nature of dwellings which they will end up managing. The major argument against this option is that it removes a great deal of initiative from individual and often very entrepreneurial bodies, which may prejudice the quality of the outcome.

Housing association capital finance

Housing association capital finance is not innately complex. In development terms, the traditional route has been to subsidise development through central grant so that affordable or social rents can be achieved, as has already been discussed. The nature of grant support has changed over the years, from the situation obtaining before the 1988 Housing Act regime whereby the level of rent dictated the grant level, to one where the grant level dictates the rent – and then on to the 2011–2015 Affordable Housing Programme, where rent expectations are given by central agencies and where grants are tailored to ensure that providers adopt a given rent regime, unless they can marshal other sources of finance to drive rents down to what they consider acceptable levels.

The pre-1988 regime took as its starting point the level of 'fair rents' – that is, rents set by a regulatory body taking account of size and amenity but not market factors. Consequently, fair rents were in most cases considerably below market levels. Such rents could in the main only support M&M, and the loan which could be raised against any surplus, taking account of the need to budget for void periods and other anticipated costs, was in most cases small indeed. The Housing Association (HAG) grant level was essentially dictated by taking the loan corresponding to the residual income after M&M costs from assumed development costs. This system was abandoned in 1989 following the 1988 Housing Act because it was essentially an open chequebook arrangement, and was replaced by a system which set grant levels and then expected housing associations to set rents which would cover not only the cost of servicing development loans equivalent to the gap between development costs and fixed grant levels (initially at around 75 per cent of total 'approved' costs) but also M&M costs. It was therefore no longer possible to insist that housing associations set fair rents, which took no account of the need to service loans; therefore rents were deregulated and all new tenancies from 1989 were assured.

The system changed somewhat after 2002, when the government introduced rent influencing via its agent, the Housing Corporation, where rents were set formulaically on the basis of local compared to national income, relative valuations and size. This dictated to a greater or lesser extent the level of grant which could be applied to developments, although associations were expected to use their own capital resources to ensure that such rent levels were achieved, along with cross-subsidy from for-sale and higher rent schemes and in many cases land at undervalue from public bodies or through the planning system.

It became clear that it would be necessary to change the approach following the austerity situation from 2010 onwards, and the 2011–2015 Affordable Housing Programme saw the introduction of the idea of affordable rents at up to 80 per cent of local market values, as already outlined. This was entirely driven by the perceived need to reduce grant input into the system to meet national expenditure reduction targets in a predictable way, although it had the odd consequence that in some areas the affordable rent was less than what the rent influencing rent would have been, due to local rental market conditions. This circumstance poses considerable constraints on housing association development, as borrowing on the back of rental levels is commonplace, and no organisation would wish to see its income constrained by rather arbitrary national criteria, however well meant. Conversely, in higher rental value areas such as London, providers have expressed the fear that outcome rents may well not be affordable to their customer base, and may not be serviceable through housing benefit or equivalent personal subsidy, given the nature of caps. If this is the case, such organisations would find themselves unable to supply the kind of product they were set up to produce, with or without the benefit of cross-subsidy. Time will undoubtedly tell.

What does 80 per cent of local market rent look like? A range of examples can be given, based on rental data from various sites, including Rightmove, and can be compared with the sort of rents that providers charge to secure and assured tenants currently (April 2012).

Let us consider the market rent for an ex-local authority two bedroom flat in Hackney, East London. On 14 April, the author found three ex-council properties on a site which ranged in rental level from £210 to £250 per week. If we apply 80 per cent to these, the range is £167 to £200 per week. This compares to the local authority average weekly rent (all types) in Hackney of just over £85 for 2011–2012 (DCLG, 2012a) which is around 40 per cent of the lowest market rent found. So, on the basis of this very limited survey, affordable rents are around twice that of social rents in that area. Given that local authorities and housing associations can charge 'affordable' rents on re-let, it is quite conceivable that flats of the same type, size and age next door to each other could have very different rents, with one up to twice as much as the other, purely because of the rental regime applied to them by the same landlord. This was the sort of incongruity that the rent restructuring regime was supposed to eliminate, and yet here it is again.

The impact of the post-2011 Affordable Housing Programme

The 2011/15 Affordable Housing Programme represents a sea change in the funding of development. It halves the resources available to assist providers to develop social and affordable housing and makes funding conditional on providers producing the new affordable product at up to 80 per cent of market rents. Its impact has been considerable. Not only are providers now producing near-market rental products along with low-cost home ownership homes, but the Affordable Housing Programme provides a precedent for further grant reductions, so it will come as no surprise when the next Affordable Housing Programme further reduces capital support. Unless there is a major rethink, or the UK economy recovers from its current ailments, there is every prospect of grant being spread yet more thinly than currently. If so, there may be a move to increase typical rents even more. There are a number of issues which arise from this. First, if rents climb to (say) 90 per cent of market levels, it is inevitable that social security benefits will take the strain, so that capital will be replaced by revenue subsidy. If this is the case, it is hard to see where the savings will accrue, and the proportion of tenants reliant on benefit will climb from the current 60 per cent average to somewhere nearer 80 per cent. At this level, given that the taper arrangements remain in the reformulation of benefit following the Welfare Reform Act, it is likely that yet more tenants will be trapped in poverty, unable to take up modest employment for fear of seeing a significant reduction in income, so high rents are hardly a work incentive. Second, and mindful of this consequence, it is likely that incentivisation schemes to encourage tenants for benefit into work will burgeon. These will very likely comprise a mix of welfare to work enabling schemes – similar to those which already exist, where providers and their partners broker apprenticeship schemes, alongside job creation initiatives and even more signposting into existing employment opportunities and creating 'mixed and sustainable' communities where those who already have work are sited next those who have none to provide positive examples of the value of work. Third, it is highly likely that the degree of cross-subsidisation from for-sale schemes will grow, along with the use of internal receipts and creative financing mechanisms such as stocks and bond issues to supplement grant, to enable home-grown reduced-rent products to cater for traditional client groups.

Scope for reform in the housing association capital area

There is considerable scope for reforming housing association capital finance and perhaps, given the changes itemised above, it is the right time to do so. If grant is to be reduced to a greater extent than currently, and housing associations still find themselves able to provide affordable accommodation, there is the need to find new products which will deliver affordable rented homes for those that need them alongside demand-side products which provide valuable cross-subsidy. One way to ensure that there remains sufficient capital in the system to provide affordable homes for rent is to provide a hand-up flexible product as standard. There has been much talk of hand up rather than hand out in recent years in the sector – that is, developing products which will lift people out of poverty rather than keeping them there.

Essentially, the principle of a hand up is to assist tenants to move out of social or affordable housing and into another sector, or to ensure that they can afford near-market rents. We have already covered the latter, but the former requires real creativity which has already been exemplified. The idea is that someone could start as a social or affordable tenant, and then 'graduate' to full renting or home ownership through a series of stages, with the surplus from the rent or capital invested in acquiring a share of the home being recirculated to produce more 'hand up' homes. This, of course, does rely upon the reinvigoration of local economies so that tenants can obtain work which will sustain such a ladder of opportunity, and a change in the way in which benefits are provided with greater work incentivisation, which is happening in the UK. Without the requisite economic uplift, it is hard to see how such a programme can be sustained, and some form of Keynesian intervention may be required to kick-start such a process.

The idea is that the home is rented first at affordable levels, which are within benefit caps, so that those with no work or low-paid work can access the system. Then, as work is found, the rent is increased incrementally but at a lower trajectory than income gain so that the tenant is better off working, whatever the income is. This might involve tailored rental solutions, so that the new rent is customised in accordance with the wage. Differential rents of this sort may be hard to model, and lenders may be averse to some of the risks entailed, principally that of unpredictability of income, although the same is true of loading income changes into the benefits system. Ultimately, the hope is that incomes will rise to the extent that they will be able to sustain the purchase of a share of the equity backed by a mortgage or similar loan, and that the property will, in the end, be converted into a full for-sale unit, with any surplus being invested into new flexible products of this sort. The incentive is clearly that purchase provides equity which can be gifted to children or taken out of the system to buy luxuries if that is what occupants wish to do, and ultimately sold at a profit. This is a form of flexible right to buy, where ownership is built into a product from the word go, and is an expectation rather than an option.

The mathematics of such a proposal are relatively straightforward, as illustrated in Table 4.2. The model assumes two properties, one of which is uplifted to 90 per cent of market rent, the other of which is subject to purchase of 50 per cent. The bottom line is the return on the combined surpluses, which in this case exceeds £104 per year, plus free capital which can be used as collateral for loans.

Use of receipts from sales

Local authorities in the UK have had a duty to sell council homes to qualifying sitting tenants at discount since 1981, under the provisions of the 1980 Housing Act. It is fair to say that sales are not what they were. Sales peaked in England at 167,000 in 1982–1983 and slumped to a low point of 2,370 in 2009–2010 (DCLG, 2012b). The reason for this relates to the difficulty in obtaining mortgage finance from 2007–2008 and to limits on discounts which meant that in practice purchase was unaffordable for the majority of tenants, and arguably by the mid-2000s the best stock had in any case been sold off.

Table 4.2 Two-property flexible purchase model

Item	Cost
Rental unit at 80 per cent of market rent	£160
Management, maintenance and loan costs per week	£150
Initial surplus from above items	£10
Increase rent to 90 per cent of market rent, conditional on job	£180
Investable incremental surplus (fourth item minus second)	£30
Purchase option	50 per cent of equity, income dependent
Value of property and initial yield	£200,000 and £100,000
Re-investment at 5 per cent yield	£10,000 per annum
Two property model	90 per cent rent and 50 per cent purchase
Annual yield year one from purchase reinvestment	£10,000
Annual yield from tailored uplift rent to 90 per cent (fifth item x 52)	£1,560
Surplus from two-property model	£11,560 per annum
Rate of return on investment at 5 per cent	£101.48

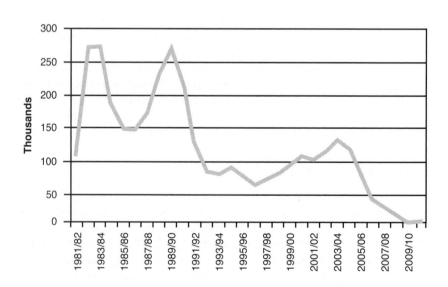

Figure 4.1 Sales under the right to buy 1981–1982 to 2009–2010
Source: Source: DCLG, 2012b.

The Right to Buy was a major plank of the incoming 1979 Conservative govern-ments' agenda, with a promise to turn the UK into a property-owning democracy. Home ownership rose from around 55 per cent in 1980 to 70 per cent by the mid-2000s, largely as a result of the policy, which has to date seen almost 1.8 million council homes sold. Figure 4.1 illustrates this trend graphically.

Initially, councils could use 100 per cent of the sales receipt to finance new capital work, not restricted to housing. So, if it cost £50,000 to build a house and the receipt from a sale was £50,000, that home could be replaced unless the council had some other use for the money. However, from the mid-1980s the government decided to restrict the amount that could be spent in any one year to 25 per cent of the receipts in the year in question, and 25 per cent of receipts from previous years. The council could therefore spend all the money from sales but over a period of time and not all at once. This was put into place to as a brake on inflation which was thought to be caused by too much money circulating too fast, as already explained in the context of monetarism. Even so, it would have been possible to back-fund the development of council housing through use of these 'cascaded' receipts, or even fund them on a buy now pay later basis, subject to the arrangement of a bridging loan. This was all stopped in 1990 following the 1989 Local Government and Housing Act 'new financial regime', which meant that councils could only ever see 25 per cent of right to buy and 50 per cent of land receipts, with the rest going to the Treasury. In 2012, there were moves afoot to enable councils to retain sufficient receipts to fund the development of new council homes on a one for one basis, and it has yet to be seen how effective this will be, but it is too little too late on the basis of sales records.

Revenue operations in the affordable and social housing sector

Revenue operations are about expenditure and income relating to current account activities, which include paying loan principal and interest, and day-to-day M&M activities. It is a simple subject. Basically, both councils and housing associations have to ensure that their income is sufficient to meet their outgoings, without any subsidy whatever. The only subsidy going into the system is personal subsidy – rents backed by housing benefit. Councils used to receive HRA subsidy, which was intended to plug a gap between notional expenditure and notional income, worked out on a formulaic basis imposed by the government. Some councils ended up getting subsidy, others paying it over to the government where notional income exceeded notional expenditure, and because rents were rising faster than expenditure, the whole system was in surplus from 2005 onwards. The main reason why councils got subsidy was the size of debts incurred through borrowing to build housing, usually on 60-year terms from the PWLB of the Treasury, as interest on debt was eligible for subsidy. So in 2011, it was decided that sufficient debt would be removed from those owing it, to be taken on by those who didn't and who had to pay into the system, so as to abolish HRA subsidy once and for all, so that councils could pay their way from rents. This is a reasonable way of doing business. After all, the debts incurred by building houses many years ago are hardly anything to do with current tenants, so why should they pay for it, and if you are landed with new debt, it is possible to reschedule it, which has to be better than paying an ever-increasing wedge of rent money to the government forever and a day. Some say that this penalises councils who have been prudent and have paid off debt over the years often through use of receipts, but you could also argue that paying off debt was the opportunity cost of developing new homes and/or undertaking major works, and that councils who chose to get debt-free were skewing their finances away from meeting the needs of current tenants – and so new debt is a lesson to be learned. Things are not as straight-forward as that, as the government assumed that councils would in fact use some receipts to pay off debt, but the principle is sound.

Stock-owning councils run a current account called the housing revenue account. It is ringfenced – that is, it cannot by law be subsidised from the council tax-collecting general fund, and it cannot be used to help fund the general fund either. Councils must aim at balancing the HRA and can only carry losses over one year.

The elements are as follows:

- Credits to HRA
    - Item 1 Rents – i.e. gross rents
    - Item 2 Charges for services and facilities – service charges on HRA properties – for example leasehold service charges and for furniture, board and laundry (note: trading income could go in here – for example HRA garages let out, or services to someone else)
    - Item 3 HRA subsidy (annual HRA subsidy determination in December, for following year) – this is now out
    - Item 4 Contributions towards expenditure (for example money from tenants for the cost of repairs which is their responsibility, financial help from the government to meet the cost of a disaster)
    - Item 5 Used to be housing benefit transfers (repealed from 2004)
    - Item 6 Transfers from the housing repairs account – some councils keep such an account within the HRA to help them focus on repairs efficiency and effectiveness
    - Item 7 Reduced provision for bad or doubtful debts – debts they expect to collect!
    - Item 8 Sums calculated by the secretary of state (i.e. notional interest on loans) – being reformed!
    - Item 9 Sums directed by secretary of state (transfers from general fund) – exceptional and only for one year
    - Item 10 Credit balance from previous year

- Debits to HRA
    - Item 1 Expenditure on M&M
    - Item 2 Expenditure for capital purposes – any money used from the HRA to finance improvements, development, etc.
    - Item 3 Rents, rates, taxes and other charges – for example rent payable on an estate office, long-term leased property
    - Item 4 Rent rebates, now out of HRA, and shifted to the general fund in 2004

- Item 5 Sums transferred under section 80(2): transfer of negative HRA subsidy to general fund – this is now out (see also Item 8)
- Item 6 Contributions to the housing repairs account – from the HRA to this specific account
- Item 7 Provision for bad or doubtful debts (rent and service charge arrears write-offs or debts they might not recover)
- Item 8 Sums calculated by the secretary of state (mainly debt financing, debt management and capital charges)
- Item 9 Debit balance from previous year

This is a fairly orderly account, but there are some items which might appear puzzling or may be in need of further explanation, and some items which definitely will need to be formulated following welfare reform from 2013.

First, look at the entry for rents, which is gross rents. The reason why gross rents are accounted rather than rents net of the housing benefit-related deduction which councils currently make is because losses through rebating are made good by payments of housing benefit subsidy which go into the general fund. So in reality, rent income is much less than this, and made good by internal adjustments. The Welfare Reform Act will see councils charging the full rent and then asking tenants to claim the housing element of the benefit from localized central government offices, to be paid to the council, just as is the case for private sector and council tenants (in 2012). It could be argued that the way in which the HRA is set out will resemble actual flows more nearly post-2013 than prior to it, as arrears will be accounted as bad debts under debit item 7, which is probably where they should go. And there will be arrears, as the minute that welfare benefit hits the tenants' pockets it is theirs to spend as they see fit, and human nature and need being what they are, there are bound to be arrears, whereas at the moment, the tenant never sees the benefit, since it is deducted before the rent is charged. Needless to say, this is a move not universally welcomed by councils, who are concerned about the impact of such arrangements on their cash flow. The same thing happened in 1981, but the government reversed the regime the following year due to protests from local authorities who found it impossible to collect all the rent due, through benefit leakage.

Item 2 relates to charges for services and facilities, and are mainly service charges on HRA properties, that is, for the management of leasehold properties. There is considerable scope for most HRAs to trade, for example by charging market rents for garages, by letting shops on estates, or providing admin and management services to other providers, although this has been relatively underexploited to date. There is no reason why councils should not establish a for-profit arms' length company to engage in market lettings and sales, which would gift the profit to the HRA as trading income, as long as care is taken to ensure that the company's activities do not fall within the general fund, from which the HRA is ringfenced.

Item 3 is the HRA subsidy (annual HRA subsidy determination in December, for following year) – this is now out, as has already been explained, but for how long? Debt readjustment following the final settlement was supposed to abolish HRA subsidy, but it must be tempting to impose and efficiency tax on councils whose HRA runs at a demonstrable surplus after paying off new debt and raising rents to affordable levels at least for part of the stock, and the government could do so at a stroke through regulation or primary legislation. Similarly, it is hard to contemplate the fate of council tenants where authorities genuinely cannot raise enough money through rents to provide a reasonable M&M service, and it may be prudent not to entirely forget subsidy, or to enable councils to subsidise their HRAs from the general fund in extreme circumstances on the basis that council housing is more than housing, and provides a social good which benefits the entire community.

Item 4 is contributions towards expenditure. As above, this includes payments from tenants for the cost of repairs which is their responsibility, and financial help from the government to meet the cost of a disaster – but not general fund contributions, due to the ringfence. Again, creative councils could direct the proceeds of a company established to service the HRA and other organisations and to engage in market housing sales and management which may benefit tenants as customers to this head, again as long as it is not regarded as general fund income.

The rest of the entries are fairly straightforward, although it should be noted that it may be good practice to keep a housing repairs account, if only to maintain a focus on repairs efficiency and effectiveness through performance monitoring a ringfenced sub-account, which is what tenants care most about, and it should be noted that in exceptional cases, the secretary of state can authorise transfers from general fund, but only for one year.

Debit entries are fairly straightforward, and highlight the need to ensure that councils maintain efficiencies and are effective in providing services, especially under the self-financing regime where there is no possibility of outside help to mask inefficiency.

Item 1 relates to expenditure on M&M functions, and is usually the most significant entry in the HRA debit side. It was noted when subsidy was discussed that such costs rose less rapidly than rents, but when rents have reached their target, even given the potential for increased income through affordable rents set on fixed-term 'flexible' tenancies, the disparity is likely to reduce, and business plans need to take account of this and consider other easy of boosting income alongside efficiency drives. One way of reducing such costs is to engage with other providers in a joint service vehicle which would manage and maintain the stock of a number of councils, which would gain from the economies of scale thus generated and expressed as savings. There are clearly investment needs here – with each authority either taking one particular aspect of the function for example back-office/information and communication systems support, or paying towards the running of a central jointly owned company which would deliver services on behalf of the group, and perhaps to others outside the partners to general additional income to be gifted to each council in proportion to their input.

Item 2 is very important, in that it accounts for expenditure for capital purposes, which broadly equates to the financing of stock improvements and new developments. If rents continue to rise at a faster rate than M&M costs, and councils choose to set new rents at 'affordable' levels, then there is no reason why this entry should not become a mainstay of development finance. It may be argued that this is dangerous since the HRA is supposed to be a landlord account to benefit existing tenants. However, it can also be argued that as soon as properties are developed they acquire a tenant who has benefited directly from such an investment decision. It can also be advanced that existing tenants would benefit indirectly through new homes being available to their sons and daughters.

Item 3 includes rents, rates, taxes and other charges for non-residential property utilised by the HRA – for example rent payable on an estate office which is not owned by the authority. It is arguable as to whether it is worthwhile leasing rather than buying offices, as there is no longer any revenue subsidy which can be set against this, and a judgement must be made about the best use of capital resources to acquire what could either be an appreciating or depreciating asset, depending on the state of the commercial property market. Commercial property has tended to appreciate in value in large urban areas over the past 50 years, so it may make sense to risk capital on acquisition on the basis that the freehold interest can be sold at some stage, or the entire asset divested when the property market is judged to have reached a peak, allowing for the relocation and possibly downsizing of other functions which it hosts.

Item 7, provision for bad or doubtful debts, is likely to be a growth industry with the welfare benefit changes from 2013, given that councils will no longer rebate rents and will rely upon the 60 per cent or so of tenants in receipt of benefit to regularly pay their rent backed by the state award. Hopefully, such losses will be offset by trading gains on the credit side of the account, but there is a real risk of on-paper bankruptcy if rental incomer cannot be sustained at a level to ensure that services can be delivered to an acceptable level and accounts remain in the black.

HRA self-financing: Financial freedoms post-2012

Let's think big picture about what self-financing could mean. We have already explored some aspects of trading, of offering services to other councils at a surplus, and of gaining economies and efficiencies through joint service vehicles, but there are larger possibilities to exploit the self-financing brave new world which councils have entered post-2012. Think of a range of products, and you will probably eventually come to the conclusion that there is more than one product of a given class which is offered commercially by the same producer, and that the price of products which are essentially doing the same thing varies according to design and market. This is also true of councils and other providers who are able to offer a suite of rents for similar-sized properties ranging from those which come out of rent restructuring to those set as a result of espousing affordable rents in relation to flexible tenancies and indeed new build and re-lets across the piece. If I were a tenant paying (say) 30 per cent more than another tenant in a similar property, I would expect to get a better service (product) than those paying less rent for a similar property. So why not offer this to reflect differential pricing? This would be equalised by spending absolutely no more on M&M but by scaling the service to reflect rents, so that non-near market properties receive a Class B service and those in other forms of near-market rent tenancies receive a Class A service. This would in fact incentivise those waiting for council housing to choose affordable rents (as long as they can afford it) and help to sweeten the pill for tenants moving from social to affordable rest on transfer or exchange. The net effect of this could be to increase income on the basis that it should cost no more to implement a management and maintenance service under these conditions that currently, as long as efficiencies are continued through and after the change process.

The price of reforming the HRA subsidy regime

Everything has its price and financial reform is no exception. Councils which became comfortable and perhaps complacent bolstered by significant sums of recycled rent money to help them pay debt and manage their stock now have to stand on their own two feet and make good any deficits which might arise. It is not a painfree process. What it does mean is that they will need to develop business stance based firmly on the twin pillars of efficiency and effectiveness, including innovation, to ensure that they provide high-quality services which customers demand. It is in some ways a shame that they are not pitted against each other in competition to manage the same stock. For example, there are 33 London authorities, of which 29 are stock owners, and which have a variable record in delivering services and improving their homes. Why so many? It is surely a historical accident, nothing more, and their geographical coverage encompasses very many different sorts of neighbourhood. Significant economies of scale could be generated by partnership working, which has already happened in some cases, and competition might well improve their edge in anticipation of being transferred lock stock and barrel to another provider.

General fund input

Not all council housing services are provided through the HRA. Some are funded through the general fund on the basis that they serve the community as a whole rather than just tenants, although local authority tenants are not barred from using these services, as they are also council tax payers. Examples include homeless persons' activities, housing aid and advice and strategy and policy operations. These are clearly not landlord functions, and rightly are not funded from rents. This separation came about as a result of the 1989 Local Government and Housing Act, in 1990 as part of the HRA ringfencing regime.

To give an indication of the scale of such funding, budgeted net expenditure for non-HRA housing in England was 2 per cent of the total grant paid to support council tax activities in 2009–2010, some £2.5 billion out of around £114.5 billion, and just 10 per cent of that expended on social care (DCLG, 2011). It is also dwarfed by housing benefit administration expenditure which in 2009–2010 was in the region of £115.5 billion including administration and payments. There has long been a debate as to whether tenants should pay for non-landlord services through their rent, but it seems that if this were the case they would be paying twice, and the complexity of reducing the council tax for tenants were this to happen probably rules out any alternative.

Scope for further revenue reform

There is scope for further revenue reform for local authorities. At the moment, we have self-financing, which will take some years to bed down, along with business plans and balance sheets showing the net worth of council assets, including housing. The reforms which could be introduced include:

- abolishing the HRA as a separate account;
- making the HRA voluntary;
- abolishing local authority housing altogether and turning the stock over to profit-making concerns;
- transferring all stock to housing associations;
- letting councils raise money as they would like and use revenue in any way they choose as long as it is resolved by council decision and accountable to tenants and other stakeholders.

We will consider these alternatives one by one. The first is tantamount to total deringfencing, and could be justified on the basis of simplicity and transparency. Council housing is just another asset which happens to be accommodation, and customers pay for it just as everyone pays towards the services of the council through the council tax. Customers who happen to be tenants would pay a bit more local tax than others to reflect the fact that they enjoy specific services, but the funding of those services need not be linked in any way to such payments. The justification for this approach is that housing is essentially a social service to be accessed by any citizen who is unable to find housing solutions in the marketplace, and is just as vital a good as policing and social services. There is no link between what is paid towards schools and the level of provision, nor between social services payments and council tax, so why should there be any link between council tenants' payments and the revenue expended on it? If more rent comes in than expenditure, fine – why not use the surplus to paint the town hall (which is a community asset enjoyed by everyone) or plant a few more trees in the park? The fact that rent is being used to pay for these facilities is in no way inconsistent with providing housing services: it all depends how the charge is marketed. The justification for levying a higher 'community charge' on tenants (who would cease to pay rent in the way we understand the term) is because they are enjoying a special category of service not enjoyed by others, although the term 'rent' would still be used in agreements in order to conform with housing legislation. It could be levied on the basis of how much it costs to manage and maintain the housing stock plus a market differential reflecting the state of the local property market, so the charge would be higher in central London than in (say) Wisbech or Newcastle. There would be total freedom on spending any surplus, although caveats could be placed on this in terms of centrally audited quality expectations, for as long as councils received general fund support, and if not, there would be reliance on the Housing Act and associated acts, for example the health and safety provisions of the 2004 Housing Act. The pros of this approach include the bolstering of local democracy and decision-making on local funds; reducing the degree of central scrutiny on local authority activities; a wholesale simplification of housing and related finance; and a community-wide incentive to maximise efficiencies in order to release extra funds to benefit everyone in the locality. The cons would include the charge of arbitrariness in relation to the charge and over-contribution of one class of resident to local services as compared to others, although this could be rebutted by pointing out that the rents are not at market levels (where this is the case) and therefore the leakage referred to simply reflects the discount offered and the fact that (arguably) such housing is a privilege and not a right.

The second possibility – that of making the HRA voluntary – would enable councils who wished to try out deringfencing to do so on a temporary basis to see if this is a better way of accounting for housing income and expenditure than other ways (for example the first option). It could even be put to the vote. Consider the matter yourself: if you were a council tenant, what would your attitude be to allowing some of your rent payment to be used to support community facilities which you may or may not wish to use? Or would you rather that it were used solely on managing and maintaining council properties, even if there is nothing wrong with either and no justification for spending surplus rent money on enhancing either the stock or the services associated with it. It would be tempting to argue for a rent reduction in this case, and this is a fair request, but it could be countered that the rent is the going rate set democratically by the council (if not by an externally imposed formula) and therefore is what it is. The pros of this approach are (as before) the democratisation of local finance and provision, and the con that a postcode lottery would develop, with adjacent councils charging similar rents delivering very different service offers, although this sits well with local democratisation and the principles of localism.

The third option, to reiterate, that of abolishing local authority housing altogether and turning the stock over to profit-making concerns is perhaps the most radical of all the notions. The HRA would be abolished entirely, and be replaced with the property revenue accounts of private landlords, who would charge the going rate for the property, with tenants unable to pay from their own resources being entirely dependent on the welfare support regime. Rents would be set so as to provide an acceptable margin over and above costs, and to provide dividends to shareholders, depending on the constitution of the company. If tenants could become shareholders, they could offset some of the additional rent level with dividends received and would therefore be very interested in the fortunes of the company. It might even lead to tenants getting more involved in housing than currently, as positive suggestions which increased the profit element would have a direct impact on their pocket, whereas less effective strategies might reduce their dividend income. This option would also take all local authority housing off the national balance sheet, along with its outstanding debts, although the sums would have to be done to see whether the benefits would be outweighed by the losses in the short, medium and long terms. It all depends upon whether rental income outweighs maintenance liability.

The fourth option is essentially wholesale stock transfer, and would remove public housing from the national balance sheet at a stroke. The advantage for housing associations would be the acquisition of significant assets with value against which borrowing could be secured, and an enhanced revenue stream. There may be savings to the public purse in that housing associations are generally more commercially minded that local authorities, and prepared to innovate to save and grow incomes, unconstrained by many of the laws and regulations which beset councils. The rationale for this option is simply that councils are local administrative bodies which have responsibilities to the public at large, and that there is no reason why they should act on behalf of a specific group of citizens who may or may not be in need of their services at all points of their lives.

The last option is far reaching and casts councils in the role of private landlords with total determination over all aspects of their stock which implies total local democratisation. Freed from any constraints imposed by central government apart from basic tenancy law, they could be totally creative as to the way in which they dealt with their assets, and there would be a direct relationship between them and their local voters, including council tenants. Granted that this might result in a postcode lottery but it exists in any case in relation to others goods and services they provide so why should housing be any different? There may be healthy competition developing between councils of similar size and locality, which might not be a bad thing in terms of driving up the quality of services provided. An additional feature – that of allowing tenants to vote with their feet and move to another council provider – may be a useful adjunct to this option which has at its heart the improvement of services through the innovation prompted by such freedoms.

The rent restructuring regime

One odd feature of housing policy over the past 20 years has been the imposition of a formula to determine the rents of social housing providers. Prior to 2002, rents in the council and housing association arenas were set largely as a matter of local policy decisions. At root, the challenge is to ensure that income covers expenditure, and how income is cut is a secondary issue. The primary concern is to get the income in, and minimise losses, which is to an extent determined by the level at which rents are set. Too high and benefit caps might be breached; a problem if 60 per cent or so of tenants are dependent in some way on government support. Too low and there is the risk that expenditure will not be met or that it will have to be set too low to deliver acceptable services and improvement to stock.

The 2002 Green Paper (DETR, 2002) contemplated the setting of rents in the social sector in a way which would reflect property values, incomes and size in a way which would iron out inconsistencies between providers purely on the basis of their identity and policies. At the time, there was (and continues to be) great debate about the difference between assured and secure rent levels, and between social rents and the private sector, and prior to the introduction of the voluntary rent restructuring regime (rent influencing for housing associations) there was a variety of easy methods in which rents were set. Some were based on a points system, where the total amount required in was cut according to the attributes of properties, others were based on relative rateable values, some were hybrid between these methodologies and yet others appeared to have no rationale at all beyond uplifting historic rents on an annual basis. The first method involved a complex calculation based on weighted attributes. It can be illustrated by a two-property system. Let us suppose that the total income required is £1,000. There are two properties in Local Authority A's system which are different in terms of bed size only. Property one has three bedrooms, and property two has two. In all other respects they are identical. Property one scored 75 points on the basis that each bedroom is worth 25 points, and property two 50 points. The total point quantum is therefore 125; 75 divided by 125 is 0.60, and 50 divided by 125 is 0.40. Therefore the rent of property one will be £1000 x 0.60 (£600) and that of property two will be £1000 x 0.40 (£400). Thus, assuming 100 per cent rent collection, the two property system will generate £1,000 per period. Any number of complexities can be included in the points system, but as long as the total adds up to the amount required it doesn't matter what factors are brought into play. A five-property scenario is somewhat harder to work out, but nonetheless transparent.

Consider the Table 4.3 and work it out for yourself!

Table 4.3 Property rents

Property	Beds	Property X bed weight	Points/total	Rent (a)
A	1	25	0.1	£769
B	2	50	0.2	£1,538
C	3	75	0.2	£2,308
D	3	75	0.2	£2,308
E	4	100	0.3	£3,007
F	5	125	0.4	£3,846
Total points		325	1.0	£10,000
Points per bedroom		25		
Income required/yr		£10,000		

Now let's make it even more complex by adding an 'age' variable into Table 4.4. Let us assume that properties fall into three age bands (10 years old, 20 years old and 30 years old). Properties which are 10 years old score twice as high as those 20 years old on the basis that they are more modern, and those which are 20 years old score twice as high as those which are 30 years old on the same basis.

An alternative methodology cuts rent by rateable values; if there were two properties in Local Authority B's system and the rateable value of the first were £2,000 per year and that of the second £1,000, and the total yield required were £10,000 per year, the rent of the first property would be £10,000 x (£2,000/£3,000) = £6,666, and the second £10,000 x (£1,000/£3,000) = £3,333.

Table 4.4 Rent calculations

Property	Beds	Property X bed weight	Points / total	Rent (a)	Age (yrs)	Property X age	Points / total	Scaled to 2	Scaled to 1	Rent (b)
A	1	25	0.1	£769	20	4	0.14	0.2	0.1	£1,099
B	2	50	0.2	£1,538	30	2	0.07	0.2	0.1	£1,126
C	3	75	0.2	£2,308	10	8	0.29	0.5	0.3	£2,582
D	3	75	0.2	£2,308	10	8	0.29	0.5	0.3	£2,582
E	4	100	0.3	£3,007	30	2	0.07	0.4	0.2	£1,896
F	5	125	0.4	£3,846	20	4	0.14	0.5	0.3	£2,637
Total points		325	1.0	£10,000	10	28	1.00	2.0	1.0	£10,000

Points per bedroom   25
Income required/yr   £10,000

	10 yrs	20yrs	30 yrs
Age variable	8	4	2
Age multiplier	2	2	2

Consider the five-property model in Table 4.3, based solely on rateable value differentials.

Table 4.5 Rateable value rents

Property	RV	Pr RV/Total RV	Rent (a)
A	£1,000	0.06897	£690
B	£2,000	0.13793	£1,379
C	£1,500	0.10345	£1,034
D	£3,000	0.2069	£2,069
E	£3,000	0.2069	£2,069
F	£4,000	0.27586	£2,759
Total RV	£14,500	1	£10,000
Income required/yr	£10,000		

Note: RV = rateable value.

It can be seen that these models produce very different results in terms of out-turn rents, and it could be justifiably argued that there should not be such a divergence, especially as the properties in question are very similar between authorities. This was the thought which motivated the development of the rent restructuring system, which was supposed to unify rents across the social housing sector: the idea was that rents in a similar area for similar properties should be the same, by a given target date. The variables selected were size, affordability and value. Put simply, affordability was worked out as average manual incomes in an area over national average incomes, size as a multiplier applied to the affordability element, and value as property values based on historic values at 1999 over average national values. The modified affordability element was multiplied by 70 per cent of the base rent, and the value element by 30 per cent to give the formula rent, and target rents were worked out by multiplying the result by an inflation factor over ten years to 2011–2012. The geographic areas were counties, so theoretically a two-bed property in county a owned by a housing association should have the same rent as a two-bed property owned by a local authority in the same county – eventually. The same was true of properties of the same size and value owned by a single housing provider. The route to bringing actual rents to target rent was known as convergence, and the process of bringing housing association rents and council rents together was termed 'harmonisation'. There were limitations placed on rent increases and caps above which rents could not go in any one year. It sounds a relatively straightforward way of doing business, and the report (ODPM, 2003) which put the system forward makes relatively easy reading, but it had odd and unwanted consequences for providers and the government.

Inflation was a key variable in limiting rents, to increases of retail price index (RPI) (per cent) + 0.5 + £2 in any one year. This was fine where RPI was positive, but negative RPI could force rents down or at least cause them not to rise, as was the case in 2010. This was because of the choice of when to measure RPI – it is measured in September, and was -1.9 per cent on the due date in 2009. This meant that social rents could only rise by (-1.9 + 0.5 + or -£2) which is -1.4 per cent + £2. If the weekly rent were £100 in 2009, the 2010 rent could only rise to £100 + (100 x -1.09 per cent + 0.5 + £2) = £101.98, even if inflation rose by the effective rent increase date (say 1 April 2010). The higher the starting rent, the worse the effect – if the rent were £200, it would be forced down to £195.20 by the limitation formula; £200 + (£200 x (-1.9 per cent + 0.5) + £2 = £195.20, £4.80 lower than the previous years' rent. This was not exactly what lenders wanted to see, who had modelled business plans relating to loans on positive inflation over (in many cases) 30 years, and several associations wrote to their regulator, the TSA, to ask to be exempted from the formula for that year. For a full explanation of the regime, see Solomou et al. (2005). Additionally, due to inflation changes over the ten-year period, it became mathematically impossible to converge rents by the due date, so the formula was modified again and again to get convergence to happen. Often the devil is in the detail with such simplifying and rationalising plans. Perhaps the affordable rent regime was introduced to help people forget about how awful the rent restructuring regime was.

Housing association revenue finance

Housing associations are companies or charities and are not governed by the rules which beset local authorities. They live on their rents and receive no external subsidy apart from housing benefit paid directly to them at the behest of tenants. The subsidy they get is capital in the form of grants, and as has already been said, they cross-subsidise capital activities via land and asset sales, including the proceeds of shared ownership schemes. They often operate commercial activities such as managing private sector properties or those of councils, providing homes for outright sale and even retail sale, and range in size from 10 to 200,000 units.

Rental income comes in the form of assured rents based on rent influencing formula and affordable rents at up to 80 per cent of local market rents. They have to cover expenditure on management, maintenance and loan repayments, where these cannot be offset by investment and/or sales income. Many associations have issued bonds or stocks to increase investment income, and others have used a variety of financial instruments for prudent treasury management ends to ensure that their surpluses and reserves work well for them.

What are the challenges which face housing associations, and what have their reactions been in an attempt to secure capital and revenue stability and growth? The challenges broadly are reductions in grant levels – as already described, and greater reliance on debt financing and cross-subsidy. It is essential to ensure that associations continue to enjoy favourable credit ratings: they must not be over leveraged with debt, otherwise lenders will not lend at favourable rates, and affordable housing programmes will not work well, or at all. There is also (in 2012) a difficult lending market, so associations have to impress to get favourable loans, which means demonstrating efficiencies and effectiveness, as well as a willingness to consider asset sales, which may not be popular with managing boards.

So what are the options for housing associations to generate capital for new homes? Issues include: joint ventures/partnerships; the increased use of market sales; further engagement with the bond markets, considering equity versus grant financing, challenged by the reduction of historic grant levels; making full use of sales receipts; taking advantage of public land release at undervalue for development; maximising tax incentives; and maximising alternative sources of government finance.

Joint ventures

This entails housing associations entering into longer term partnerships with developers to provide affordable homes. It typically involves housing associations taking on the social/affordable rented and shared ownership element of large mixed tenure schemes. Such arrangements share the development risk between partners, and provide housing associations high degree of control on design and location of properties. This approach means housing associations taking on more sales-risk.

Market sales and group restructuring

Another option is to increase the amount of homes built for outright sale, and use the profits generated to reinvest in new affordable homes. Associations are able to develop for outright sale and remain charitable – mainly by creating for-profit subsidiaries, however, care must be taken to protect the charitable status of housing associations (for tax reasons) when taking this option.

Utilising the bond market

Bonds are financial instruments whereby the provider incurs a future debt and is obliged to pay interest, and repay the principal at a later negotiated date ('maturity'). Bond holders acquire a creditor stake in the company. They have been utilised over the past five or so years by housing associations to supplement grant and traditional borrowing – especially since the 2007 credit crunch. This allows associations to diversify their sources of debt funding. An example is where the large UK-wide housing association Places for People issued 'retail bonds' in June 2011. This targeted private individual investors rather than corporate and institutions. Housing associations also issue bonds targeted at institutional investors, but there is always going to be a choice between these, based on their perception of which gives best value for money to investors.

Equity versus grant financing

Some housing associations generate funding through the release of shares; and equity is used to build more homes for sale or for rent. This route is currently limited to the for-profit group members. There would need to be regulatory change to be more generally applicable, as it might affect charitable status. The advantage is that, as previously, there is reliance on traditional lending, and shares often offer better returns than more traditional investments

Taking advantage of tax reforms

Housing associations currently benefit from lower levels of value added tax (VAT) in several areas, although until recently, full VAT was paid on repairs and maintenance. Due to successful lobbying by the sector, there was a VAT reduction for associations in the 2012 budget, which enabled housing associations to invest more in affordable homes delivery and put money into social sustainability ventures, as well as non-core functions such as job creation and apprenticeships. Shielding non-charitable housing associations from corporation tax would also be beneficial in terms of affordable homes development, although this has not materialised at the time of writing. The trade body for housing associations, the NHF, lobbied hard for further VAT reductions in the 2012 budget, and may yet succeed in modifying the corporation tax rules in favour of associations. A principal feature of the VAT reforms was the VAT cost-sharing exemption, implemented from summer 2012 by tax authorities. At the time of writing, guidance was yet to be given but could reduce the sector's tax burden by tens of millions of pounds. Many housing associations work in partnership when developing or managing homes, and specifically back-office functions, to gain efficiencies through economies of scale. Effectively, the individual associations 'buy' services from the cost sharing group (CSG), which has to charge VAT.

Housing association accounts

Housing associations have to keep business accounts and to present them to their boards and regulator on a regular basis. They are not in themselves complex, and the main ones are the income and expenditure account, balance sheet and cash flow account. Housing associations are required by the HCA – now the regulator for all registered providers including housing associations – to keep various accounts, which are scrutinised annually by their internal and external auditors. Guidance to associations on the preparation of accounts is given in the NHF/Accounting Standards Board Statement of Recommended Practice (SORP) for registered social landlords, and the HCA requires a series of accounts quarterly, as detailed in its quarterly financial returns, known as the FV3.

The balance sheet records the assets and liabilities of the association at a point in time, usually a quarter day, or at the financial year-end (for example 31 March). Assets include the book value of the properties it owns, which is their market value less any grant liability outstanding, the value of any land and office accommodation, and other durable assets such as non-leased company cars and equipment. Liabilities include the amount of debt outstanding (the capital sum, and any capitalised interest – that is, interest rolled up into the loan sum), and depreciation – the amount of the value of assets 'used up' in the year.

The income and expenditure account includes all credits and debits associated with the properties currently managed and the organisation as a whole, and includes turnover – all revenue income for the year, mainly rent and service charges, but not interest; operating costs – the costs of running the organisation, including staff costs, depreciation, maintenance and repairs, bad debts and overheads; interest payable and receivable; and surpluses – for the year, transferable to the organisation's reserves, and surpluses before taxation, showing tax deducted on activities, and the value of any grants received against tax.

The third set of accounts is the cash flow statement for the quarter and forecasts for the next three quarters. A cash flow statement details movements of cash into and out of the organisation. Examples of cash inflows include creditor items include interest received, grants received, sales income, loan advances and fixed assets purchased. Examples of cash outflows include interest paid, corporation tax paid and loan principal paid; and cash flows are stated as net cash flow – that is, cash in minus cash out.

The accounting figures for the current period are usually compared in the statement with equivalent entries for the previous period, to show whether the organisation has made relative financial gains or losses. This is an excellent indicator of the financial health of the organisation and is standard accounting practice. Key performance indicators include measures of financial health used by lenders and regulators. Viability indicators include the liquidity ratio, which is the ratio between current assets and current liabilities, which indicates whether the association can pay its way in the short to medium term. Interest cover is another measure of health, and indicates the degree to which interest payable is covered by the annual surplus. Another key measure is the gearing ratio, which is the ratio of loans to assets, and is an indicator of the ability to borrow more. Other measures include efficiency measures such as unit housing management and maintenance costs, average staff costs/employee and rent arrears as proportion of gross rent.

Housing associations and affordable rents

As has been noted earlier, housing associations developing during and after the 2011–2015 Affordable Housing Programme are expected to develop affordable rented accommodation among a suite of other products, as part of the government's desire to develop more housing for less public resource. As has been stated several times, affordable rents are chargeable at up to 80 per cent of local market rents, and are associated with assured shorthold and other fixed-term housing tenure products which are offered by housing associations post-Localism Act 2011. The logic is straightforward: higher rents mean the ability to borrow more against the development and to minimise grant input. The problems associated with affordable rents are related to their interaction with housing benefit caps: in some areas of London, such rents have proved to be debilitating in exceeding or nudging the top of the cap, with serious affordability implications. It should be noted that the new definition of affordable housing in PPS3 is:

> Rented housing let by registered providers of social housing to households who are eligible for social rented housing. Affordable rent is not subject to the national rent regime, but is subject to other rent controls that require a rent of no more than 80 per cent of the local market rent.

By 'national rent regime' is meant the rent influencing regime which has already been discussed. The new definition has caused some concerns in progressing existing 'planning obligation' agreements due to the differences between this and the previous definition of 'affordable', and there were restrictions on the ability of housing associations to convert re-lets to affordable rents. In early 2011, the HCA decided that associations could only convert half their re-lets to affordable tenure, and this was broadly welcomed by housing associations who were in many cases worried that a more significant percentage would be unsustainable in relation to the incomes of tenants. It is also notable that just under half of the 2011–2014 Affordable Housing Programme resources have been devoted to the affordable programme, with the remainder (£2.3 billion) being used to support the social housing development plans already put forward by associations. It will take some time before affordable housing dominates the housing association rental scene.

There are some controls on the level of rent that can be set, and the market rent element is that informed by the Royal Institute of Chartered Surveyors' (RICS) assessment of market rent levels, and maximum increases of RPI + 0.5 have been required by the HCA, so the affordable product is much more constrained that a full market option. Most housing associations have decided to offer affordable rents on the basis of fixed-term tenancies, although they can also offer them on lifetime assured tenancies, and some have suggested that the affordable rent option is a natural step towards alternative tenure options – for example home ownership either full or shared. Having got used to the idea of paying a higher rent, many tenants will question the logic of paying rent for a property they will never own as opposed to buying into an asset which in normal conditions appreciates and could constitute a step on the home ownership ladder to full ownership. Similarly, it might induce them to acquire properties through the right to acquire if it applies to the tenancies associated with affordable rents. It is too soon to say what the impact of the affordable rent regime might be on tenants and housing associations. Clearly, it has the potential to generate healthy cash flows for associations, but equally there must be the worry that arrears will mount and hence threaten sustainability of such arrangements, as well as the interaction between the affordable rent levels and the welfare benefits regime. If tenants cannot afford affordable rents, then inevitably cash flows will be threatened and development programmes put in jeopardy. If this comes at a time of adverse sales through a difficult mortgage market in particular and credit market in general, the prognosis for housing association health will not look particularly favourable.

Income-generation possibilities

Housing associations have spent much time and effort in developing businesses to supplement rental income, and to ensure that they have sufficient capital to develop as they wish. Among the products offered, running services for other bodies is a significant offer, with associations managing short-term lease properties for local authorities as well as procuring them for fee, managing sheltered housing schemes, managing private rented accommodation for landlords, acting as development agents for other associations and councils, providing training and job experience for a variety of clients for a fee, and a variety of other market or semi-market options. In line with demographic changes in the UK, several housing associations offer retirement housing at near-market rates, used to cross-subsidise other activities, or as self-funding initiatives. For example, the Anchor Trust provides retirement properties for sale in addition to rental opportunities on a mainly leasehold basis, involving the investment of investing sales proceeds from owner-occupiers to pay for services, with some schemes offered on a shared ownership basis. An example of lettings at near commercial rents to a niche market is found in Thames Valley Housing Association's Fizzy Living scheme, whereby the association set up a commercial subsidiary to buy 1,000 homes for private rent. It launched Fizzy Living to let at market rent levels to young professionals in South East England, and its initial programme saw 63 one- and two-bed flats let to this group in Epsom, Surrey. It was funded from the association's equity, at £30 million, and attracted £50 million from pension funds and other institutions to finance the acquisition of 1,000 new build properties over three years. Blocks of 60 to 50 units have been let by Fizzy Living, and all profits are returned to the group to cross-subsidise affordable housing starts. The plan is to ensure that Fizzy Living turns into £15 million turnover organisation. Ultimately, the association will transfer it to a tax-efficient real estate investment trust, to continue to cross-subsidise affordable housing programme. The new subsidiary is expected to raise £120 million from banks on the basis of its assets. This income gain is in addition to economies and efficiencies which have reduced management costs from 35 per cent to 25 per cent of rental income. The example shows how efficiencies plus income generation can raise money to supplement grant shortages and keep development programmes on track (Inside Housing, 2012).

Housing associations are increasingly letting properties at market rents or for sale – often through subsidiaries – often to cross-subsidise other products. An example is Sovereign Housing Association's acquisition of 84 homes to let at market rents in the West Country of England, with 34 purchased in 2010 and 50 in 2011. The purchases were acquired through Sovereign Living Limited, a trading subsidiary. They have experienced lettings in a declining home ownership market, with plans to acquire further properties for market renting.

Subsidy alternatives in the housing association sector

The primary method of assisting housing associations to develop affordable homes has been via the provision of grant, and affordability has hitherto been guaranteed by regulating through the rent influencing regime and through the limit of 80 per cent on affordable rents, so that most will be within the reach of the lower paid in employment, and those reliant upon housing benefit, which are not exclusive categories. However, there are perfectly respectable alternatives to this regime. There is the option of revenue subsidisation, although this is unlikely to be favoured at any time soon due to the inherent uncertainties associated with employment levels, compared to the certainty of planned capital support. Another option is to reduce grant yet further so that the strain is taken by the housing benefit regime – this might be objected to in a similar fashion as the first alternative, and finally there is the withdrawal of all subsidy to let housing associations rely upon their own resources and public land sold under value to achieve their ambitions.

Housing benefit and local housing allowances

Housing benefit is a personal subsidy paid by the state to assist with the cost of paying the rent, and is subject to a means test as well as withdrawal with earned income. Currently it is paid as a separate benefit alongside others (for example job seekers allowance and employment support allowance), and subject to its own caps and rules. The principal form of housing benefit is an allowance to help pay the cost of private and social rents. The former is known as local housing allowance because it is relativised to rent levels in the local area – the so-called broad market rental areas which are supposed to represent areas with similar rental characteristics. The latter is known as housing benefit. The rules are very similar, but have been subject to significant changes in terms of level and eligibility over the years, and from 2013 they will be integrated gradually into the new order universal benefit system. In essence, housing benefit works by comparing personal incomes to a standard applicable amount related to the income support threshold, and then reducing the payment from that point in line with increases in income – currently, 65p is withdrawn for every £1 earned above the threshold – until the payment is zero. There are also complex rules concerning the impact of non-dependents living in a household, who are assumed by the system to be contributing a sum to towards the rent, and rules on savings levels which debar benefit.

Some forms of housing benefit are paid directly to tenants and others are deducted at source. Currently, councils deduct the housing benefit element at source and receive subsidy from central government to help make up the loss of rental income, whereas housing association tenants receive housing benefit either directly or in the form of a payment to landlords depending on choice or financial circumstances, or rent arrears status. All forms of housing benefit will be subject to reform following the implementation of the Welfare Act 2011, which will see the abolition of hundreds of different welfare benefits and an integrated payment capped at (currently, in October 2012) £26,000 per household per year or £500 per week for a couple or lone parent and £350 per week for a single adult, the level of net earnings of lower-quartile working households, the principle being that no one should be better off on benefits than in work. In practice this will mean in most cases that housing benefit will be reduced once other elements have been assessed to ensure that the cap conditions are met. Some groups (for example pensioners) will be shielded from the full rigours of the new system, but it represents a sea change in the way that benefits are assessed and delivered, and has attracted not a little controversy in relation to the impact of the new housing credit system on lower-income working households in areas where private rents are relatively high, among others.

The impact of affordable rents on housing benefit expenditure and households

Affordable rents are set at up to 80 per cent of market rents, and are generally higher than previous social rents worked out according to the rent restructuring formula. It might therefore be thought that the impact of new affordable rents would be to increase the housing benefit bill, which would be an unwelcome outcome for central government. It depends on how benefits are viewed: grants given to housing associations and other registered providers to provide affordable housing are not repayable in most cases apart from in the case of shared ownership; once it is paid it is gone, whereas housing benefit varies according to the income of households as well as the rent for which they are liable, so if the economy improves, theoretically housing benefit costs should decrease, although the converse is also true. So if you are a government which believes that employment and wages will increase without jacking up rents, housing benefit-based subsidy is by far the more attractive option. The national bill for housing benefit is huge and volatile – it was in the region of £18.5 billion in 2010–2011, an increase of £1.3 billion from the past year (Inside Housing, 2011), and the government has tried many ways of stabilising it, although its fortunes relate largely to demographics – people in rentals withdrawing from the employment market with inadequate pensions by reason of age and the fortunes of that market. Capping will help to reduce some of that volatility, but not entirely. Most affordable rents will be comfortably within the cap, although they may not be genuinely affordable when other household costs are taken into account, which had been an area of concern raised by those within and outside the housing profession since the changes were mooted.

Welfare reform and housing

Social and affordable housing products are targeted at poorer households who find it difficult or impossible to compete in the market place for rented or owner-occupied accommodation. It makes no sense to create products which are not affordable to the target group, nor to design a benefits system which undermines the principle of affordability, and so they should always be within the reach of the lower paid in employment. They should also support households who wish to work, and commence on a low wage. Rents should therefore be set with other essential household costs – food, heating, travel etc. – in mind, so that households are able to budget effectively to meet their needs. It would be hard to set tailored rents for each household, and so affordable rents should take account of typical household expenditure patterns and requirements, which currently they do not.

The key aspects of welfare reform concerning housing are the changes to the housing benefit regime, to be called housing credits, the overall cap on benefit and changes to conditionality. Housing credits will apply to all forms of rented accommodation, and the assessment and levels will be based on existing formulae. If total credits exceed a cap, then the housing element will be scaled back to stay within the total amount for which the household is eligible, to a minimum of 50p. The idea is that households should be able to budget within a finite amount bearing some similarity to the budgets of lower-paid families in employment. The reality is that many will be priced out of the market in popular areas such as London, which raises the issue of how cities' infrastructural needs – cleaning, lower-paid administrative work, postal deliveries etc. – will be met if people cannot afford to travel form lower-rent areas or sustain higher rents close to their places of employment.

One of the other controversial aspects of the reform is the decision to limit housing support to accommodation which is deemed to be the correct size and to penalise under-occupancy. Under-occupiers in the social rented sector will be treated much the same as those claiming local housing allowance, in that there will be a 14 per cent cut if there is under-occupancy by one room, and 25 per cent for two rooms, which will apply just to working people, but is expected to affect something like 670,000 social and affordable tenants (Turn2Us, 2012). Take the case of someone who has succeeded to a tenancy – it may have been their home for many years, with friendship groups and family networks in place, and the effect of the cap will be to force them to reconsider and possibly move somewhere smaller – not something which those able to compete in the market place need to consider in most cases.

Councils will be able to mitigate some of the effects of the cap by making discretionary housing payments, but these will be supported by local income, and they may find they cannot afford to do so. There will also be a duty for councils to provide housing options advice to those who find themselves unable to afford to rent locally which in some cases may mean finding the best way to move to a cheaper area – a form of geographical social engineering, which has seen some councils suggesting moves to the Midlands and the north of England from London! The issue then becomes: will jobs be available for movers and if not, will this not simply increase the level of dependency in society?

References

DCLG (Department of Communities and Local Government), (2011) *Local Government Statistics, England, no 21.* London: DCLG.

DCLG, (2012a) Housing Statistics Live Table 702: Local authority average weekly rents from 1988/89. Available at: www.communities.gov.uk/housing/housingresearch/housingstatistics/housingstatisticsby/rentslettings/livetables/, viewed 1 April 2012.

DCLG, (2012b) Housing Statistics Live Table 670: Social housing sales: Local authority stock sold through the Right to Buy scheme, by region. Available at: www.communities.gov.uk/housing/housingresearch/housingstatistics/housingstatisticsby/socialhousingsales/livetables/, viewed 1 April 2012.

DETR (Department for Environment, Transport and the Regions), (2002) *Quality and Choice – a Decent Home for All.* London: DETR.

Inside Housing, (2011) Housing Benefit Bill rises by £1.3 billion, London: Inside Housing.

Inside Housing, (2012) Thames Valley eyes private letting plan. Available at: www.insidehousing.co.uk//6520395.article, viewed 13 September 2012.

London and Quadrant, (2011) L&Q launches dedicated construction subsidiary. Press release, 10 January. London: L&Q.

ODPM (Office of the Deputy Prime Minister), (2003) *A Guide to Social Rent Reforms in the Local Authority Sector.* Norwich: HMSO.

Shelter, (2010) *CSR Briefing 2010.* London: Shelter.

Solomou, W., Wright, P. and Whitehead, C., (2005) *Understanding the rent-restructuring formula for housing association target rents*. Rent Briefing paper 4: Cambridge: Dataspring.

Turn2Us, (2012) Benefit changes timetable. Available at: www.turn2us.org.uk/information__ resources/benefits/news_and_changes/benefit_changes.aspx?page=16619, viewed 6 May 2012.

5 Housing law

Keywords: *introduction to housing law; housing law in context; introduction to the English and other UK legal systems; homelessness and allocations; Decent Homes and the 2004 Housing Act fitness system; landlord and tenant – public sector; landlord and tenant – private sector; repairs and maintenance; consultation and regeneration; human rights; standards and regulation; Localism Act; scope for housing law reform.*

Introduction

Housing law is a vast subject, and this book can only hope to cover the rudiments, although there is ample reference to legislation elsewhere in context. It is necessary to regulate the balance of power between landlords and tenants, if only for clarity, transparency and to rectify the obvious imbalance of influence between the parties. Law is essentially a regulatory and normative system which reflects the views of established society as regards the rights and wrongs of human conduct, and housing illustrates quite a few of these areas. Consider the position of landlord and tenant in an unregulated context: landlords could demand any level of rent they pleased, and evict summarily on non-payment, and tenants could refuse to pay the rent for any number of reasons free from regulated enforcement. There has always been some form of law regulating the behaviour of landlords and tenants: it is wholly justifiable, and there is little point in contemplating at great length what the world would be like without it.

The main branches of housing law concern the relationship between landlord and tenant (contract law in the main, although the law of tort, public law and criminal law do come into the picture), the law of property as it relates to ownership, and that relating to the condition of property. There are also important areas of the law which relate to access to housing, homelessness and resident involvement. This chapter will look at key themes only, and suggest further reading and study so that readers can acquire a full and useful knowledge of the subject.

Classifying law is very important. There is a distinction between public international law (PIL) and private international law. PIL deals with the conduct of states and international organisations and their relations, for example, treaties, decisions of International Court of Justice, European Union (EU) law, etc. This has clear relevance to housing, for example, the way in which the EU defines a public body and how it may influence the way on which housing associations operate. We may contrast this with private international law, essentially the way in which the laws of one state are applied to cases brought in another country.

Then there is the distinction between public law – concerned with the constitution and functions of public or governmental organisations (for example councils), the relationship between public organisations and citizens, and the state's relationship with individuals and private law, which relates to the legal relations between ordinary people. It is also important to consider the legal position of corporate bodies and property rights, including transfer rights, when examining housing law and its operational significance.

Criminal law concerns the policing, controlling and punishing certain forms of conduct which the state finds intolerable, for example, theft, and unlawful eviction. There are several housing elements in this area, as landlord and tenant disputes have a habit of turning nasty. In contrast, civil law includes whole of private law and all of public law except criminal law, and deals with the rights and obligations existing between individuals. The two main branches of civil law are the law of contract, regulating agreements between parties which are voluntarily entered into and which are intended to have legal consequences, for example a tenancy contract, and tort, which covers breaches of duty imposed by law rather than voluntary agreement, for example, trespass, nuisance, slander and negligence.

Common law is judge-made law; essentially this gives rise to a series of rules applied by courts in their deliberations, and an essential doctrine is that of *Stare Decisis* – standing by previous decisions, the modern form of which is binding precedent, which includes case law. Then there is the law of equity: in the Middle Ages, the monarch would hear appeals against legal decisions and consider them on the basis of fairness and conscience, which developed into the modern law of equity. The lord chancellor's office was established to deal with equitable remedies, for example injunction (an order to restrain someone from committing a wrong) and specific performance (an order to force a defendant to fulfil their side of the bargain). Equity provides a 'gloss' to common law.

Common law helps judges interpret statute law, which is that law which is brought about by acts of parliament. The acts are known as primary legislation, and secondary legislation includes orders, statutory instruments, regulations which are mode by parliament and ministers of state and which interpret and operationalise statutes.

English law contrasts with that in most other countries, in that there has been a continuous evolution of that system. There is also no codification, in distinction to many European countries and the US. The reason for this is the absence of the influence of Roman law, unlike the position on the continent, which is perhaps odd given the length of time that the Romans occupied the British Isles. There is also the doctrine of being innocent until proved guilty, unlike the case in many other countries.

In the UK, the courts are the main method of settling disputes, and there are courts which deal only with criminal matters and those which deal with civil issues, as well as first instance (original) and appellate courts. The whole court service is administered by Her Majesty's Courts and Tribunal Service (HMCTS), and the object is to ensure that citizens receive timely and effective access to justice.

In addition to courts of law, justice is administered through the tribunal system. This area of law is often referred to as administrative justice, is embodied currently in the tribunals courts and Enforcement Act 2007 system, and concerns the activities of public bodies. It consists of a number of important areas, which, to simplify, includes judicial reviews – a procedure to enable citizens to challenge the decisions of public bodies, for example where the timetable or process of consultation has not been followed. It is concerned with matters which are *Ultra Vires* (beyond the powers of public authorities); unreasonableness; and proportionality (acts out of proportion to the harm it seeks to avoid). The Human Rights Act 1998 also allows challenges to public authorities. Remedies include mandatory (or *Mandamus*) – an order to do something; quashing, which nullifies an *ultra vires* decision; and prohibition, which can order a body not to act unlawfully.

Sources of law include European law, legislation passed by parliament, delegated legislation – that is, law which is made by lesser public bodies on behalf of the state, such as local authorities which are themselves creatures of statute, judge-made law (principally case law) and custom – law which has been passed down from time immemorial. To clarify, European law is supreme, and governs the operation of law in member states, and finds its origin in the Treaty of Rome, modernised through the Treaty of Lisbon in December 2009. The EU law institutions include the European Commission, European Council, The Council of Ministers, Court of Justice of the EU and the General Court. Its sources include treaty articles; regulations; directives; and decisions in the Court of Justice of the EU. Decisions made there are directly applicable to English law, or directly effective, which means that it is achieved by order. Some EU laws have vertical direct effect, that is, they are enforced from state to state, and others have horizontal direct effect – that is they are enforced from individual to individual.

Parliamentary legislation is a major source of law and of great importance to housing. Primary legislation is the term given to acts of parliament. An act begins life as a bill, of which there are two types: public (alters the law, and can be a government or private member's bill), and private (brought by a local authority to give local powers for example compulsory purchase to assemble a development area). It should be remembered that although it is often said that parliament is sovereign, it can be challenged by EU law which is supreme, and acts can be repealed.

The passage of a bill to legislation:

The first stage is the 'Whitehall' stage, where the bill is researched, following a ministerial announcement or some other policy imperative, usually emanating from the manifesto of the party which formed a majority and forms the government of the day. There then follows the proposal: the official consultation: a green paper setting out the rationale for the bill: and then a white paper which is more or less the finalised draft bill.

Having been drafted, the bill then goes to the 'Westminster stage' for debate and scrutiny by both houses (i.e. the Commons and the Lords). It then receives its first reading and second reading. It then progresses to the committee stage, from thence to the report and consideration stages, and finally to the third reading and royal assent. The bill then becomes an act, but is generally brought in according to a timetable. For example, the Welfare Reform Act 2012 will be brought in stages commencing in April 2013.

Statutes can be classified in a number of ways. They can be consolidating statutes bringing a number of cognate acts together but proposing little new, such as the 1985 Housing Act which brought together the 1980 Housing Act, the 1977 Housing (Homeless Persons) Act and a number of other minor laws. The 1996 Housing Act consolidated much of the 1985 Housing Act, including all the law relating to homelessness (Part VII of the 1996 Act) and everything relating to allocations (Part VI of the 1996 Act). The 1996 Act has in turn been modified by the Homelessness Act 2002, which inserted new or changed clauses into the earlier legislation. It can be seen from this that English law is essentially evolutionary in form and progress.

Other acts are codifying acts, which propose a new regime, for example, the 2004 Housing Act, which replaced the old fitness for human habitation tests by ones based on the risk of harm to households in relation to property defects.

Delegated legislation is very important in English law: examples include ministerial regulations ('statutory instruments') which interpret given law, for example, the raft of regulations associated with the Welfare Reform Act 2012, which operationalise the pronouncements in that act and give clarity to local authorities who will be administering large chunks of it; orders in council (Privy Council); local authority byelaws (these must be must be *intra vires* (within their powers) and reasonable); and rules made by the Supreme Court and county courts.

The Scottish law system is slightly different from the English and Welsh equivalents, although much UK-wide legislation is tested out in Scotland before being fully applied to England and Wales. There is insufficient scope in this volume to discuss the minutiae of Scottish law, but it is in essence similar in that persons are presumed innocent until proven guilty, and housing legislation is more or less identical, apart from ownership issues. It may be said that the English law system, which has evolved over centuries and adapted itself to societal mores, and which is the model of law adopted in most Commonwealth countries, is in many ways superior to the codified law systems on the continent and in the US because it is a living organism, whereas the codified systems have to be amended and amended again to make sense of societal change, albeit keeping the essence of their codes intact. It has also proved very difficult to erase or weaken some fundamental aspects of codes which would not have been written by any sane person if they were to be drafted today. The US Constitution preserves the right to bear arms, and perhaps no more need be said on this subject, as this book may have an international readership, other than the fact that firearms may also have an offensive and unprovoked use.

Another key feature of English law is judge-made law. Cases are considered by courts in the light of legislation and also common law, a vast array of cases which relate to the one in question, and which are used as a precedent in deciding the rights and wrongs of the case in hand. Case law is, then, built up from a pool of precedents i.e. previous court decisions. The so-called doctrine of binding precedent applies to legal proceedings, which is essentially the rule of binding precedent – if a precedent is a decision given by a court to which there is a right of appeal from the court in which it is cited, it is binding, although there are some limited circumstances under which judges can avoid precedent.

Homelessness and allocations

In this section, we discuss Parts VI and VII of the 1996 Housing Act ('the Act'), as modified. Part VI deals with allocation of council homes and Part VII deals with homelessness.

Homelessness and housing need

Homelessness is the most acute form of housing need, but not the only type. Others include living in overcrowded condition, in unfit or unsuitable housing, accommodation which is hard to afford without going without basics. It should be noted that, under Section 167(2) of the Act councils must give 'reasonable preference' in allocations directly or via nominations to people who are homeless – this includes people who are intentionally homeless, and those who do not have a priority need for accommodation, as well as those living in insanitary or overcrowded housing or otherwise living in unsatisfactory housing conditions.

Homelessness is a particularly serious and numerous housing condition; in 2008–2009 alone, around 21,515 people were accepted as homeless by councils in England – that's 2.5 households per 1000, and in that year, councils made around 113,000 decisions on homelessness – of these, about half (around 53,500) were that applicants were homeless and in priority need. They also decided that around 33,000 weren't homeless and gave them housing advice.

Homeless people end up in a variety of accommodation options, that is there if any duty towards them at all. DCLG statistics from 2010 show that in England alone, as at 31 March 2009, there were 2,450 households in bed and breakfast, 5,170 in hostels (including women's refuges), 10,480 placed temporarily in council or housing association property, 37,450 in private leased accommodation (rented by the council or a housing association from a private owner), and 8,450 in other forms – including 'homeless at home'. That's 64,000 households – well over 150,000 people.

There is evidence that homelessness is falling, perhaps aided by the policy to offer preventative advice and options, as shown in the Figure 5.1.

It is hard to give an authoritative explanation for this – the basic duties have not changed that much over the years. Is it genuinely that fewer people are homeless these days or is it due to the way that applicants are dealt with and advised? In some areas, councils are very effective at enabling people to find their own solutions – for example through access to the private rented sector, low-cost home ownership, or simply persuading them to hang on until a suitable offer can be made.

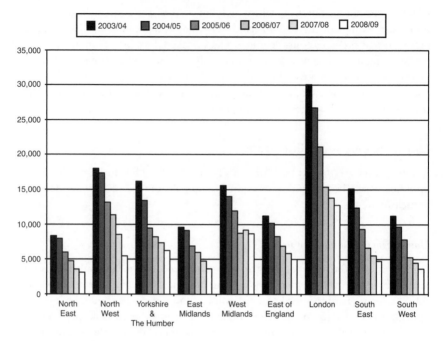

Figure 5.1 Homelessness acceptances, 2003–2009
Source: DCLG, 2010a.

Additionally, trends in temporary accommodation usage are improving as Figure 5.2 shows.

This sort of follows from Figure 5.2, although there will always be a lag between homelessness acceptance rates and temporary accommodation usage.

Reasons for homelessness vary significantly (see Figure 5.3), and by far the majority of cases in England relate to parental evictions. This may relate to the street mythology that if parents evict a pregnant daughter or one with children, then they will get a council house or flat before more or less anyone else. Unfortunately, the reality is that many of these cases will find themselves in temporary accommodation, and not particularly salubrious accommodation at that, until duty can be discharged through the private or social housing sectors – eventually.

Ask yourself the following questions: why is parental eviction the main category? Why do parents evict their children (i.e. the underlying causes)? Can housing stress cause violence, and if so, how? Why do assured shorthold tenancies lead to homelessness (hint: think of security of tenure compared to a secure or assured tenancy)?

A short history of homelessness

As has already been pointed out, homelessness is the tale of the deserving and the undeserving poor, and the legislation has its origins in the Poor Law, promulgated

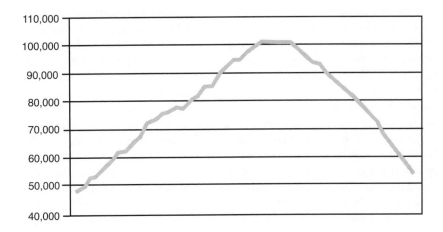

Figure 5.2 Trends in temporary accommodation, quarter 1 1998 to quarter 4 2009
Source: DCLG, 2010.

in Elizabethan times, and lasting until 1948. Assistance was targeted at the 'respectable poor' of the parish, with workhouses as a stop-gap temporary solution, and help was forthcoming only if the applicants were judged to be deserving by local board of guardians. There was no 'free lunch'; you had to work for your board in both senses of the word. The Poor Law system remained in existence until the emergence of the

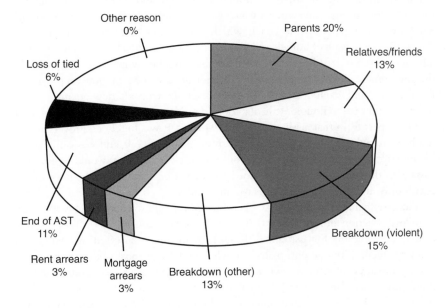

Figure 5.3 Reasons for homelessness
Source: DCLG, 2010b.

modern welfare sta   ; Poor Law remained on statute
book until 1967. R\   ...une of the Poor Law approach include the
emergence of friendl\   ...ues providing financial assistance; trade union assistance
for members; the substitution of government-sponsored employment opportunity
and other 'self-help' initiatives for workhouse provision; state pensions and national
insurance; and the interwar extension of unemployment insurance system for all
except self-employed persons.

The 1948 National Assistance Act was a prime mover in homelessness law. Passed
by the 'welfare statist' Labour government of Clement Attlee, it formally abolished
the Poor Law system, and gave local authorities the responsibility to provide accommodation and services to people with disability or mental health problems (so-called
'Part Three accommodation'). It also placed an obligation on local authorities to
carry out an assessment of need for anyone who might require residential care. Under
section 21 of the National Assistance Act 1948 local authorities have a duty to
support those who have a local connection with their area who are in need of
accommodation and services by reason of age, disability or some other substantial
reason. The legislation has not been abolished, and sometimes is used in connection
with destitute asylum seekers.

Lead-up to the 1977 Housing (Homeless Persons) Act

In 1974, homelessness began to be seen as a housing issue. The government of the
day said that councils should transfer responsibility for assisting homeless people
from social services to housing departments. Shelter and other charities complained
about the inhumane treatment of homeless families, and there was considerable
media interest in the issue: witness *Cathy Come Home* (a TV film written by Jeremy
Sandford and directed by Ken Loach, which came out in 1966), which helped raise
the profile of the issue of homelessness and which was watched by 12 million people.
The act, which started life as a private member's bill but which was taken over by
the government, defined homelessness and priority need, focused more on provisions
for families, and excluded most homeless people without dependants from a
statutory right to be housed. It had a code of guidance, as there was little relevant
case law apart from that arising from the 1948 Act. It was highly controversial – as
has been noted previously, it started as private member's bill, and was only passed
because opposition insisted on a 'local connection' clause before it would support the
passage of the bill, an echo of the Poor Law regime of assistance to the poor of the
parish only, and its framework remains intact today.

The essential duties, which have been carried forward to modern legislation, are
as follows (section numbers below refer to the 1996 Housing Act): If a person is
homeless, is eligible for assistance (through nationality – inserted in 1996), is in
priority need, is not intentionally homeless and has a local connection, or no
connection anywhere, the receiving council has a duty to secure accommodation for
them (s. 188: see also s. 193(1)). Note that this does not imply that council housing
will be offered – the duty can be discharged through the private sector, or via nominations to housing associations.

Where a person is found to be homeless, in priority need, not intentionally homeless but with a local connection elsewhere, the council where local connection falls has the duty to secure accommodation (s. 193(1)). Where a person is homeless, in priority need, but intentionally homeless, the council has a duty to secure temporary accommodation only (for example for three months). Intentionality means that the person has done something or has omitted to do something (for example pay the rent) which has caused the homelessness through their own fault (s. 191). Where a person is homeless, but has no priority need, the duty is to provide advice and assistance only (s. 190(3)). All of these have been transferred to Part VII of the Housing Act 1996, as amended principally by the 2002 Homelessness Act.

The current law: Part VII 1996 Act and 2002 Homelessness Act

HOMELESSNESS AND THREATENED HOMELESSNESS?

Someone is homeless if they have nowhere that they have a right or permission to occupy (what's the difference?), or they have such a right but can't exercise it (think of a case where this might apply) (s. 175).

Accommodation is only available for occupation if it is available as a home for the person together with any other person who it is reasonable to expect to live with them (for example as a member of their family) (s.176). It is not reasonable for a person to continue to live somewhere where it is likely that they or someone who it is reasonable for them to live with would run the risk of domestic or other violence (s.175(3)).

Councils have a duty to provide advisory services. This includes free advice and information about homelessness, and the prevention of homelessness; often this is delivered through housing options and advice services. Councils can give grants/loans, rent premises, second staff, to third parties – including voluntary agencies – advising on their behalf, for example Shelter and Citizens' Advice Bureaux.

A local housing authority or social services authority must take note of guidance issued by the secretary of state. Guidance was first issued in 1978 to accompany the Housing (Homeless Persons) Act 1977, and later guidance reflects a mass of case law. In relation to making inquiries, if it has reason to believe that applicant may be homeless or threatened with homelessness, council must make inquiries to find out whether there is a duty and what it is, and when they have done so, they must tell the applicant what it is in writing, and applicants have the right to ask for a review of the decision (s. 202).

There is an interim duty to accommodate in case of apparent priority need. If the council has reason to believe that an applicant may be homeless, eligible for assistance and have a priority need, it must make sure they he or she has somewhere to live pending the decision on what duty it has (s. 188).

ELIGIBLE?

The Allocation of Housing and Homelessness (Eligibility) (England) Regulations 2006 make it clear who is eligible or otherwise in relation to homelessness applications. The principle is that refugees with leave to enter or remain in the UK, people with exceptional leave to remain without recourse to public funds, or those habitually resident in the UK are eligible for housing assistance under the homelessness legislation. Those who had to leave Montserrat after the volcanic eruption of 1995 and subsequent events of this nature are also eligible. Those subject to immigration control are entitled only to minimal help, which may extend to arranging private accommodation. The eligibility rules on European Economic Area nationals are complex and beyond the scope of this book.

PRIORITY NEED

The following qualify: a pregnant woman or someone she lives with or who it is reasonable to expect that she might live with; a person with whom dependent children reside or might reasonably be expected to reside with (for example the father); someone who is vulnerable through old age, mental illness or physical disability or other special reason, or with whom such a person lives or might reasonably be expected to live (for example a carer), and someone homeless or threatened with homelessness because of an emergency (for example flood, or fire) (s. 189(1)).

WHAT IS INTENTIONAL HOMELESSNESS?

This is doing or failing to do something which results in losing the home, for example failure to pay the rent; but the person must know what they are doing! Leaving home if it is reasonable to stay also counts as intentional homelessness. An important point is that if someone is homeless, in priority need but intentionally homeless they are only entitled to short-term housing to allow them time to find somewhere else to live (s. 191). Duties towards intentionally homeless persons vary: for priority need cases, it is to secure somewhere to live for a time to allow them a reasonable amount of time to find somewhere, and give advice and assistance to help them do so. In the case of those not in priority need, the duty is to give advice and assistance 'as considered appropriate in the circumstances' to help them find somewhere to live.

LOCAL CONNECTION

The local connection clause was controversial when the 1977 law was passed, and was inserted at a late stage. This is a direct reference to the Poor Law which has already been described – the principle that assistance should only be given to the poor of the parish. Local connections arise because of past or present residence there, where residence is or was by choice, because of employment in the area, through of family associations, or other special circumstances. However, a person is not employed in a district if serving in the regular armed forces, and councils can make a judgement as to where the connection lies. If someone does not have a connection with the council they approach, but do have somewhere else, the council will in most cases refer the person to that area unless they run the risk of violence there or if there is some other special reason not to.

Applicants have the right to have the decision on homelessness reviewed, although this must be requested within 21 days of notification of the decision. The review can be in relation to the decision as to whether or not the person is homeless, on eligibility, and on the suitability of the accommodation offered. There is a right of appeal to the county court on points of law.

ACCOMMODATION

Councils can discharge their accommodation duties towards homeless persons in a number of ways. They can provide it themselves, making an allocation under Part 6 of the Housing Act 1996, or through another agency – for example, through the offer of housing association accommodation via a nomination, or through the private sector. The latter is increasingly common, and was strengthened under the Localism Act.

Other aspects of the legislation include duties to protect a homeless person's possessions, usually by providing storage facilities, the duty for other organisations to cooperate with the housing authority – for example, housing associations and social services departments. Giving false information under the act is punishable by a Level 5 fine.

The 2002 Homelessness Act made some important changes to the legislation. It widened the priority categories, for example, to 16 and 17 year olds, and those aged between 18 and 21 leaving care, as well as imposing a duty on councils to carry out a homelessness review and devise a homelessness strategy, with an emphasis on preventing homelessness through timely advice and interagency working. This emphasis was strengthened in the 2006 guidance published by the government, which stressed the importance of advice on social security benefits, household budgeting, tenancy support services and family mediation services. It also highlighted the importance of signposting to more specialist advice such as debt management, health care and coping with drug and alcohol misuse where needed. Good practice includes explaining the various housing options that are available, which can include advice and assistance (for example legal advice or mediation with a landlord) to enable them to stay in the current home; financial assistance (for example rent deposit or guarantee) to obtain private rented accommodation; assisting with an application for long-term social housing via a housing waiting list or choice-based lettings scheme; or advice on how to apply to another social landlord for accommodation. It also imposed a duty on local authorities to devise homelessness strategies and service reviews.

TEMPORARY ACCOMMODATION

Councils have an interim duty to accommodate homeless applicants while they are making enquiries, and also a duty to house homeless households who are eligible, in priority need but intentionally homeless for a reasonable time to help them make their own arrangements. There are many forms of temporary housing, although rightly there are restrictions on using bed and breakfast hotels for families with children except in emergency. Such accommodation can range from hostels, although these are less common than 20 years ago, private sector lets, property which has been leased from private owners commonly between three to five years and regular social housing let on a short-term or non-secure basis. Some housing associations procure and /or manage such accommodation for councils in return for a fee. The availability of such accommodation and sustaining such tenancies has been seriously affected by the caps on housing benefit which have arisen under recent welfare reforms, which has led to a shortage of private accommodation for this purpose in many higher-demand areas. One form of accommodation which is controversial is the applicant's own home – in many cases, councils endeavour to persuade the families of those applying as homeless to continue to accommodate in the existing home until somewhere suitable can be found, during which time they are still regarded as homeless under the legislation. It could be said that in many cases, their actual circumstances are identical to those who are in such accommodation but who have not taken the homelessness route – and this raises issues of equity between housing needs groups.

ALLOCATING PUBLIC SECTOR ACCOMMODATION

The main source for the law relating to allocations in relation to local authorities is Part 6 of the Housing Act 1996. Public resources should be allocated fairly and in relation to need, and this part seeks to guide councils in this area. The concept of need has already been discussed, but it revolves around the definition of 'reasonable preference categories'. Another major point is that choice must feature in allocations systems, although under shortage conditions this choice is often more notional than real. In essence, the reasonable preference categories are as follows:

- people who are homeless – this includes people who are intentionally homeless, and those who do not have a priority need for accommodation;
- people in insanitary or overcrowded housing or otherwise living in unsatisfactory housing conditions.

The Housing Act 1996 section 167(2) was amended by the 2002 Homelessness Act to include the following new groups:

- young people who at risk (particularly those aged 16 through 17 years or with a background in the care of the local authority social services department);
- homeless applicants who were previous members of the armed forces;
- those recently released from prison or youth custody;
  people who need to move on medical or welfare grounds, including disability;
- people who need to move to a particular part of the council's area, where failure to meet that need would cause hardship (to themselves or to others).

It should be noted that councils can also take account of the need to attract workers to an area or financial means when allocating properties.

When councils devise their points or banding schemes, they should consider what weight to give to these aspects of housing need, although being in more than one needs category may not give additional priority through accumulation, something made clear in the Ahmad case (Ahmad, R. (on the application of) v. London Borough of Newham [2008] EWCA Civ 140). In this case, an applicant applied to Newham under their choice-based lettings scheme. The application was from a housing association property in an attempt to find somewhere larger to meet the family's needs. The essence of the case is that the family tried to claim cumulative need on the basis of being on a transfer list and also satisfying one or more of the reasonable preference criteria, but it was decided on appeal by the House of Lords that it was no longer necessary to house those in greatest need first – for example, those falling under several of the priority needs categories.

It is important to draw attention to some other aspects of allocations law. There are cases where priority can be taken away – for example, where the household has committed anti-social behaviour, or where there is a history of serious rent arrears. This seems reasonable to preserve some degree of order on local authority estates or at least not to make the situation there worse, but does raise the question of how those in these categories should be dealt with in terms of relieving housing need. It does, however, have the effect of incentivising good behaviour through eligibility for social housing – eventually!

Another aspect of allocations reformed by the Localism Act is that councils can reduce priority under allocations schemes if they believe that the applicant has enough resources to buy or rent a property in the market. This sounds rational, but raises the issue as to how long the judgement period should be, and the council's knowledge of market conditions on which to base such a decision, since strategic housing market assessments can become out of date quickly, and income may rise or fall over a period especially if (for example) the applicant is an agency or casual worker, and no one is unemployment-proof under recessional conditions.

Notably, the s. 167(2) of Part 6 of the 1996 Act gives additional preference in allocations systems to a number of categories within the reasonable preference groups, including: those owed a homelessness duty as a result of violence or threats of violence likely to be carried out and who as a result require urgent re-housing, and those who need to move because of urgent medical reasons. There is some discretion over the interpretation of these terms, but 'violence' is interpreted in terms of victims of domestic violence; victims of racial harassment amounting to violence or threats of violence; same sex couples who are victims of harassment amounting to violence or threats of violence; and witnesses of crime, or victims of crime, who would be at risk of intimidation amounting to violence or threats of violence if they remained in their current homes.

The 2002 Homelessness Act made some important changes to allocations systems, in that it facilitated choice-based lettings schemes (s. 167 1A); it gave local authorities the power to refuse allocation in cases of serious anti-social behaviour (s. 106A), and made it clear that councils cannot exclude applicants not resident in the borough, but that local connection can increase relative priority. It also set transfer cases on a level playing field with new applicants (s. 159(5)) and repealed the duty to keep a housing register. Choice-based lettings, based on broad needs bands with priority usually assigned within these on the basis of the date when cases entered the system, is now widely used as a system of determining need and ordering re-housing, although there are some councils who still use a points-based system without banding, even though the Labour government aspired that all councils in England should have plans in place to introduce such a system by 2005.

In April 2005, the legislation was amended by order to give additional focus to those with medical requirements seeking social housing. Section 167(2)(d) of the 1996 Act provides that people who need to move on 'medical and welfare' grounds must be given reasonable preference for an allocation. It also embodied the intention to ensure that disabled people with access needs are given appropriate priority for social housing, influenced by the Disability Discrimination Act 1995). The 2005 changes also introduced the idea of accessible housing registers, where properties are earmarked for those with 'relevant access needs', and suggested that councils should consider adapting properties to meet such need if those which are appropriately designed are not available.

In 2009, statutory guidance was published, entitled *Fair and Flexible* (DCLG, 2009), which is still current, although it should be read in conjunction with the relevant provisions of the Localism Act. It stated that local authority allocation schemes must support those in greatest housing need i.e. reasonable preference is still paramount. This has been reinforced in the Localism Act. Special mention and emphasis was given to those who have experienced homelessness. It made it clear that equal weight need not be given to each reasonable preference category – for example, if overcrowding is the most significant problem, its relief should be prioritied in allocations policy. It stated that all authorities should consider whether there should be a need to grant 'additional preference' to some reasonable preference groups with urgent housing in the light of local circumstances. It reinforced the previous guidance, that people who are homeless or placed in temporary accommodation under the homelessness legislation should continue to be entitled to reasonable preference for social housing, as well as stressing the importance of meeting equalities duties:

> [Councils must] ensure that it is compatible with the requirements in the equality legislation. In particular, as well as the other duties to eliminate unlawful discrimination, local authorities are reminded that they are subject to a duty to promote equality of opportunity and good relations between people of different racial groups, as well as a duty to promote equality of opportunity between disabled persons and other persons, and between men and women.
>
> (DCLG, 2009, p. 11, para. 21)

This has now been overtaken by the 2010 Equalities Act, although it has the same consequences for allocations systems.

Fair and Flexible stresses the need to give greater choice and wider options for prospective tenants than embodied in existing choice-based lettings approach, giving a choice not just of property location, but of tenure, for example low-cost home ownership and private rented alternatives. It suggests that allocations policies should be set within an enhanced housing options approach – that is, the provision of joined-up advice and information on tenure alternatives, as well as mobility out of the area, and it repeated the Hillsian mantra of the importance of creating more mixed and sustainable communities through allocations policies.

One of the big themes of the document, which was carried forward by the Coalition government, is that housing authorities should promote greater social and economic mobility through their allocations systems. It envisaged that choice-based lettings schemes should be developed on a regional or sub-regional basis, and nationally. Another big theme is making better use of the housing stock, which means giving existing tenants who are under occupying social housing appropriate priority for transfers. Finally, it lays greater emphasis on ensuring that scarce accessible and adapted accommodation is prioritised for people with access needs, and suggests personal support, incentives and financial payments to encourage people who under-occupy family-sized homes to downsize, along with incentives to vacate adapted homes and mitigate overcrowding in situ.

Support for people in work or seeking work is also a key theme, which it suggests could involve using local lettings policies to ensure that particular properties are allocated to essential workers or to those who have skills which are in short supply, regardless of whether they are currently resident in the authority's district. Additionally, or alternatively, a council could choose to give some preference to existing tenants who are willing to move to take up training opportunities – for example where council has identified a need to address skills shortages and worklessness as part of their skills strategy.

The cumulative preference rule (or rather rule-out) is emphasised, the relevant case being Ahmad v. London Borough of Newham in the House of Lords in 2009. What came out of this was that there is no requirement for local authorities to frame their allocation scheme to provide for cumulative preference (to give greater priority to those falling under more than one reasonable preference category); that it is neither unlawful nor irrational to determine priority between people within the reasonable preference categories on basis of time on register; that it is acceptable to give greater priority to one reasonable preference group than another; and that it is acceptable to give priority for allocation of a limited number of properties to existing tenants outside the reasonable preference categories. The broad implications of this case are that it is open to local authorities to determine between applicants in the reasonable preference categories by waiting time alone; councils can now devise simpler more transparent allocations systems, now that 'cumulative preference' is removed; and in terms of 'local connection', there is nothing to stop local connection as a policy priority, provided that overall the scheme continues to meet the reasonable preference requirements.

Waiting time was a feature of pre-points system housing registers. The author recalls a time in the early 1980s when he worked as a housing advisory officer in a shire district where applicants for council housing were told that the only criteria for being on the waiting list were not to be a home owner, be over 18, and to live or work in the district; and that they would be housed after a wait of approximately two and a half years. He also remembers getting on a fast bike and telling applicants who had mere months to wait that the district had changed to a points system, and that they would probably have to wait years depending on their circumstances, and perhaps have to make their own arrangements. Now, post-Localism, time served on a list is once again a factor which can be taken into account along with need and local connection, but it is in no sense a primary characteristic. It is used as a simple way of determining priorities between people in the same needs band, and it is now possible to give more weight to it than hitherto following the Ahmad case.

Decent Homes and the 2004 Housing Act fitness system

We now turn to the 2004 Housing Act and the fitness system used to determine whether properties are habitable or otherwise. To recap, councils and housing associations were told to get their homes decent by 31 December 2010 (remember the 2000 Housing Green Paper); the target has now been extended for a number of authorities. The Decent Homes Standard is a minimum standard that triggers action to improve social housing. It is a standard to which homes are improved. As constructed, the standard allows all landlords to determine, in consultation with their tenants, what works need to be completed, and in what order, to ensure the standard is met.

The Decent Homes Standard has four criteria which are:

1.   It meets the current statutory minimum standard for housing (i.e. the dwelling should be free of Category 1 hazards under the HHSRS, 2004);
2.   It is in a reasonable state of repair;
3.   It has reasonably modern facilities and services;
4.   It provides a reasonable degree of thermal comfort.

The standard was revised in 2006 when the HHSRS was introduced through Section 9, 2004 Housing Act, to replace the unfitness standard as the statutory minimum standard. The HHSRS is the government's approach to the evaluation of the potential risks to health and safety from any deficiencies identified in dwellings.

The HHSRS is founded on the logical evaluation of both the likelihood of an occurrence that could cause harm, and the probable severity of the outcomes of such an occurrence. It relies on the informed professional judgements of both of these to provide a means of representing the severity of any dangers present in a dwelling. The assessment using the HHSRS is based on the condition of the whole dwelling (ODPM, 2006a).

The HHSRS concentrates on threats to health and safety. It is generally not concerned with matters of quality, comfort and convenience. Also, the system is about the assessment of hazards in relation to the potential effect of conditions – the form of construction and the type and age of the dwelling do not directly affect an assessment. However, these matters will be relevant to determining the cause of any problem and so indicate the nature of any remedial action. The relevant DCLG guidance for public sector landlords also applies to other registered providers, principally housing associations. The guidance recommends the need to incorporate HHSRS into their stock condition surveys.

To be decent, all homes in the social sector should be free of Category 1 hazards. If the landlord is about to embark on a programme of work, housing managers should consider whether there are any Category 1 hazards that need to be included in the refurbishment works. There are 29 Category 1 hazards, and they include: dampness, excess cold/heat; pollutants for example asbestos, carbon monoxide, lead; lack of space, security or lighting, or excessive noise; poor hygiene, sanitation, water supply; accidents – falls, electric shocks, fires, burns, scalds; and collisions, explosions and structural collapse. Each hazard is assessed separately, and if judged to be 'serious', with a 'high score', is deemed to be a Category 1 hazard. All other hazards are Category 2 hazards.

Inspections are essentially carried out in the traditional fashion, i.e. a physical assessment of the whole property during which deficiencies (faults) are noted and recorded. When an inspector finds a hazard, two key tests are applied – what is the likelihood of a dangerous occurrence as a result of this hazard and if there is such an occurrence, what would be the likely outcome? It is this which gives rise to the category judgement (ODPM, 2006b).

The use of the HHSRS in stock conditions surveys is to determine which properties have Category 1 hazards in relation to the vulnerability of those living in the dwellings; this will prioritise remedial action. Examples of hazards which might be Category 1 in relation to vulnerable elderly occupants are: a broken stair-rail; trip hazards – high threshold to negotiate to get out of a door; and a substandard heating system (risk of hypothermia). The key aim of an inspection is to minimise the chances of any unacceptable hazards and comply with the HHSRS. The HHSRS takes the form of an inspection of the property on a room-by-room basis, checking all the elements, fixtures and fittings. A check is carried out of the common parts (for example, stairs and shared rooms and amenities), as well as outside the building, looking at the external elements, and the yards/gardens and paths. The inspector will record any deficiencies, disrepair or anything else that may give rise to a hazard.

Deficiencies hazards

The purpose of the check is to assess whether any of the deficiencies and faults contribute to any one or more of the 29 hazards specified in the guidance. The key questions are: do the deficiencies increase the likelihood of a harmful occurrence, or do they increase the severity of the harm?

Remedial action or work is then specified in relation to the output, and a decision taken as to what needs to be done to remedy deficiencies and to reduce risks as low as reasonably practicable. A timetable is then devised for works to be undertaken. Some action may be very urgent where an immediate risk to current occupiers is identified, others may be less urgent. A record of the programme of works is made, and the date when works are finished is recorded. There then follows a review, to ensure that hazards identified during the inspection have been removed or minimised. Re-inspection is also part of the regime; how frequently this needs to be done depends on the age and type of property, and whether there has been any change of occupants. Some elements or facilities will need to be checked more frequently than others or when required by law (for example, gas appliances) or by an accreditation scheme.

Principles of the HHSRS (paragraph numbers refer to Appendix III of the 2006 guidance) include:

- 1.12 The underlying principle of the HHSRS is that any residential premises should provide a safe and healthy environment for any potential occupier or visitor.
- 1.13 To satisfy this principle, a dwelling should be designed, constructed and maintained with non-hazardous materials and should be free from both unnecessary and avoidable hazards.
- 1.18 For the purposes of the HHSRS, the assessment is solely about the risks to health and safety. The feasibility, cost or extent of any remedial action is irrelevant to the assessment. Some deficiencies, such as a broken stair tread or a leaking pipe may be quickly, easily and cheaply remedied, but while such deficiencies are present, the threat to health or safety can be considerable.

The four HHSRS classes of harm

The classes of harm used for the HHSRS are based on the top four classes of harm as identified in a risk assessment procedure for health and safety in buildings. This identifies seven classes of harm, but only the top four are used for the purposes of the HHSRS as these are harms of sufficient severity that they will either prove fatal or require medical attention and, therefore, are likely to be recorded in hospital admissions or general practitioner records. They are:

- Class I covers the most extreme harm outcomes, including: death from any cause; lung cancer; mesothelioma and other malignant lung tumours; permanent paralysis below the neck; regular severe pneumonia; pPermanent loss of consciousness; 80 per cent burn injuries.
- Class 2 covers severe harm outcomes, including: cardio-respiratory disease; asthma; non-malignant respiratory diseases; lead poisoning; anaphylactic shock; crytosporidiosis; legionnaires disease; myocardial infarction; mild stroke; chronic confusion; regular severe fever; loss of a hand or foot; serious fractures; serious burns; loss of consciousness for days.
- Class 3 covers serious harm outcomes, including: eye disorders; rhinitis; hyper-tension; sleep disturbance; neuro-pyschological impairment; sick building syndrome; regular and persistent dermatitis, including contact dermatitis; allergy; gastroenteritis; diarrhoea; vomiting; chronic severe stress; mild heart attack; malignant but treatable skin cancer; loss of a finger; fractured skull and severe

concussion; serious puncture wounds to head or body; severe burns to hands; serious strain or sprain injuries; regular and severe migraine.

- Class 4 includes moderate harm outcomes which are still significant enough to warrant medical attention, including: pleural plaques; occasional severe discomfort; benign tumours; occasional mild pneumonia; broken finger; slight concussion; moderate cuts to face or body; severe bruising to the body; and regular serious coughs or colds.

The hazard groups (Appendix III, Annex D, p. 49) are classed as follows:

- A Physiological requirements: Hygrothermal conditions
- B Psychological requirements: Space, security, light and noise
- C Protection against infection: Hygiene, sanitation and water supply
- D Protection against accidents: Falls, electric shocks, burns, scalds, and building-related collisions

The effect of conditions on health can be illustrated by considering hygrothermal conditions, including damp and mould growth. This category covers threats to health associated with increased prevalence of house dust mites and mould or fungal growths resulting from dampness and/or high humidity. It includes threats to mental health and social wellbeing which may be caused by living with the presence of damp, damp staining and/or mould growth. The most vulnerable age group in terms of potential for harm is all persons aged 14 years or under.

Hazards which impact on psychological wellbeing include crowding and space. This category covers hazards associated with lack of space within the dwelling for living, sleeping and normal family/household life. There is no specific age group or other category which are deemed to be more affected than others. Lack of space and overcrowded conditions have been linked to a number of health outcomes, including psychological distress and mental disorders, especially those associated with a lack of privacy and childhood development. Crowding can result in an increased in heart rate, increased perspiration, reduction of tolerance, and a reduction of the ability to concentrate. Crowded conditions are also linked with increased hygiene risks, an increased risk of accidents, and spread of contagious disease. Relevant matters relating to overcrowding affecting likelihood and harm outcome include a lack of living area of an adequate size for the household or potential household; the lack of a separate kitchen area of adequate size; the lack of a separate, or an appropriately sited, or sized personal washing area, and no door to the personal washing area or lock on door or glazed door.

In terms of bedroom space, some of the issues pointed up under the HHSRS include an inadequate number of bedrooms for the household or potential household, inadequately sized bedrooms, and bedrooms which are inappropriately sited – for example, next to a cooking area.

One of the issues often brought up when discussing health and safety in the context of the 2004 Housing Act is the hazard of falling on stairs, which is age related. It includes falls over guarding (balustrades) associated with the stairs, steps or ramps. However, it does not include falls over guarding to balconies or landings, and nor does it include falls associated with trip steps, thresholds or ramps where the change in level is less than 300 millimetres. The most vulnerable age group is all persons aged 60 years or over. In relation to hazard assessment, all stairs, steps and ramps associated with the dwelling should be taken into account. This includes the internal stairs, stairs for exclusive use of the dwelling occupants, common stairs, external steps, fire escape stairs and any ramps. It is the overall likelihood of a fall that is assessed. This should take account of the frequency with which each might be expected to be used.

Landlord and tenant – public sector

An understanding of public sector landlord and tenant law is essential for housing practitioners: it is an area of law which has changed significantly following the passage of the Localism Act. What follows is an overview of the different tenure types and conditions, and attention should be paid to relevant case law and amendments to the primary legislation.

The essential forms of social housing tenancy are the secure tenancy for council tenants and housing association tenants before January 1989, and the assured tenancy for housing association tenants after January 1989. There have been modifications since the Localism Act, in that local authorities and housing associations can create flexible tenancies of up to five years, and housing associations can create assured shorthold tenancies in cases other than temporary lets, which used to be the restriction. There is also the introductory tenancy form for starter council tenants and the probationary form for starter housing association tenants, both of which are discretionary but which are both widely used. Councils can also grant non-secure tenancies, in temporary accommodation mainly, where they do not wish to grant security of tenure and wish to move the tenant out in order to prevent silting up.

Before the 1980 Housing Act, council tenants had contractual tenancies, determined by one months' notice to quit, with possession on no or limited grounds. Prior to 1980, housing association tenancies were in the main regulated under 1977 Rent Act, and subject to fair rents. Following the 1980 Housing Act, council and housing association tenants became secure tenants, with housing associations let at fair rents. Following the 1988 Housing Act, new housing association tenants after January 1989 were assured tenants. For such tenants, there was no fair rent, due to the new financial regime needing to generate rents to cover loan repayments under the mixed funding development regime and M&M costs. When the 1996 Housing Act came into force, councils and housing associations could let initially on introductory and probationary tenancies.

There are fundamentals which need to be established at the outset. Tenancies confer rights to reside in the property, whereas licences confer permission to occupy only. An example of a tenancy is a secure tenancy, where the tenant has exclusive possession of the property, has the right to exclude the landlord, and the accommodation is self-contained and let at a rent. An example of a licence is hostel accommodation in the case that occupants may share living accommodation as well as cooking and washing facilities, even if they have their own rooms and a key to these. Much depends on the nature of the arrangement, and the distinction is not always clear cut. Another example of a tenancy is the excluded occupier tenancy – in this case, the tenant has keys to a room/flat in a property also occupied by the landlord and pays rent, right to notice to quit and court order, although possession will always be granted. This can be compared to a licencee, where the occupant has the use of a room, probably no key, receives personal services for example cleaning; where the landlord can enter room, where there is no rent but an occupation charge, no security of tenure, limited notice to quit and no court order is needed to evict.

Secure tenancies

The source of law for secure tenancies is Part 4 of the 1985 Housing Act, as amended by the 1988 and 1996 Housing Acts, and the 2011 Localism Act. Secure tenancies must meet the tenancy condition; the tenant must be an individual and occupy the dwelling as his or her only or principal home. If there are joint tenants, each must be an individual, and at least one of them must occupy the dwelling house as his or her only or principal home. The landlord must be a local authority or other designated public body. Housing associations are unable to create new secure tenancies.

Exclusions include long tenancies (over 21 years and other limited types); introductory tenancies; premises occupied as a consequence of employment; tenancies granted pursuant to a local authority's duties to provide temporary accommodation for homeless and asylum purposes; tenancies of agricultural holdings and licensed premises; tenancies to which the Landlord and Tenant Act 1954 (Part 2) applies (so-called business tenancies); student lettings and sublets. Secure tenancies are entitled to take in lodgers, but the tenant may not sublet or part with possession of part of the dwelling house without the landlord's consent. Consent cannot be unreasonably withheld, but if the tenant sublets or parts with possession without consent, the tenancy ceases to be secure and cannot become secure again. This would give rise to a ground for possession

In relation to rent, secure tenancies are not subject to any restrictions on rent which can be charged, although in practice the rules of the rent restructuring regime are a guiding principle, which if adopted, determine target rents through a formula based on relative value and relative incomes modified by bed size, subject to caps and limits on rises.

Grounds for possession

The grounds are to be found in Schedule 2 Housing Act 1985, and fall into three categories: grounds 1 to 8 are discretionary, that is, the court must be satisfied that it is reasonable to make the possession order. Grounds 9 to 11 are mandatory: the court must be satisfied that suitable alternative accommodation will be available for the tenant. Grounds 12 to 16 are discretionary, and in these cases, the court must be satisfied that it is reasonable to make the possession order and that suitable alternative accommodation will be available.

Summary of repairing obligations and improvements

The tenants' obligations include internal decoration, and putting right any damage caused by them. The landlord is responsible for most other repairs, including any problems with the roof, guttering, windows, doors and brickwork. They also have to ensure that the plumbing, gas and electricity are working safely. In terms if improvements, written permission is required from the council first. The council cannot refuse certain improvements without a good reason. The tenant can obtain compensation for money spent on improvements on leaving, to a current (2012) maximum of £3,000.

Assured tenancies

Assured tenancies were introduced by the Housing Act 1988, with important changes made by the Housing Act 1996 with effect from 28 February 1997. This is the default form of tenancy for housing association tenants after 15 January 1989, and most housing associations adopted the Housing Corporation model guidance which contractually introduces several concessions which do not exist for private assured tenancies. To qualify as an assured tenancy, the property must be let as a separate dwelling; the tenant must be an individual (not a company); and the tenant must occupy the dwelling-house as his/her only or principal home. Assured tenancies are not subject to any restrictions on rent which can be charged, but most housing associations have adopted the rent influencing regime model as a condition imposed by their regulator, although his does not apply to post-Localism Act flexible tenancies or assured shorthold tenancies.

An assured tenancy can only be brought to an end by the landlord obtaining a court order. A periodic assured tenancy may only be determined with a court order for possession upon establishing one of the statutory grounds (see Schedule 2 Housing Act 1988), and a Section 8 notice required is required to obtain possession. As well as being in the prescribed form (SI 1997/194 – Form 3), it must specify the ground(s) on which the landlord is seeking possession; lay out particulars of the ground(s); state the date after which proceedings may be commenced (this date is no earlier than two weeks after service of the notice – however certain grounds have differing time periods); and state that proceedings will not be begun later than 12 months from the date of service of the notice. The grounds for possession are contained in Schedule 2 Housing Act 1988. The grounds fall into two categories: grounds 1 to 8 are mandatory, that is, if the ground is proven, the court must make the possession order, whereas grounds 9 to 17 are discretionary – that is, if the ground is made out, the court will make the order only if it is reasonable to do so.

Housing association use of assured shorthold tenancies

The assured shorthold tenancy form is still used mainly for temporary accommodation arrangements by housing associations, and the agreement is arranged for a time period of six months, but may be agreed for a longer period, for example for 12 months. The tenant is allowed to remain in the property for the initial fixed period, usually six months, and in accordance with the Housing Act 1988 and in an assured shorthold tenancy, the landlord is granted the right to possess the property after the initial six month period of time, subject to the service of a Section 21 notice.

Introductory tenancies

This is a 12-month probationary tenancy after which council tenants may become a secure tenant, provided they meet the conditions of their tenancy agreement. They can be evicted easily after a notice to quit, and there is no discretion available to the court. Introductory tenants cannot exchange their tenancy with any other tenant, or transfer the tenancy, unless they are ordered to by a court or in other very rare circumstances. They cannot exercise the right to buy (however, the period of introductory tenancy may count towards the right to buy), take in lodgers or sublet all or part of the property, or make improvements to the property without the council's permission.

Their rights include that to be told about introductory tenancies and the council's duties to repair, and to be consulted on housing matters and kept up to date about any changes that affect introductory tenancies. Their obligations are to pay the weekly rent, keep the property clean and decorated, respect their neighbours and not cause a nuisance, make sure that anyone living at or visiting the property does not cause a nuisance, keep the garden in a neat and tidy condition, allow council work-men into the property to carry out inspections and repairs, and to give their landlord four weeks' notice to end the introductory tenancy. Reasons used to seek possession and evict introductory tenants include where the tenant fails to pay the weekly rent, or consistently pays rent late, where the tenant causes, or allows visitors to cause, a nuisance or annoyance, and where the tenant moves out and rents the home to someone else. An introductory tenant becomes a secure tenant automatically 12 months from the date tenancy started or the date the tenant moved in (whichever is later), unless the council decides to grant flexible tenancies under the provisions of the Localism Act, as will be discussed later. This transition will exist as long as the council has not started action to evict tenant during the 12-month period. Councils can decide to extend introductory tenancy for a further six months.

Probationary tenancies

Housing associations can make use of starter tenancies, which are based on assured shorthold tenancies. This use could involve all their properties in a number of local authority areas, or one or more defined estates or set of neighbouring streets. The rights of probationary tenants are restricted. There is no security of tenure, as with an assured tenancy, no right to assign, no right to transfer, no right to take in lodgers, no right to make improvements (a probationary tenant can apply to improve their property but if they move out during their probationary period, they have no right to statutory compensation), no right to buy (although their time as a probationary tenant does count for discount purposes), and no right to vote prior to transfer to a new landlord.

Recovering possession of a secure tenancy

In order to regain possession of a property, the landlord has first to serve a notice of seeking possession, then obtain a court order for possession, and then obtain a bailiff's warrant for eviction if the tenant does not acquiesce. The principal grounds have already been mentioned, but it is worth examining a few in detail. Grounds 1 to 6 are discretionary:

- Ground 1 Rent arrears or breach of obligation. In this case, the tenant is in arrears with payment of rent or has breached an obligation of the tenancy, and it is a discretionary ground.
- Ground 2 Nuisance and behaviour. The tenant or person residing in or visiting the dwelling house has either caused nuisance or annoyance to a person residing, visiting or otherwise engaging in lawful activity in the locality; or been convicted of using the dwelling-house or allowing it to be used for immoral or illegal purposes, or been convicted of an arrestable offence committed in, or in the locality of, the dwelling-house.
- Ground 2A Domestic violence. The dwelling was occupied by a married couple or couple living together as husband and wife and one or both of the partners is a tenant of dwelling, one partner has left because of violence or threats of violence by the other towards them or an occupying member of their family, and the court is satisfied that the leaving partner is unlikely to return. The court must be satisfied that the main reason for the partner leaving was the domestic violence (Camden LBC v. Mallett [2001] 33 HLR 204).
- Ground 3 Condition of premises. The condition of the dwelling-house or any of the common parts has deteriorated owing to acts of waste, neglect, or default of the tenant or a person residing with the tenant. If the latter is a lodger or sub-tenant the court must be satisfied that the tenant has failed to take reasonable steps to ensure their removal.
- Ground 4 Condition of furniture. The condition of furniture, provided by the landlord, has deteriorated owing to ill-treatment by the tenant or a person residing with the tenant. If the latter is a lodger or sub-tenant the court must be satisfied that the tenant has failed to take reasonable steps to ensure their removal.
- Ground 5 Misrepresentation by tenant (original tenant only). The tenant, or someone acting on his behalf, was guilty of a fraudulent misrepresentation in obtaining tenancy. Landlord must prove that: the statement was false, the tenant knew that the statement was false, or was reckless to its truth, and this induced the granting of the tenancy.
- Ground 6 Improper assignment. The tenancy was assigned to the tenant by way of exchange under s. 92 Housing Act 1985, and a premium was paid in relation to this assignment.

The following grounds are mandatory, but the landlord must provide alternative accommodation:

- Ground 7 – dwelling let in consequence of employment where the tenants behaviour is incompatible with that purpose

- Ground 8 - The dwelling was made available whilst the tenants home was being renovated and the original home is now available again
- Ground 9 Overcrowding. The dwelling-house is so overcrowded that the landlord is guilty of an offence.
- Ground 10 Demolition. The Landlord intends, within a reasonable time of obtaining possession, to carry out demolition, reconstruction or major works on the property. These works cannot reasonably be carried out with the tenant remaining in possession.
- Ground 10A Redevelopment. The landlord intends, within a reasonable time of obtaining possession, to dispose of the dwelling under a statutory redevelopment scheme.

The following grounds are discretionary, and the court must be satisfied that other accommodation will be made available:

- Ground 11 Charity. The landlord is a charity and the continued occupation by the tenant would conflict with the objects of the charity.
- Ground 12 Employment. The dwelling-house forms part of a building used mainly for purposes other than housing and the tenancy arose in consequence of the tenant's (or a predecessor's) employment by the landlord or local authority. That employment has ended and the landlord requires the dwelling-house for another employee of the landlord or local authority.
- Ground 13 Property adapted for disabled. The dwelling-house has features (different from normal houses) making it suitable for a disabled person and there is no longer such a person residing in the dwelling-house, and the landlord .requires it for occupation by such a person.
- Ground 14A Accommodation for special groups. The landlord is a housing trust which lets dwelling-houses only to persons with special housing needs and the tenant is not such a person, or has been offered a secure tenancy of other premises, and the landlord requires the dwelling-house for such a person.
- Ground 15 Accommodation for special needs. The dwelling-house is one of a group of such properties let out to persons with special needs (there being facilities and services for such people nearby) and the tenant is not such a person, and the landlord requires the dwelling-house for such a person.
- Ground 16 Succession (size of premises). The dwelling-house is more extensive than reasonably required by the tenant and the tenant succeeded to the tenancy under s. 89 Housing Act 1985 and a s. 83 notice was served between 6 and 12 months after the date of the previous tenant's death.

Demoted tenancies

The demoted tenancy was introduced by the Anti-Social Behaviour Act 2003. It enables councils and housing associations to deal more effectively with anti-social behaviour. It is a two-stage regime entitling such landlords to apply to demote an otherwise secure tenancy; and then, during this demoted period, the landlord may seek possession of the property as of right, subject to statutory procedure. The court will not make a demotion order unless it is satisfied that the tenant or person living in or visiting the property has engaged or has threatened to engage in conduct to which s. 153A or 153B of the Housing Act 1996 applies, and that it is reasonable to make the order. Qualifying conduct includes: conduct which is a nuisance or annoyance conduct which is capable of causing nuisance or annoyance to any person, and directly or indirectly relates to or affects the housing management functions of the landlord; and conduct arising from an unlawful use of the premises – conduct where someone has used or threatened to use the housing accommodation (owned or managed by the landlord) for an unlawful purpose, for example any conduct amounting to a criminal offence (such as drug dealing, running a brothel or harbouring stolen goods).

Housing associations and assured tenancies

Housing associations can create assured and assured shorthold tenancies. An assured tenancy is a periodic tenancy under the meaning of the 1988 Housing Act (as amended), and used to be the default form of private sector tenancy until the passage of the 1996 Housing Act, which made the assured shorthold form the default. There are fewer rights than those applying to the secure form, for example, the absence of the right to buy or to form a tenant management organisation, and there are more mandatory possession grounds.

Most of the grounds for possession are designed with the private sector in mind, and are rehearsed here in full and should be read in conjunction with the section concerning private sector tenancies. More detail is given in the section dealing with private sector lets.

Mandatory grounds/notice period:

1.   Returning owner-occupier/two months
2.   Mortgagee requiring possession/two months
3.   Tenancy proceeded by holiday let/two weeks
4.   Educational institutions/two weeks
5.   Returning minister of religion/two months
6.   Demolition or reconstruction/two months
7.   Death of a tenant (no succession)/two months
8.   Two months (eight weeks) rent arrears/two weeks

Discretionary grounds:

9.   Suitable alternative accommodation available/two months
10.   Some arrears of rent due/two weeks
11.   Persistent arrears of rent/two weeks
12.   Breach of any other terms of tenancy (not rent)/two weeks

13. Damage caused by waste default or neglect of tenant/two weeks

14. Nuisance and 14a domestic violence/0 weeks

15. Deterioration of furniture/two weeks

16. Tied accommodation/two months

17. False information or misrepresentation/two weeks

Private sector tenancies

There are several different types of private sector tenancy, and security of tenure depends on the date the tenancy started. There has been a tendency to reduce security of tenure over the past 20 years to make the sector more attractive to private investors and deflect a degree of housing need away from limited social housing. It is very important in addressing the requirements of niche groups – for example, young people leaving college and starting out on career, students, mobile workers, holiday and short-term business lets, company lets, etc. It is rarely seen as a long-term option, unlike the case 100 years ago. Rents are generally substantially higher than in the social/affordable rented sector.

The assured shorthold tenancy has been the default form since the 1996 Housing Act, replacing the assured tenancy as the default since the 1988 Housing Act. Prior to this, private landlords created regulated tenancies – sometimes known as Rent Act 1977 tenancies or fair rent tenancies. There are also licences – permissory arrangements – for example lodgings, informal arrangements to stay with friends or relations.

Regulated tenancies

There are still regulated tenants around – those whose tenancy began before January 1989. In fact, most lettings by private landlords which began before 15 January 1989 are regulated tenancies under the rent acts, unless the landlord and tenant live in the same house. It does not matter whether the letting is furnished or unfurnished, and there are significant rights concerning the amount of rent that can be charged, along with a high degree of tenure security. The rent must be within the Rent Act rateable value limits. A property will almost always be within the Rent Act rateable value limits if its rateable value today is £1,500 or less in Greater London, or £750 or less elsewhere. The rent must be more than two thirds of the rateable value of the property on the 'appropriate day'. The 'appropriate day' is either 23 March 1965, if the property had a rateable value then, or, if it did not, the date on which it was given one. Properties at rents lower than this prior to 1988 Housing Act are 'controlled tenancies', although almost all controlled tenancies were converted into regulated tenancies by the Housing Act 1980.

Regaining possession

There are 19 grounds for possession. Cases 1 to 10 are discretionary cases, and cases 11 to 20 are mandatory cases. There are two other grounds for possession which are not 'cases' as such: 1) the court can grant possession if it thinks that it is reasonable and suitable alternative accommodation is or will be available for the tenant; and 2) the other ground for possession is that there is statutory overcrowding in the property, as defined in the Housing Act 1985.

Discretionary grounds:

- Case 1: the tenant has not paid the rent, or has broken some other term of the tenancy
- Case 2: the tenant has caused a nuisance or annoyance to neighbours, or has been convicted of immoral or illegal use of the premises
- Case 3: the tenant has damaged the property or allowed it to become damaged
- Case 4: the tenant has damaged the furniture
- Case 5: the landlord has arranged to sell or let the property because the tenant gave notice that he or she was giving up the tenancy
- Case 6: the tenant has assigned or sublet the whole of the property without the landlord's consent
- Case 7: no longer exists
- Case 8: the tenant was an employee of the landlord and the landlord requires the property for a new employee
- Case 9: the landlord needs the property for himself or herself or certain members of his or her family to live in and that greater hardship would not be caused by granting the order than by refusing to grant it – but this does not normally apply if the tenant was a sitting tenant when the landlord bought the property
- Case 10: the tenant has charged a subtenant more than the Rent Act permits

Mandatory grounds (in the following cases, the order cannot be postponed for more than 14 days, except where it would cause exceptional hardship, when the maximum is six weeks):

- Case 11: the landlord let his or her home with the intention of returning to live there again
- Case 12: the landlord let accommodation to which he or she intends to retire
- Case 13: the accommodation was let for a fixed term of eight months or less, having been let for a holiday at some time during the previous 12 months
- Case 14: the accommodation was let for a fixed term of a year or less, having been let to students by a specified educational institution or body at some time during the previous 12 months
- Case 15: the accommodation was intended for a member of the clergy and has been let temporarily to an ordinary tenant
- Case 16: the accommodation was occupied by a farm worker and has been let temporarily to an ordinary tenant
- Case 17: when some agricultural holdings were amalgamated, accommodation previously occupied by a farm manager has been let temporarily to an ordinary tenant

- Case 18: the accommodation was previously occupied by a farm manager, widow or widower and has been let temporarily to an ordinary tenant
- Case 19: the property was let on a protected shorthold tenancy and the shorthold term has ended
- Case 20: the landlord was a member of the regular armed forces at the time the letting was made and intended to live in the house at some future date

Succession

Under the Rent Act 1977, as amended by the Housing Act 1988, the tenancy will pass to the tenant's spouse, or someone living with the tenant as husband or wife, who will become a Rent Act statutory tenant provided he or she was living with the tenant at the time of his or her death. If there is no such person, a member of the tenant's family who has lived with the tenant for at least two years immediately before the death of the tenant will be able to succeed to an assured tenancy. There can be no more than two successions. For a second succession, i.e. a family member taking over from a spouse, the same rules apply but the second successor must also have been a member of the original tenant's family. Note that in the case of secure and assured tenancies, there is only one statutory succession.

Regulated tenancies are subject to a fair rent. It is a rent which is worked out by a rent officer or rent assessment committee according to the rules in the Rent Act 1977. All fair rents are recorded in the local rent register. The rent officer must consider all the circumstances except the personal circumstances of the landlord and the tenant; the state of repair of the house or flat, its character, locality and age, how much furniture is provided and what it is like, and any premium lawfully paid. The rent officer must ignore: any disrepair for which the tenant is responsible; any improvements that the tenant has made which he or she did not need to under the terms of his or her tenancy. The rent officer must assume that demand for similar houses or flats available for letting in that particular area does not greatly exceed supply, i.e. that the rent would not be forced up by shortage. Tenancies starting on or after 28 February 1997 are automatically shorthold tenancies unless special steps are taken to set up an assured tenancy. Tenancies which started or were agreed before 28 February were automatically assured tenancies unless a special procedure was followed to set up a shorthold tenancy.

Grounds for possession

The following are mandatory grounds, and elaborate on those given in the previous section:

- Ground 1: Notice must be given before or at the start of the tenancy that possession might be recovered on this ground or the court is of the opinion that it is just and equitable to dispense with the requirement of notice and (in either case):
  - (a)   at some time before the beginning of the tenancy, the landlord who is seeking possession or, in the case of joint landlords seeking possession, at least

one of them occupied the dwelling-house as his only or principal home; or

(b)   the landlord who is seeking possession or, in the case of joint landlords seeking possession, at least one of them requires the dwelling-house as his or his spouse's only or principal home.

- Ground 2: The dwelling-house is subject to a mortgage granted before the beginning of the tenancy and:

  (a)   the mortgagee is entitled to exercise a power of sale conferred on him by the mortgage or by s. 101 of the [1925 c. 20.] Law of Property Act 1925; and

  (b)   the mortgagee requires possession of the dwelling-house for the purpose of disposing of it with vacant possession in exercise of that power; and

  (c)   either notice was given as mentioned in Ground 1 above or the court is satisfied that it is just and equitable to dispense with the requirement of notice.

- Ground 3: The tenancy is a fixed-term tenancy for a term not exceeding eight months and:

  (a)   not later than the beginning of the tenancy the landlord gave notice in writing to the tenant that possession might be recovered on this ground; and

  (b)   at some time within the period of 12 months ending with the beginning of the tenancy, the dwelling-house was occupied under a right to occupy it for a holiday.

- Ground 4: The tenancy is a fixed-term tenancy for a term not exceeding 12 months and:

  (a)   not later than the beginning of the tenancy the landlord gave notice in writing to the tenant that possession might be recovered on this ground; and

  (b)   at some time within the period of 12 months ending with the beginning of the tenancy, the dwelling-house was let on a tenancy falling within paragraph 8 of Schedule 1 to this Act.

- Ground 5: The dwelling-house is held for the purpose of being available for occupation by a minister of religion as a residence from which to perform the duties of his office and:

  (a)   not later than the beginning of the tenancy the landlord gave notice in writing to the tenant that possession might be recovered on this ground; and

  (b)   the court is satisfied that the dwelling-house is required for occupation by a minister of religion as such a residence.

- Ground 6 (summary): The landlord is seeking possession or, if that landlord is a registered housing association or charitable housing trust, a superior landlord intends to demolish or reconstruct the whole or a substantial part of the dwelling-house or to carry out substantial works on the dwelling-house or any part thereof or any building of which it forms part.

- Ground 7: The tenancy is a periodic tenancy (including a statutory periodic tenancy) which has devolved under the will or intestacy of the former tenant and the proceedings for the recovery of possession are begun not later than 12 months after the death of the former tenant or, if the court so directs, after the date on which, in the opinion of the court, the landlord, or in the case of joint landlords, any one of them became aware of the former tenant's death.

- Ground 8: Both at the date of the service of the notice under section 8 of this Act relating to the proceedings for possession and at the date of the hearing:
  (a)　if rent is payable weekly or fortnightly, at least eight weeks' rent is unpaid;
  (b)　if rent is payable monthly, at least two months' rent is unpaid;
  (c)　if rent is payable quarterly, at least one quarter's rent is more than three months in arrears; and
  (d)　if rent is payable yearly, at least three months' rent is more than three months in arrears (for the purpose of this ground 'rent' means rent lawfully due from the tenant).

The following grounds are discretionary:

- Ground 9: Suitable alternative accommodation is available for the tenant or will be available for him when the order for possession takes effect.

- Ground 10: Some rent lawfully due from the tenant:
  (a)　is unpaid on the date on which the proceedings for possession are begun;
  (b)　except where subsection (1)(b) of section 8 of this Act applies, was in arrears at the date of the service of the notice under that section relating to those proceedings.

- Ground 11: Whether or not any rent is in arrears on the date on which proceedings for possession are begun, the tenant has persistently delayed paying rent which has become lawfully due.

- Ground 12: Any obligation of the tenancy (other than one related to the payment of rent) has been broken or not performed.

- Ground 13: The condition of the dwelling-house or any of the common parts has deteriorated owing to acts of waste by, or neglect or default of, the tenant or any other person residing in the dwelling-house and, in the case of an act of waste by, or neglect or default of, a person lodging with the tenant or a subtenant of his, the tenant has not taken such steps as he ought reasonably to have taken for the removal of the lodger or subtenant.

- Ground 14: The tenant or a person residing in or visiting the dwelling-house:
  (a)　has been guilty of conduct causing or likely to cause a nuisance or annoyance to a person residing, visiting or otherwise engaging in a lawful activity in the locality; or
  (b)　has been convicted of: (i) using the dwelling-house or allowing it to be used for immoral or illegal purposes, or (ii) an arrestable offence committed in, or in the locality of, the dwelling-house.

- Ground 15: The condition of any furniture provided for use under the tenancy has, in the opinion of the court, deteriorated owing to ill-treatment by the tenant or any other person residing in the dwelling-house and, in the case of ill-treatment by a person lodging with the tenant or by a subtenant of his, the tenant has not taken such steps as he ought reasonably to have taken for the removal of the lodger or subtenant.

- Ground 16: The dwelling-house was let to the tenant in consequences of his employment by the landlord seeking possession or a previous landlord under the tenancy and the tenant has ceased to be in that employment.

- Ground 17: The tenant is the person, or one of the persons, to whom the tenancy was granted and the landlord was induced to grant the tenancy by false statement made knowingly or recklessly by:
  (a) the tenant; or
  (b) a person acting at the tenant's instigation.

Assured shorthold tenancies

This is the default form of private sector tenancy. In the case of an assured shorthold tenancy, the landlord can regain possession of the property six months after the beginning of the tenancy, provided that he or she gives two months' notice requiring possession. The landlord can charge a full market rent for an assured or an assured shorthold tenancy. Under the 1996 Housing Act, tenancies starting on or after 28 February 1997 are automatically shorthold tenancies unless special steps are taken to set up an assured tenancy. An assured or shorthold tenancy may either last for a fixed number of weeks, months or years – called a fixed-term tenancy, or run indefinitely from one rent period to the next – called a contractual periodic tenancy. In the case of a fixed-term assured shorthold tenancy, the landlord will only be able to seek possession during the fixed term if one of grounds for possession of an assured tenancy – 2, 8, 10 to 15 or 17 – apply and if the terms of the tenancy make provision for it to be ended on any of these grounds.

In the case of an assured shorthold tenancy on a periodic basis, the landlord has an automatic right to possession at any time after the first six months, provided he or she has given two months' notice requiring possession. Shorthold tenancies which started or were agreed before 28 February 1997 had to have an initial fixed term of at least six months. Shorthold tenancies starting on or after 28 February do not.

Assured tenancies and assured shorthold tenancies – rights and obligations/repairs

Unless the tenancy has a fixed term of more than seven years, the landlord is responsible for repairs to the structure and exterior of the property, to baths, sinks, basins and other sanitary installations and to heating and hot water installations, plus, in the case of flats or maisonettes, other parts of the building or installations in it which he or she owns or controls and whose disrepair would affect the tenant. The landlord is required to ensure that all gas appliances are maintained in good order and that an annual safety check is carried out by a recognised engineer – that is, an engineer who is approved under Regulation 3 of the Gas Safety (Installation and Use) Regulations 1998. The landlord must keep a record of the safety checks and issue it to the tenant within 28 days of each annual check. He or she is not responsible for maintaining gas appliances which the tenant is entitled to take with them at the end of the letting.

Tenants' rights

There is a right to 'quiet enjoyment' and the landlord should ask the tenants' permission before he or she enters the premises. The landlord cannot evict without a possession order from the court. If the landlord sells the freehold of the property the tenant will retain any rights they have to remain in the property, as the tenancy will be binding on any purchaser. Matters such as whether pets can be kept, satellite or cable television or Internet broadband etc. installed, should be negotiated at the outset of the tenancy and included in the terms of the tenancy agreement.

Ending the tenancy – the section 21 Notice (s. 21 1996 Housing Act)

When an assured shorthold tenancy comes to the end of the fixed term, the landlord can end the tenancy but must have given two months' notice that he or she requires possession. If the tenancy started on or after 28 February 1997, the landlord has a right to repossess the property without giving any grounds for possession at any time after any fixed term comes to an end or at any time during a contractual or statutory periodic tenancy, provided it is at least six months since the start of the original tenancy. The notice must be in writing.

Tenancies and licences

Tenancies exist where there are rights to reside in the property, whereas licences confer permission to occupy only. The distinction is not always clear cut. An example of a tenancy is a restricted tenancy where the tenant has keys to room/flat in a property also occupied by landlord and pays rent, and has a right to notice to quit and court order. A licencee has occupancy of room, probably no key, receives personal services for example cleaning, the landlord can enter the room, there is no rent but an occupation charge, no security of tenure, limited notice to quit and no court order is needed. As ever, it is for the court to decide whether an arrangement is a licence or tenancy.

Repairs and the law

One of the great advantages of being a tenant as opposed to being an owner-occupier is that the landlord is responsible for most repairs to the dwelling. This is a complex area of the law, but one which practitioners need to have a firm grasp of.

Disrepair is an area with significant statute and case law, and is defined as the deterioration of an element. there is an implied obligation to repair the property if already in disrepair at start of tenancy. There is no liability to put in new items which were never part of the building – these are improvements not repairs. An example of such an issue is damp. Many older houses were not built with a damp-proof course – damp can give rise to disrepair, but there is no obligation to put in a damp-proof course even though may be best way to deal with problem!

Statutes

Relevant statutes are:

- Defective Premises Act 1972 – duty of care on landlords to keep tenants reasonably safe from injury;
- Landlord and Tenant Act 1985 – landlord must keep structure and fabric in good repair (from 1961 Housing Act);
- Housing Act 1985 – consolidates previous legislation regarding council repairing covenants;
- Environmental Protection Act 1990 – statutory nuisance;
- Housing Act 2004 – HHSRS and action by councils regarding houses in multiple accupation.

Implied covenants

The landlord must keep in repair and proper working order: the structure and exterior of the dwelling-house (including drains, gutters and external pipes); installations in the dwelling-house for supplying water, gas and electricity and for sanitation (including basins, sinks, baths, sanitary conveniences – but not other fixtures, fittings and appliances for this purpose); and installations in the dwelling-house for space heating and heating water.

These covenants apply to all lets of dwellings made on or after 24 October 1961 for a term of less than seven years (s. 13 Landlord and Tenant Act 1985). Any express (written) covenant seeking to pass liability for repairs specified by s. 11 of that acts invalid. Under s. 12(2) a county court may authorise contracting out of repairs function of reasonable looking at all terms of the lease. It should be noted that the term 'lease' is legally identical to 'tenancy' in this context.

They apply to the following premises: rented premises; common parts, provided the property let (to anyone) after 15 January 1989 – as long as disrepair affects enjoyment of dwelling or common parts (for example, shared hallways and staircases in blocks of flats); and if the lessor has control of whole block (s. 116 Housing Act 1988).

Tenant's liability

Tenants must treat the property in a tenant like manner – doing jobs around the house that any tenant would do. Remedies against tenants include: specific performance – an equitable remedy and a decision for the court, but it is unusual for court to order this against a tenant. It is more likely that the landlord will seek to evict the tenant or to enter the premises (with proper notice and avoiding breaches of quiet enjoyment) to effect repair and seek damages.

Consultation and regeneration

It is a shame that those endeavouring to regenerate areas should feel it necessary to abide by a shoal of legislation enforcing consultation. It should surely be a matter of natural justice and politeness to consult those whose homes lie in the path of a bulldozer before flattening dreams and aspirations due to some grandiose scheme deemed necessary by politicians and social engineers. Thank goodness there are laws which regulate such matters, or else residents would be entirely disempowered, although there are not a few examples of where this has happened despite the existence of legal protection.

The statutory basis for consulting local authority secure tenants is to be found in s. 105 Housing Act 1985. Contexts include major changes in housing management delivery, or of the housing management organisation, for example moving from a decentralised office approach to centralised delivery or vice versa; moving to a different way of allocating housing; outsourcing a function/functions; and transfer of management (for example TMO or ALMO or another registered provider). Separate legal conditions apply to consultation on proposed changes in stock ownership (for example large-scale voluntary transfer).

In relation to regeneration, here referring to major redevelopment of an estate (part or in whole), this may involve Section 106 and core strategy consultations. It entails a significant disruption to lives of residents – including decanting and compulsory purchase routes to displace leaseholders and freeholders. It may also involve changes in housing management and/or the identity of the landlord, and may involve consultation via a third party or contracted party – for example, through a TMO or an independent adviser who may be subcontracted via an ALMO or TMO to discharge the council's consultation duties.

Duty to publish details of consultation arrangements

Practice varies considerably, as illustrated in the following case law. In Short v. Tower Hamlets LBC [1985] 18 HLR 171, Tower Hamlets agreed to conduct an exploratory marketing exercise with a view to selling an estate. The court held that councils did not need to consult tenants about this as it did not substantially affect them and was not (yet) a matter of housing management. In the case of R v. Hackney ex Bourbour (June 2000 Legal Action 24) CA, Hackney Council planned to dispose of six tenanted estates. Group 6 included an estate where the applicant was a secure tenant. Consultation included a ballot of all the Group 6 estates as a whole. Applicants claimed there should have been a separate ballot of the Stamford Hill estate. The application was dismissed. It was decided that the method of consultation was for council to decide, no ballot was required and nothing in the act required separate consultation of every block or estate. It was also found that there had been a substantial delay in the tenant's application, and that estates had not been clustered to 'rig' the ballot.

Large-scale voluntary transfers

A large-scale voluntary transfer cannot proceed without a tenants' ballot. Tenant consultation usually addressed by the local authority and the new landlord. It involves agreeing a formal transfer consultation document that includes legally enforceable commitments on tenancy rights, rent guarantees, investment in the stock, representation on the board of management and proposed housing policies.

Legal basis for consultation on regeneration schemes

Under Section 105 of the Housing Act 1985, local authorities must maintain arrangements as they consider appropriate relating to consultation on matters of housing management, which include those which in the opinion of the landlord authority relate to the management, maintenance, improvement or demolition of dwelling-houses. Methods could include: public meetings, website information, surveys, focus groups, engagement with stakeholder groups, inviting input into a residents' charter and into a development brief, and ensuring proactive and genuine involvement in any planning measures for example a masterplan, core strategy, development plan pocuments – especially in the examination in public stage.

Issues which should be thoroughly consulted on, and involve stakeholders in meaningful dialogue in, include tenants' home loss payments and disturbance allowances, the nature of temporary tenancies on decanting, gaining possession, the form of any new tenancy granted in a new or refurbished property, rent levels and terms of conditions in the new tenancy (what if it is an assured tenancy held from a housing association?), and the impact of the new affordable tenancy regime if this is the path the council wants to go down.

Human rights

Human rights legislation has a significant effect on housing provision and management. The 1950 European Convention on Human Rights (ECHR) is a binding international agreement that the UK helped draft, and informs the Human Rights Act 1998.

Since coming into force on 2 October 2000, the Human Rights Act has made rights from the ECHR enforceable in UK courts. The act gives people a clear legal statement of their basic rights and fundamental freedoms. The key principle of the act is that wherever possible there should be compatibility with the Convention rights (DCA, no date).

The Human Rights Act is about giving further effect to rights in the ECHR. The rights of a person accused of a crime to question witnesses may need to be balanced against the rights of victims and vulnerable witnesses. The wider interests of the community as a whole may also need to be taken into account. This idea is reflected in the way that many of the Convention rights are written. The Human Rights Act ensures that the supporting judgements of the European Court of Human Rights are fully available to UK courts. It also ensures that parliament has to reflect carefully, in considering proposed legislation, on the question of where the balance lies between the individual's rights and the needs of the wider community. The Human Rights Act requires UK courts to respect laws passed by parliament. It allows a higher court to declare that a law cannot be given a meaning compatible with the Convention rights. Parliament can then decide whether and how to amend the law. Thus the act balances the rights and responsibilities of the law-making and judicial parts of the UK constitution, leaving the final word to the democratic process.

The Human Rights Act means that Convention rights and responsibilities form a common set of binding values for public authorities right across the UK. Public authorities must have human rights principles in mind when they make decisions about people's rights, and human rights must be part of all policy-making. It requires all UK law to be interpreted and given effect as far as possible compatibly with the Convention rights. Where it is not possible to do so, a court may quash or disapply subordinate legislation (for example regulations or orders) or, if it is a higher court, make a declaration of incompatibility in relation to primary legislation. This triggers a power allowing a minister to make a remedial order to amend the legislation to bring it into line with the Convention rights.

It is unlawful for a public authority to act incompatibly with the Convention rights. The Human Rights Act allows for a case to be brought in a UK court or tribunal against the authority if it does so. However, a public authority will not have acted unlawfully under the act if, as the result of a provision of primary legislation (such as another act of parliament), it could not have acted differently.

Under the Human Rights Act there are absolute, limited and qualified rights. Absolute rights include the right to protection from torture, inhuman and degrading treatment and punishment (Article 3), the prohibition on slavery and enforced labour (Article 4) and protection from retrospective criminal penalties (Article 7). Limited rights include the right to liberty (Article 5) which is limited under explicit and finite circumstances, set out in the ECHR itself, which provides exceptions to the general right. Qualified rights include the right to respect for private and family life (Article 8), religion and belief (Article 9), freedom of expression (Article 10), assembly and association (Article 11), the right to peaceful enjoyment of property (Protocol 1, Article 1) and to some extent the right to education (Protocol 1, Article 2).

The articles particularly relevant to housing are articles 8 and 11. Under Article 8, you have the right to respect for your private and family life, your home and your correspondence. Article 8 is an example of a qualified right in the ECHR. What this means is that there is a framework in place against which any interference with your rights by the state may be justified. In general, your right to a private life means that you have the right to live your own life with such personal privacy as is reasonable in a democratic society, taking into account the rights and freedoms of others. Any interference with your body or the way you live your life needs to be justified. Your right to respect for family life includes the right to have family relationships recognised by the law. It also includes the right for a family to live together and enjoy each other's company. Unmarried mothers are always covered by 'family' and foster families may be. Under Article 8, you have the right to enjoy living in your home without public authorities intruding or preventing you from entering it or living in it. You also have the right to enjoy your home peacefully. This may mean, for example, that the state has to take action so that you can peacefully enjoy your home, for example, to reduce aircraft noise or to prevent serious environmental pollution. In this context, your 'home' may include your place of business. It is worth noting that the right is 'tenure blind'.

Under Article 14, freedom from discrimination, discrimination means treating people in similar situations differently or those in different situations in the same way, without proper justification. You cannot be denied equal access to them on grounds of your 'status'. The structure of Article 14 means that you need to be able to identify another Convention right in order to make use of the non-discrimination protection. This should be read in conjunction with the Equalities Act 2010. Discrimination is prohibited on the grounds of sex, race, colour, language, religion, political or other opinion, national or social origin, association with a national minority, property or birth. Article 14 also protects from discrimination on the grounds of 'any other status'. This includes sexual orientation, whether you were born inside or outside a marriage, disability, marital status and age.

Protocol 1, Article 12 is also highly relevant to housing. You have the right to the peaceful enjoyment of your possessions, which means that public authorities cannot usually interfere with things you own or the way that you use them. All sorts of things can count as property, for example, land is property, as is a lease on a house or flat. Even entitlement to a social security benefit can be property, and companies, individuals, legal owners, beneficiaries, trustees and corporations can benefit from this right. There is the right under this article to peaceful enjoyment of property without interference. You have the right to use, develop, sell, destroy or deal with your property in any way you please. The right to protection of property means that public authorities cannot interfere with use of property unless there is a law that lets them do it and unless interference is justified.

The European Court of Human Rights is the enforcement machinery of the ECHR, and hears complaints from individuals or states about alleged breaches of ECHR rights and freedoms by countries that belong to the Council of Europe.

Horizontal and vertical effects

Horizontal effect is a term often used to describe the impact of the Convention rights in legal relations between two private parties. It is distinguished from vertical proceedings brought by an individual to enforce obligations owed to him by the state. The main effect of the Human Rights Act is vertical, principally affecting cases between individuals and state or public authorities rather than disputes between private parties. However, the act requires all legislation, as far as possible, to be read and given effect compatibly with the Convention rights.

Judicial review.

Judicial review refers to legal proceedings by which administrative decisions or actions by, for example, a government department can be challenged before the courts on the grounds that they have been made invalidly or are unlawful or irrational. Judicial review may result in the matter complained of being overturned, and a decision having to be retaken.

Standards and regulation

The TSA was the social housing regulator which introduced six regulatory standards in respect of social housing providers and was launched in December 2008, to replace the regulatory arm of Housing Corporation. It has now been abolished by the Localism Act 2011, with most of its powers transferred to the HCA. The new standards to evaluate performance for registered providers, which still exist came in 1 April 2010, and cover housing associations and stock-owning local authorities, but not ALMOs. Non-stock-owning ALMOs are not directly subject to regulatory scrutiny by TSA, but the client councils are responsible for their performance. There is a tenant focus running through the regulations, with local variations in service delivery via negotiation with tenants. The TSA standards were effective from 1 April 2010, and involvement runs throughout policy and strategy-making and regulation/monitoring. The regulatory code has strengthened requirements to consult and involve tenants. There are local offers on service delivery levels, which had to be negotiated with tenants and be in place by 1 April 2011. The six standards relate to: tenant involvement and empowerment; home; tenancy; neighbourhood and community; value for money; and governance and financial viability. Local offers are agreements on expected service levels, involvement and scrutiny. The HCA monitors organisations against these. Local offers apply to standards on tenant involvement and empowerment, home, and neighbourhood and community. They require evidence of negotiation and engagement, regardless of the outcome.

Some of the standards

The tenant involvement and empowerment standard includes standards on involvement and empowerment, customer service and choice, equalities and diversity, tenants with additional support needs and complaints. The home standard includes measuring the quality of accommodation, to decent homes plus. It also examines the cost-effectiveness of repairs and maintenance. The tenancy standard and neighbourhood and community standards include standards on allocations, rent and tenure, but there is no debate with tenants on this, and no local offer. The neighbourhood and community standards major on local area cooperation, and anti-social behaviour, and this one has a local offer. The value for money standard shows how expenditure has been prioritised in relation to each of the standards and in the delivery of local offers, and in meeting other needs, for example investment in new social housing provision. Its purpose is to show how the organisation has ensured that value for money has been secured and tested. It also contains plans and priorities for delivery of further value for money improvements, and there is no local offer associated with this one. Under the governance and financial viability standard, the organisation must adhere to all relevant legislation. It must comply with governing documents and all regulatory requirements, and must be accountable to tenants, the TSA and relevant stakeholders. It must also safeguard taxpayers' interests and the reputation of the sector, and have an effective risk management framework. Registered providers are required to manage their resources effectively to ensure their viability is maintained. There is no local offer on this one, and does not apply to councils.

Localism Act: scope for housing law reform

The Localism Act 2011 received Royal Assent on 15 November 2011, and is one of the most important pieces of legislation to affect housing since 1996. It brought into play major changes to the planning regime which have affected housing delivery and it has increased local (neighbourhood) input into planning strategies, policies and deliverables, although there is a presumption in favour of development. There were also major changes to the Section 106 and community infrastructure levy regimes. Closer to home, there were major changes to housing policy relating to homelessness, tenancy types, allocations, housing mobility, complaints systems and housing finance. It also confirmed new models for local authority governance, including crucially the elected mayor and cabinet model. It also abolished the TSA and brought in changes to the compulsory purchase order regime. It will be dealt with fully in Chapter 7, but the main influence has been the introduction of flexible tenure, increasing the needs basis of social housing tenancies.

Tenancy strategies

Under s. 150 of the Localism Act, councils in England must prepare and publish a strategy (a 'tenancy strategy') which sets out matters to which the registered providers of social housing for its district (mainly housing associations) must have regard to when putting together policies relating to the kinds of tenancies they grant, the circumstances in which they will grant a tenancy of a particular kind, where they grant tenancies for a fixed term, the lengths of the terms, and the circumstances in which they will grant a further tenancy on the coming to an end of an existing tenancy.

Flexible tenure

These are essentially variants of the secure tenancy form for local authorities, and have a duration of not less than two years on a fixed-term basis. They are introduced by Section 154 of the Localism Act. Such tenancies are determinable by four weeks' notice by the tenant (Section 107c Housing Act 1996 as inserted) and the landlord can seek possession of such a tenancy (under Section 107d) simply by showing that the flexible tenancy has come to an end, after service of six months' notice and a statement that the landlord does not intend to grant another tenancy at the end of the flexible tenancy period. The must also be not less than two months' notice that possession is being sought. Under section 107e, the tenant may request a review of the decision not to grant a further tenancy, and if the landlord has failed to carry out a review of the tenancy, the court can refuse to grant possession. Section 155 enables councils to grant flexible tenancies following year-long introductory tenancies, and also after demoted tenancies. Section 163 enables housing associations to grant assured shorthold tenancies following the expiry of demoted tenancies and Section 164 enables them to grant assured shorthold tenancies more generally than hitherto. Before the passage of the act, housing associations only granted assured shorthold tenancies on temporary accommodation used for homeless persons. Again, the term is for at least two years. There is no right to acquire attached to such tenancies, and the notice requirements are similar to those of council flexible tenancies.

Scope for further tenure reform

The next step could be just one flexible tenure for social and affordable housing tenancies. This would finally confirm social and affordable housing as welfare housing, a hand-up to assist people until they have the means to rent privately or buy on a part- or full-ownership basis.

References

DCLG (Department for Communities and Local Government), (2009) *Fair and Flexible: Statutory Guidance on Social Housing Allocations for Local Authorities in England*. London: DCLG.

DCLG, (2010a) Table 770 Statutory homelessness: decisions taken by local authorities under the 1996 Housing Act on applications from eligible households, England. Available at: www.communities.gov.uk/documents/statistics/xls/2102063.xls. viewed 6 June 2013.

DCLG, (2010b) Table 774. Statutory homelessness: households accepted by local authorities, as owed a main homelessness duty, by reason for loss of last settled home, England, 1998 to 2013. Available at: https://www.gov.uk/government/statistical-data-sets/live-tables-on-homelessness, viewed 6 June 2013.

DCA (Department for Constitutional Affairs), (no date) Guide to the Human Rights Act, available at: http://webarchive.nationalarchives.gov.uk/+/www.dca.gov.uk/peoplesrights/human-rights/pdf/act-studyguide.pdf, viewed 1 September 2012.

HHSRS (Housing Health and Safety Rating System), (2004) Operating Guidance Housing Act 2004: Guidance about inspections and assessment of hazards given under Section 9. London: DCLG, available at: www.communities.gov.uk/documents/housing/pdf/142631.pdf, viewed 1 September 2012.

ODPM (Office of the Deputy Prime Minister), (2006a) Housing Health and Safety Rating System: Enforcement Guidance, Housing Act 2004. Part 1: Housing Conditions. London: ODPM.

ODPM, (2006b) Housing Health and Safety Rating System:- Enforcement Guidance, Housing Act 2004. Part 1: Housing Conditions. London: ODPM. Available at: www.communities.gov.uk/documents/housing/pdf/safetyratingsystem.pdf, viewed 1 September 2012.

6 Housing regeneration and development

Keywords: *Introduction to housing regeneration and development; the elements of regeneration – social, economic, physical and environmental; why is regeneration required?; how to do and not to do regeneration; case studies; resident involvement in housing regeneration; the role of government and its agencies; the role of change agencies; assessing success and failure; the future of regeneration; introduction to housing development, the enabling and production of new-build housing for rent and for sale; the strategic planning process, how many homes are needed?; the affordable housing requirement; housing needs surveys and strategic housing market assessments; planning policy implications; focus on Section 106 and the community infrastructure levy; critical analysis of registered housing providers – problems and prospects; the privatisation of development; the importance of sustainability; environmental sustainability; economic sustainability; social sustainability; the importance of planning; core strategies and planning guidance; development planning – pre- and post-Localism; brownfield and greenfield development; design – layout and dwellings; density; design matters; focus on lifetime homes; form of building contracts and contract management; resident involvement; conclusion – the future of development.*

Introduction

Housing development is the creation of new stock or the remodelling of existing stock so as to produce dwellings of an acceptable standard for sale or rent. Regeneration generally involves the demolition of existing stock, in part or in whole, on an area basis, and its replacement with new dwellings along with the refurbishment of existing ones. It can therefore be seen that the scope of regeneration is wider than that of development. It also includes the notion of social and economic interventions to regenerate not just homes but also communities. This chapter will examine the nature of housing development and regeneration, and explore their scope and limitations.

The elements of regeneration – social, economic, physical and environmental

Regeneration is a portmanteau term which needs unpacking. It is perhaps helpful to visualise a neighbourhood which stands in need of regeneration. Picture an inner-city area where terraced housing built in the late nineteenth century dominates, where the homes fail the Decent Homes standard, and where many of the dwellings are unoccupied through abandonment or a conscious policy of removing tenants where the local authority has re-housed them, and where many have been declared unfit for human habitation. The area may be characterised by low employment levels and high relative poverty, with higher than average infant mortality and lower than average life expectancies. There may be relatively low educational attainment, and many of the younger people may be not in employment, education or training. Each of these elements can be addressed by regeneration plans. The area may have few parks or open spaces, and relatively few facilities for community activities, not to mention a dearth of shops and educational facilities.

Regeneration has social, economic, physical and environmental aspects. In relation to the visualised area, it may be necessary to look at the social mix in the area – to encourage a range of household types, as well as to provide social facilities such as well-stocked libraries and educational facilities which will provide younger people with a better start in life, and to provide adult education. It may also be necessary to provide recreational facilities, as well as parkland to encourage healthy living, along with GPs' surgeries in the form of a health 'hub'. In economic terms, if the area lacks sources of employment, it may be prudent to encourage firms to relocate in or near the area depending on its size, to help provide work for those living there, or to provide training facilities to help residents into work elsewhere. In physical terms, it may be necessary to demolish many of the dwellings which are judged beyond economic repair, to improve or remodel those which have some hope of providing decent housing, and to develop new homes. Physical regeneration could also extend to the environment, with the provision of recreational space (which also serves a social aim), and attention to public furniture such as benches as well as to hard and soft landscaping features so the area presents well. Such improvements may draw would-be owner-occupiers back into the area, so thought should be given to the appropriate tenure mix to achieve this, perhaps through introducing some form of lower-cost home ownership into the development mix. Environmental improvements relate not only to external improvement via hard and soft landscaping, but also to energy-efficient solutions with as small a carbon footprint as possible. All of this can form part of a 'master plan' for the area, a form of planning brief which will inform the local development plan. The object of the exercise would be to transform an area which has high levels of dereliction and decay, where people do not wish to live, into an area which is attractive as a place to live and work, and which coheres as a community.

One essential ingredient in such a regeneration approach, alongside necessary funding, is that local people should be consulted on their vision for the area. It must be remembered that areas are places where people live, and have in many cases dwelt for some time, who have a stake in the area, and unless their aspirations are taken on board, there is the very real risk of failure as the 'solutions' will be rejected by local people and plans opposed, which may result in delay and frustration of such plans for the right reason. This can be done through surveys, master-planning exercises and 'planning for real' over a reasonable period of time, perhaps longer than envisaged in planning legislation, to win hearts and minds. Regrettably, this attention to detail is often missing in major regeneration schemes, where consultation may be just tokenistic.

Why is regeneration required?

The idea of regeneration has been presented in a fairly stark manner, examining a notional neighbourhood which exhibits serious decay and where some form of solution is obviously required, and where the temptation to bulldoze the lot has been avoided. It may be useful to formalise the matter by considering (under each head) why regeneration may be necessary. Consider the lists below, which identify the need for regeneration, with (a non-exhaustive list of) symptoms of decay stated:

- Social:
  - No 'sense of community';
  - No community leadership from within;
  - High levels of social deprivation measured in educational, income and savings, anti-social behaviour and related terms;
  - Adverse labelling of the area by people outside as well as within the area (for example as a 'sink' estate or 'dreadful enclosure');
  - Low levels of civic engagement;
  - High levels of vandalism and petty crime.

- Economic:
  - Low incomes;
  - Higher than average dependency on state benefits;
  - Low levels of employment;
  - Low levels of savings;
  - Presence of loan sharking;
  - No or few workplaces within the community or within reasonable proximity;
  - Low levels of owner-occupation;
  - Failing shops/lack of retail outlets.

- Physical:
  - Relatively high proportion of dwellings which fail Decent Homes standards;
  - Older poorly maintained stock;
  - Boarded-up dwellings;
  - High proportion of dwellings which exhibit HHSRS hazards;
  - Thermal inefficiency as a major feature of dwellings;
  - Neglected 'feel' to the area – littering, broken walls, damaged trees, vandalism, etc.

- Environmental:
  - Lack of green space;
  - Neglected green areas;

- Poor-quality hard and soft landscaping;
- Heavy traffic to part of the area;
- Polluted ground;
- Few trees and bushes, or inappropriately sited vegetation;
- Few gardens and other private green space.

Add your own instances to the foot of each list.

The notion of regeneration is not a new one. In the early 1960s, large areas of inner-city Victorian slum dwellings were cleared by municipal authorities and replaced by tower blocks and council maisonettes and flats in a quest for better living conditions and indeed the rise of council development can be attributed to regeneration. It must be remembered that the roots of council housing stem from a desire to attack health issues, and that the garden city pioneers in the first part of the twentieth century were aiming at producing balanced communities well ahead of Hills. However, what counts as regeneration depends on what is in the mind of the regenerator. The motivation for regeneration must always be unearthed. If the mindset is one which aims at generating communities with higher spending power and with a fair proportion of economically active and aspirational individuals, then it is highly likely that the regeneration will include a reasonable proportion of owner-occupied and even private rented dwellings in the mix; and if the intention is to create an area of affordable housing where lower-income households will be the primary beneficiary, then council or housing association dwellings for rent may be in the majority. The vision for regeneration may be partly or even wholly political, which may explain why in some cases, owner-occupied dwellings replace those for municipal rent on the basis of anticipated voting patterns. There is no such thing as politically neutral regeneration, and it should be axiomatic that the views of those who will be affected by regeneration should count when such plans are proposed.

To a certain extent, the planning system does enable local views to be taken into account, and the Localism Act, with its revivication of parish bodies and the introduction of neighbourhood planning bodies (to be discussed in Chapter 7) should ensure that local views are taken into account when such plans are formulated. Typically, a local authority will devise a master plan for an area as a first step to planning regeneration. A master plan is essentially a plan for a large area – such as a town centre – which establishes a development framework for infrastructure, buildings and public realm and presents how the town centre might look in the future. Typically, local authorities commission architect and planning practices to put together a master plan for an area, based on the political, social and economic aspirations of local and sometimes national politicians.

What, then, are the essential components of regeneration?

Vision

There has to be a vision for the area which is worked through and takes into account the existing strengths of the area as well as its weaknesses. The vision should be owned not only by local politicians and specialists but by the people it will affect. Consultation should not be tokenistic or short term, and local people should be on regeneration master-planning panels, along with other stakeholders. They should be able to engage in planning for real events at the outset, and there should be surveys to gauge local sentiment. Unless this happens, there will rightly be opposition from the outset due to the democratic deficit. Resident advisers should be independent of the proposer, and their comments should be taken seriously if based on other engagements, and they should be selected by those who stand to lose most from remodelling. The advantages and disadvantages of various options should be thoroughly and carefully explained, so that genuine choices can be made. The vision should encompass, social, environmental, physical and economic dimensions, and every effort should be made to keep existing communities together if that is the local sentiment. Tenure mix should be subjected to local scrutiny and decision-making, in line with costing – cross-subsidy may well be something that needs to be factored in, but it should be remembered that this does not necessarily entail an over-dominance of owner-occupied dwellings on the site itself. The cross-subsidy could come from somewhere else, perhaps an area developed for owner-occupation on a site currently undeveloped or with another use (for example industrial usage, where the *raison d'etre* for that form of industry has passed, or where it is incompatible with residential development). Thought should be given to the need to provide shops, roads, schools, nurseries, health centres and other provision that communities require so that the community recreated is truly sustainable, and thought should be given to how the community will develop over the years. It may, therefore, be necessary to develop lifetime homes so that people do not have to move at later stages of their lifecycle, but can continue to enjoy the fruits of the development when into retirement, or when they are less able-bodied than currently, as well as making provision for the existing demographic realities. This extends to ensuring that developments do not contain steep slopes so that those who are wheelchair-bound or who otherwise have mobility challenges are not excluded from the benefits of the development.

Cost-effectiveness

It is essential to consider the means by which the development will come to be: it may well be that it will be necessary to cross-subsidise the social and affordable units through sale of some of the land to private developers, and if so, thought should be given to which parcels of land should be included in such a proposition, and their relationship to existing and planned dwellings.

Economic sustainability needs to be built in

Local employment possibilities will help keep communities together, therefore developments should contain places of work wherever possible if they are not already located in proximity to sources of employment which will last. It is unacceptable, or should be, to develop housing in the absence of economic opportunity, as this may consign residents to long term unemployment or under-employment. Reliance on the retail sector alone is unlikely to fit the bill, as service jobs are typically poorly paid.

Alongside these considerations, training opportunities to enable local residents, current and future, to take advantage of economic activity need to be in place. It would be worth conducting a skills audit of local people to help steer the economic aspect of regeneration, along with aspirations, as long as it is backed up by action in the foreseeable future, given that many regeneration proposals are long term, some over 20 or so years.

Environmental quality

Surveys show that the quality of the surrounding environment is a major determinant of the way people rate the area in which they live. This is not surprising: the area is a life environment as much as the dwelling and is used by residents for a number of purposes – to travel to work, to shops, to enjoy as a vista and as a place of recreation. Therefore attention should be given to hard and soft landscaping, and to retain features which are appreciated currently such as mature trees and green spaces which are used, as well as buildings of some character which help identify the area as a place. The concept of place is important – as highlighted in Edward Relph's seminal work on the subject (Relph, 1976). In that work, Relph contrasts places which have some authenticity and meaning, such as Chelsea riverside, with places which could be absolutely anywhere, for example an anonymous shopping mall or low-rise estate of anodyne buildings lifted from a pattern-book of a national developer. There is undoubtedly some subjectivity in the notion of place, but sensitive landscaping can make all the difference. Hard landscaping could be creative – for example, a ship which used to be moored in the river nearby could be docked on dry land and form a centrepiece to a housing development, and a group of trees could form the focus of a housing area, along with existing hedges and perhaps a wildlife field. It is here where the views of local residents can make a real difference to the quality of the environment.

The role of government and its agencies

What is the role of government and its agencies in promoting and managing regeneration? The government sets the planning agenda, so attention needs to be given to the sort of legislation which will enable those who wish to regenerate areas in a responsible manner to do so. The relevant legislation is to be found in the town and country planning acts and in associated government circulars. Section 215 of the Town and Country Planning Act 1990, for example, enables a council to serve a notice on occupiers adjoining an area to clear an area of undesirable development where it may negatively affect a development, and even to undertake the works themselves. This power can be used to remove eyesores, and has been used effectively in many regeneration projects. Examples of usage include requiring old industrial units to be demolished, regenerating urban shopping frontages and addressing over-grown gardens (DCLG, 2005a).

Local authorities have had a significant impact on regeneration. A prime example of this is the mayor of London/Greater London Authority's guidance contained in the *London Design Guide* (LDA, 2010), building on the *Mayor's Housing Strategy* (Mayor of London, 2010). Importantly, developers need to take cognisance of these publications as a condition of getting planning permission.

So regeneration must be responsive to local plans and national directives. It must contain a coherent vision, and must involve local people along with other stakeholders in the conversation.

The regeneration of Glasgow

Glasgow is Scotland's largest city, and was once a significant manufacturing and maritime centre. Its wealth was built on ship building and trading, and Clydeside was one of Britain's major ports and ship manufacturing areas. In common with many other cities in Europe which relied upon heavy industry, its fortunes declined after the Second World War, mainly due to competition from the emerging Far East economies, and, like many other cities, it has yet to find its metier. Its housing stock has been affected by this decline, as well as its infrastructure, thus leading to plans for regeneration in all the senses discussed.

The key to regeneration here is economic stimulus, and Glasgow Corporation has prepared an economic development strategy, which tries to sustain economic growth and spread its benefits widely among citizens. In addition, 12 strategic projects have been identified to progress regeneration in the metropolitan area. The economic regeneration plan spans ten years from 2006, and its ambition is to make Glasgow 'a world-class city achieving its potential to deliver sustainable wealth and well-being for all its citizens' (Business in Glasgow, no date). This entails attention to three values: first, to become more specialist, innovative and productive. This makes sense because early action in this area could lead to the city cornering the market, for example, in the development of high-tech navigation equipment or specialist maritime equipment. This is not in the actual plan, but purely to illustrate the concept. Innovation and productivity do not necessarily go hand in hand, but if the innovation is marketable, it may well lead to economic growth both directly and as a result of that innovation and also through economies of scale and linkage between cognate industries – the sort of multiplier effect which is notable when oil refineries are developed and spawn a range of petrochemical industries ranging from oil, gas and petrol to paint and plastic.

Second, the vision is to share prosperity between all Glasgow's citizens. It is obvious that if employment is increased along with wages, the local retail sector will also benefit, along with other services aimed at the local population, which will in itself create and sustain more employment (the trickle-down effect). This means the development of the secondary, tertiary and quaternary sectors in concert. In housing terms, this effect could give rise for greater demand for owner-occupied housing and home improvements, thereby stimulating the construction industry, as well as for new builds to cope with demand from incoming workers plus natural growth.

Third, the alignment of the business, physical (including infrastructural), cultural and social environment to ensure that innovation and growth can be supported better. This entails the development of high-quality affordable homes, as well as education and training opportunities so that the benefits of growth can be spread vertically as well as horizontally.

The vision is supported by an action plan for regeneration. In essence, the corporation realises that Glasgow is now a predominantly service industry-based community, with the majority of the 400,000 or so jobs in that sector, and with less than one in ten in manufacturing or utilities. There is a significant national and local government administration contingent within this sector. As with all sound plans of this type, the authors have performed a SWOT analysis, which is essential in understanding the political, economic and social environment against which regeneration will take place. Strengths include business/economy – a growing knowledge economy and strong business, tourist and cultural environments among others; people – increasing graduate presence, and improved deprivation figures; place – good connectivity, investment in the housing and health sectors, and high city-centre performance, as well as a sense of 'place'). Weaknesses include relatively low productivity levels, an overreliance on public-sector employment, a culture of low aspiration and dependency, and the 'image' problem, as well as vacant and derelict land. Opportunities include continued globalisation, along with the development of niche sectors and brands, an increased demand for skill and talent, and continuing residential demand, along with investment in learning and health infrastructure. Threats include increased global competition along with sharp cuts in public expenditure, important given the large size of the public sector in the city, an increase in the dependent-population ratio, a decline in the small business sector, and the inability to sustain the gains from regeneration activity. The strengths and opportunities outweigh the weaknesses and threats, which gives a firm basis for the promotion of the regeneration plan.

Having decided that the regeneration strategy will not be defeated by internal and external threats, the plan then goes on to spell out the aspirations which will form the basis of performance management. It is formulated in terms of baseline (current) conditions and aspiration and then the gap between the two: for example, the baseline employment rate was 9 per cent below the Scottish average, and the aspiration is to be at the average figure. The gap is quantified at 50,000 jobs. Average earnings are based at 5.3 per cent of the UK average, and the aspiration is to get to the average. Labour productivity is in the 34th quartile, 34 out of 35 – and the aspiration is to reach the second quartile, which entails bridging a gap of 43 per cent in terms of productivity. A review panel was also set up to measure progress and make adjustments where necessary.

The result of this careful planning should be the wholesale regeneration of the social and economic fabric of Glasgow, and it reaches beyond the city's geographical boundaries: it is envisaged that Edinburgh and Glasgow, which form the Scottish central urban belt, should grow together to create a city region which will compete with the larger world cities in terms of economic and social productivity. This probably makes sense, as the growth of one of these cities may be at the expense of the other.

If the plan succeeds, individuals will be able to spend more on housing, which should increase demand for that commodity, as well as having more income to improve their homes. Increased business rates yield will almost certainly mean more capital available for housing renewal and even new build. The financial resource will be added to by increasing domestic rate monies as more properties are built: a virtuous circle of development.

The role of change agencies

A change agency is an organisation or individual which acts as a catalyst for development. An example is the HCA, which provides finance and guidance to registered providers of housing, and another is the mayor of London/Greater London Authority. Individual consultancy firms often act as change agents, commissioned by corporations to develop regeneration plans, based on their experience in this field. Ove Arup Ltd is just such an organisation. Its master-planning service includes urban regeneration energy infrastructure concept planning and utility planning management. It has been involved in drafting regeneration plans in Stratford, East London, anticipating the development of Olympics legacy sites there. It has also drafted regeneration plans for Stoke on Trent, a Midlands town which has lost most of its manufacturing industry and poses particular challenges. This regeneration has a housing aspect to it: RENEW North Staffordshire is a pathfinder area of low-demand housing and the challenge includes tackling low housing demand and abandonment (Ove Arup, 2007). A logical approach is taken to developing the area using an area regeneration framework (ARF). The first stage is a baseline assessment, which involves identifying the background issues, informed by a consultation event with major stakeholders including residents. Second, and building on this, is the 'vision and objectives' stage, which in turn leads to the 'developing the options' stage, which involves not only research into the socioeconomic variables, but engagement with stakeholder groups. This leads to the last stage which that of developing the final ARF, which involves testing the draft interventions to see if they are sound.

Focusing in on the housing aspects, a major objective is to provide a range of housing opportunities in terms of location, size, type and tenure. The Ove Arup (2007) report pulls no punches in describing some of the problems, as well as some of the positive features of the pottery towns. For example, the high quality of some of the civic buildings in Burslem is praised, although the potteries which once sustained the town have vanished, and there is considerable dereliction in the surrounding area. The Etruria Valley is described as an area of major dereliction, characterised by low-grade storage and waste-deposal facilities and presenting a significant challenge. Recommendations flowing from the baseline report include the encouragement of mixed-housing developments to increase housing demand and promote sustainable communities, and it is recommended that housing development be undertaken on brownfield sites which would improve the environment and displacement of undesirable and outmoded industrial activities. Attracting younger people back to the area is key to the strategy, and along with a business and industry package, it is suggested that affordable housing should be prioritised to enable and encourage move-back and to stem out-migration. Impacts on neighbouring housing markets must be considered.

The delivery plan is a logical sequence, starting with visible development to gain community enthusiasm for the programme, proceeding to major land assembly, and then to ensure that there is continuity of industry and built form between each of the settlements so that everyone gains. The regeneration proposals are phased, with phase one (2008–2011) concentrating on the rejuvenation of Burslem town centre, with the development of up to 500 new residential units. Phase two includes non-residential developments – regenerating the derelict potteries sites including the famous Royal Doulton. This will be accompanied by the development of a new canal side residential area. Phase three involves the development of up to 1,223 new build units in the area, once the economic regeneration has been deployed to secure jobs in the area. The draft regeneration plan is worth reading as a succinct and forceful example of a well-crafted regeneration proposal (Ove Arup, 2007).

Assessing success and failure

What does success look like? It might be better to ask what failure looks like: an area characterised by identikit monotonous flats which could be anywhere; ersatz shopping centres with anodyne chain stores and the anywhere feel of fast-food outlets; false authenticity, such as a model galleon, and the odd bit of vernacular architecture outside the regional context; along with some muzak to keep you awake as you sip your latte and watch the...well, whatever. It's a no on many levels. But why? It feels safe, it is immediately unidentifiable, but it is ultimately unchallenging and lacks any sense of place beyond the theatrical. This may seem rather jumbled, but take time out to imagine your own private hell of anodynity. Success or failure resides in the mind and eye of the beholder, and especially of those who will have to live in the vision as it becomes reality. This should not be forgotten in the enthusiasm to fly from drawing-board to actuality.

Success means a number of things:

1. The scheme makes an economic contribution to the area, either by introducing a new source of income for local people or by supplementing an existing source, or replacing a source which has disappeared.
2. The scheme makes a social contribution to the area, through a variety of means, which could be through the creation of a mixed-tenure environment, the provision of education facilities, or other social facilities which enrich the life of the community.
3. The scheme makes an environmental contribution to the area, through a variety of measures, including soft landscaping, sustainable vegetation planting, perhaps communal heating, recycling facilities and zero-carbon or low-carbon development.
4. The scheme is an improvement in these terms on what went before – otherwise the scheme will have failed.

The future of regeneration

Regeneration has a bright future. There are plenty of opportunities for it – most cities have an area which used to be viable economically but is no longer, or a patch of housing which is decaying, or an area of derelict brownfield or redfield land. In all cases, it is absolutely necessary to discover local sentiment, albeit qualified, to ensure that what is produced does not alienate existing residents who have a significant stake in the area, and without moving them away if they do not wish to leave.

Housing development

In this book, 'development' means the creation of affordable housing for rent and for sale. Before 2011 development entailed the construction of dwellings at affordable rents, that is, rents at rent restructuring levels, along with homes for low-cost and outright sale. Post-2011 it means the development of dwellings let at up to and including 80 per cent of market rents, along with low-cost homes. It usually involves some form of external or internal subsidy – capital or revenue. External subsidy involves social housing grant sourced from the HCA, and internal subsidy can involve cross-subsidy of council rented housing from sales capital receipts – from land, open market or low-cost ownership housing or both. It can also involve 'in-kind' subsidies – Section 106 deals with land or housing transfers to a third party from the planning system.

Who develops?

Registered providers (a term introduced by the 2008 Housing and Regeneration Act) are the key developers in the UK. A registered provider is a housing provider registered with the HCA. Registered providers include housing associations, stock-retention councils, ALMOs which are developing housing, some private developers, and local housing companies or trusts. Registration gives the possibility of receiving social housing grant but doesn't guarantee it.

Basic principles of subsidy

The basic principles can be explained as follows:

Calculate capital subsidy – a simple example is: work out (a) the cost of developing a property and take from this sum (b) any money you can put into it yourself (if any) and work out the equivalent loan (c) for example (a) = £200,000, (b) = £80,000, (c) = £200,000 - £80,000 = £120,000; work out the loan repayments (d) for example £120,000 over 30 years at 4 per cent interest only = approximately £400 per month; estimate the cost of managing and maintaining the property plus major repairs, improvements and contingencies (for example uninsurable losses + insurance costs) (e) for example management at £100 per month + maintenance at £100 per month + contingencies at 10 per cent = £20 per month = £220 per month. Add (d) and (e) i.e. £400 + £220 = £620 per month (f); work out the affordable rent (g) (for example £220 per month); finally, work out the capital subsidy finance needed as whatever grant is equivalent to a loan which (f) – (g) would support (i.e. £400) = £120,000. Revenue subsidy is, guess what? It's £400 per month or £4,800 a year.

Housing markets and supply and demand

It is important to consider the impact of housing markets on development possibilities, since dysfunctions in such markets explains the reason why affordable housing occurs at all. Given stable demand, you can increase prices by restricting supply (increasing scarcity) if the consumers are good for it (i.e. there is 'effective demand' for it). They'll pay. Put another way, if something which is 'effectively demanded' becomes scarcer, people will be prepared to pay more for it or to outbid others to get it.

Much depends on demand elasticity (willingness to pay more) – how far will consumers stretch to buy it? If air were only available on the market, it would be pretty demand elastic. Think about it. If the price gets too high, depending on willingness to pay more, demand may fall, and prices will adjust downwards to prevent market collapse.

Application to housing markets

Home ownership is the aspiration of many in work. Here is a scenario for you to consider. In Area A there are twice as many vacant homes for sale as in Area B. The population levels and characteristics are identical, as are aspirations, income and savings levels. All other things being equal, which area will have the higher house prices? People decide to move from one area to the other. If they move from area B to Area A, what will the effect on each local for-sale housing market be? Here's a twist. What will the effect on each local private rental market be, assuming that there is an identical amount of suitable rented housing in each area?

The answer is that Area A would be expected to be cheaper to buy a house in, due to the higher ratio of available properties to those demanding them. If people decide to move from Area B to Area A due in some degree to house prices, as long as there is work available, demand in Area B will reduce, so house prices in the area will reduce. Area A will experience an increase in demand, therefore house prices in that area should increase. It is entirely possible that house prices in both areas would be roughly equivalent on a like-for-like basis, and if this were the main reason behind migration, movement would slow down or possibly cease.

That said, there are many more factors than population relocation which explain variations in housing and land prices. Some of them relate to the nature and quality of the land – for example, some land will be designated as a site of special scientific interest and will be prohibited from development. Other land may be in an area of outstanding natural beauty, and therefore subject to very strict planning control, which may thereby increase the price of land. Some land may be redfield – that is, heavily polluted, which may reduce the price of the land although the cost of remedying defects may well equal the discount. Others relate to location – land which is at the edge of a city may be more valuable than that further away, due to the accessibility to work and infrastructure, and that near the centre of a city may be more valuable still, due to competition for the commodity. The designation of land for planning purposes will also have a bearing on its value – if it is designated as industrial land it may have less value (if there is no more industry or demand from that quarter) than a similar parcel designated for residential use.

Similarly, house prices will be affected by more than population pressure and effective demand, although these are likely to be the most significant factors. Some of these include the quality of the build, size of plots, proximity to city centres and historic factors.

The enabling and production of new build housing for rent and for sale

Local authorities are the principal enablers of new build housing, through the planning system. They have as duty to estimate the need for housing over a period of time, and to allocate land for that purpose, and also have a direct role in the construction of homes as well as indirectly through partnership working with housing associations and other developers. They can also enable lower-cost housing by selling land at undervalue, although this needs to be justified by receiving nomination rights or some other benefit which will account for the discount given, as councils have a duty to obtain best value for their assets. They can also gain housing through the Section 106 process (Section 106 of the Town and Country Planning Act 1990), where they can induce a developer to share their profits with the community through negotiation, and pass housing or land to a third party.

The strategic planning process, how many homes are needed?

Strategic planning can be described as determining how many homes are required, when and where. There are different geographical scales which apply, for example, regional planning (for example the Mayor's London Spatial Plan, and regional planning authority planning frameworks i.e. regional spatial strategies), and local plans – devised by county councils, single-tier authorities and district councils. We should also include plans devised by neighbourhood forums following the Localism Act.

The role of planning in affordable housing development

Planners are supposed to devise clear planning policy, and are assisted by legislation and guidance in so doing. An example is the definition of affordability and affordable housing. Affordability is defined in the Planning Act 2008 as 'the ability of households or potential households to purchase or rent property that satisfies the needs of the household without subsidy' and affordable housing, for the purposes of planning, includes social rented and intermediate housing. Further clarity was delivered in the

National Planning Policy Framework, which replaced the definitions in Planning Policy Statement 3 (DCLG, 2011b). In the guidance, social rented housing is defined as that owned by local authorities and private registered providers (as defined in Section 80 of the Housing and Regeneration Act 2008), for which guideline target rents are determined through the national rent regime. It may also be owned by other persons and provided under equivalent rental arrangements to the above, as agreed with the local authority or with the HCA.

By contrast, affordable rented housing is let by local authorities or private registered providers of social housing to households who are eligible for social rented housing. Affordable rent is subject to rent controls that require a rent of no more than 80 per cent of the local market rent (including service charges, where applicable). It also stipulates that affordable housing should include provisions to remain at an affordable price for future eligible households or for the subsidy to be recycled for alternative affordable housing provision (DCLG, 2012).

The role of planning in housing delivery also involves the following: setting affordable housing targets – authority wide; setting site-capacity thresholds (above which a proportion of affordable housing will be sought); and setting site-specific targets (indicative affordable housing targets for each residential site or mixed-use sites which incorporates a residential component) taking into account the impact of affordable housing on site viability. Another role is to define provision which is not on the application site – not all gain via Section 106 (more to come on this) need be taken on-site, but questions of what, where, when and how come into play. For example, affordable housing on another site or financial contribution in lieu must be used to provide affordable housing. Finally, planning may endeavour to secure affordable housing in perpetuity – development plans should set this out where appropriate.

Strategic planning involves different geographical scales. It encompasses regional planning (for example the Mayor's London Spatial Plan, which will survive; Regional Planning Authority planning frameworks i.e. regional spatial strategyies, which will be replaced by joint local authority plans, local plans, and in the future, community-based plans). Examples of regional planning include sustainable communities plans. An instance is the Thames Gateway development plan, which includes the expansion of settlements in the M11 corridor towards Stansted, and expansion plans for Ashford and the enhancement of Milton Keynes. This plan is aimed at assisting the management of economic growth and provision of housing and related infrastructure.

Development control

Local authorities at the lower tier are responsible for granting planning permission. Local authorities can make three basic decisions: they can grant planning permission – either detailed or in outline; give conditional planning approval; or they can reject, which carries the right to appeal. Major schemes may be subject to a planning inquiry, on the basis of size and impact on the existing developments and communities. Councils employ enforcement planners to ensure that developments are built to plan parameters.

The affordable housing requirement

Whatever the scale of development envisaged, and certainly in respect of any strategic planning, it is essential to try to determine how many affordable homes will be needed. This involves estimating the amount and type of housing needed and which can be supplied by the market, taking account of incomes and savings levels in relation to house prices, and the cost of providing for the remaining households. Realism is essential here, since the available finance will clearly limit the number of homes which can be developed with an element of public subsidy, and these days the quantum of public money available is considered prior to development targets. Having done this, it should be possible to identify how much land is required in the right areas to meet the implied targets. Finally, it is essential to determine the most cost-effective way of supplying good-quality housing.

In order to estimate the quantum of housing required, local authorities commission housing needs surveys and housing market assessments. Basically, the process involves estimating the formation rate of new households – independent and 'hidden households', that is those living with another household (for example, with parents, relations or friends, and adding the net effect of in- and out-migration). It can therefore be said that the 'housing requirement' of an area is equal to the total amount of housing needed by households in an area at a given point in time, projected into the future on the basis of household formation and migration trends.

A basic formula for determining the affordable housing requirement is: new households forming minus households no longer requiring housing plus inflow (in-migrating households) minus outfolw (out-migrating households plus households no longer requiring housing). An assumption must then be made about the number of households who will be able to afford to buy or rent in the market. This is complex, but involves trying to generalise from a representative sample of households endeavouring to make provision in the market in terms of incomes and savings against lower-quartile (or some other measure of relatively low) house prices and rents. Data can be gathered from primary and secondary incomes surveys, and house price data from estate agents' websites or the Land Registry, although there are several organisations which provide this form of data, as well as government sources. Such estimates are just that and are not reliable beyond a few years, due to the unpredictability of market demand which relies largely on the fluctuating state of the economy.

This is a simplified formula which could be used to try to estimate affordable housing demand. The number of new and existing households whose requirements cannot be met through the owner-occupier market can be assessed by comparing average incomes, multiplied by standard lender multiples, plus an assumption about average savings levels, to the average cost of property plus other acquisition and moving costs, broken down into bed-sizes. A similar exercise could be conducted in respect of rented property.

This quantum can be compared with the number of homes it is likely that will be produced for the affordable housing market. Taking estimated need from estimated supply, if the figure is positive, this indicates the amount of affordable supply required, and a negative figure (which is most unlikely) indicates that there is no affordable housing requirement in the area.

A note on housing market assessments

As has been said, HMAs can provide valuable insights into housing markets now and in future. They can provide a fit-for-purpose basis to develop planning and housing policies by considering characteristics of the housing market, how key factors work together and probable scale of change in future housing need and demand. Their general outputs include the identification/ definition of housing market areas, the quantity and percentage of market housing required, including low-cost home ownership, and the percentage of affordable housing required, divided into social rented and intermediate housing. Data used include primary and secondary data, although secondary data is usually the main supporting source, with primary data used to validate and further explain the information and assessment obtained from secondary data. Examples of primary data include that relating to levels of housing need – overcrowding, need for adaptations, hidden homeless (for example sofa surfers), local affordability information (income, savings, etc.), aspirations, preferences and concerns of local residents, and private-rented sector rent levels, along with local housing allowance cap data. Secondary data include data to support demography and household type analysis relevant to estimating current housing need including census data, population mid-year estimates, and NHS registration data.

This will help provide a picture of population by ethnicity, age and numbers of households by type (for example families, couples, lone parents, etc.), tenure and household representative rates, migration estimates, and household formation rates in general.

Focus on Section 106 and the Community Infrastructure Levy

It is impossible in a book of this size to do justice to the planning system, but it is essential to consider the impact of two very important enablers to social and affordable housing development, namely Section 106 and the Community Infrastructure Levy. The underlying principle of both of these is that developers should contribute something to the communities in which they work, from the profits they will make from their activities. One reason is that whenever something is developed, it excludes another form of development – for example, building a supermarket excludes the possibility of using the site for housing, unless flats are built over the shop or adjacent to it as part of the deal. Section 106 can be seen as an attempt to have the cake and to eat it too – as a developer may be persuaded to gift land or housing on-site or off-site to a housing association and thereby enable affordable housing development after all.

Section 106 of the Town and Country Planning Act 1990 (as amended by the Planning and Compensation Act 1991) provides that planning authorities can negotiate with a developer, a process initiated either by the applicant on the basis of an outline or worked-through proposal, or authority, to secure some community gain from varying the detail but not the spirit of the constraints of the development plan. The benefits of Section 106 include cash or in-kind contributions towards a range of infrastructure and services including local roads and public transport, and they can be used to create or improve public assets such as public spaces, community facilities, as well as affordable housing through a third party to the negotiations, for example a housing association. Section 106 agreements have been highly effective – in London, boroughs secured between £155,000 and £35 million from Section 106 agreements signed between 2005 and 2007, and it was estimated that nationally, the value of gains was around £2.5 billion per year, with a £100–£200 million a year expectation in London as a whole. Money from Section 106 deals were spent on affordable housing; new open space or environmental improvements; new roads and transport capacity and health and education facilities (London Assembly, 2008). Section 106 is subject to a necessity test – local authorities should not seek a contribution through a planning obligation unless it is necessary to make development acceptable; relevant to planning; directly related to the proposed development; fairly and reasonably related in scale and kind to the proposed development; and reasonable in all other aspects (DCLG, 2005b).

The use of planning obligation must be governed by a fundamental principle that planning permission may not be bought or sold. It is therefore not legitimate for unacceptable development to be permitted because of benefits or inducements offered by a developer which are not necessary to make the development acceptable in planning terms. Similarly, planning obligations should never be used purely as a means of securing for the local community a share in the profits of development, i.e. as a means of securing a 'betterment levy'. In other words, Section 106 must be transparent and inspectable. It is, however, possible to prescribe the nature of the development to achieve planning objectives – the guidance already referred to says that a requirement through a planning obligation for the provision of an element of affordable housing in residential or mixed-use developments with a residential component should be in line with local development framework policies on the creation of mixed communities.

Mitigating the impact of a development is another legitimate aim of Section 106, for example where a proposed development is not acceptable in planning terms due to inadequate access or public transport provision, planning obligations might be used to secure contributions towards a new access road or provision of a bus service, perhaps coordinated through a travel plan. It is also possible to use Section 106 to compensate for any loss or damage caused by a development – planning obligations might be used to offset through substitution, replacement or regeneration the loss of, or damage to, a feature or resource present or nearby – for example a landscape feature of biodiversity value, open space or right of way. There must be some relationship between what is lost and what is to be offered, if it is not possible to provide an exact substitution. It is reasonable to seek to restore facilities, resources and amenities to a quality equivalent to that existing before the development. ructure levy is a betterment tax , based on the difference between the value of the land before and after development. This is charged by local authorities, and can be used to pay for infrastructure such as roads, health centres and park improvements. Following the Localism Act it can be used to pay for anything which supports development. This will be discussed further in the following chapter.

A critical analysis of registered housing providers – problems, prospects and the privatisation of development

This book focuses on registered providers of housing as developers, but in many cases they do not operate alone and are reliant on private-sector developers. Many housing associations engage private developers to actually build the dwellings, and enter into design and build contracts to do so. In so doing, the quality of the product might not be exactly what is required in terms of meeting housing need – for example, they may have cut corners to produce homes which are not adaptable to lifetime standards or built to those standards from the outset, due to the need to make an acceptable profit. They may also have to develop schemes where the proportion of outright sale properties or low-cost units is greater than they would otherwise wish in order to cross-subsidise the rented element. Even the rent yield from affordable rented housing may not be enough to make a scheme dominated by rented housing stack up. Another limitation is that their programmes are highly constrained by public subsidy, which depends on the macroeconomic views of whatever government happens to be in power. In austerity Britain, this means having to make do with a lot less subsidy than is required to build sustainable developments which will stand the test of time, or be at all adequate to meet housing need in the quantity required.

The importance of sustainability

To be sustainable means to last, and there is little more important in a development than it should stand the test of time. There is little point in developing housing stock unless it will provide suitable homes for people throughout its useful build life, considering the size of the outlay required to produce homes. There are several dimensions to sustainability, the principle of which are environmental sustainability, economic sustainability and social sustainability.

Environmental sustainability

This means ensuring that the materials the dwellings are built from are provided from environmentally sound sources, which means using renewable resources wherever possible and practicable. It also means that the dwellings should have as small a carbon footprint as possible. A carbon footprint is the emissions of greenhouse gases produced by an event, person or product. Greenhouse gases include methane and carbon dioxide. Such gases can be emitted through land clearance, producing fuel or food, and the production of buildings. Once the dwelling is produced, its carbon footprint will be defined largely by the fuel which will be burned in heating the home, so it is essential to ensure that any appliances produce as little carbon emissions as possible. Carbon emissions have the effect of increasing the rate of global warming. Solar power, the use of communal heating systems, and the use of other natural sources such as wind power, geothermal power and photovoltaic cells are examples of low-carbon solutions to providing electric power. The Kyoto Protocol has been signed by 37 countries and commits them to reducing the emission of carbon dioxide, methane, nitrous oxide, sulphur hexafluoride, and two groups of gases (hydrofluorocarbons and perfluorocarbons). The UK is a signatory to Protocol. There have been several more conferences which have been aimed at committing industrialised nations to reducing greenhouse gas emissions since the date of the Kyoto Protocol in 1997. The last United Nations Climate Change conference (at the time of writing in July 2012) was held in Durban, South Africa in 2011, and was notable in that it included so-called developing nations such as China and India who made conditional commitments to limit the emission of greenhouse gases.

Economic sustainability

Economic sustainability means several things but can be reduced to three essentials. Buildings should have as low maintenance costs as possible, and should be manageable within a relatively tight budget for those who live in them. They should also represent good value for money in terms of the procurement and production price. Another aspect of economic sustainability relates to the occupant: homes should be affordable as well as built in areas where there is the prospect of work – otherwise occupants may be condemned to long periods of worklessness and benefit dependency, which is in no one's interests. Yet another is ensuring that the development will be relatively cost effective to maintain over its lifetime, and that it will be economic to manage, which may relate to location vis-à-vis housing management offices where possible. Another way of looking at economic sustainability which is complementary to the approaches already enumerated is that the building yields a reasonable rate of return. In affordable housing terms, this may mean ensuring that the rent yield is not eroded by growing M&M costs, and stays more or less constant over the life of the dwelling.

Social sustainability

Social sustainability is hard to define but could denote a situation whereby the dwellings built actually help to foster a sense of community. Much depends upon the vision of society engendered. If, for example, you conceive a well-balanced society as one where young and old, disabled and able-bodied and people of all races and ethnic origins live happily together, this may imply a development with a mix of dwelling sizes, with an external environment fostering play and other recreation, as well as level land to aid mobility. At the very least, a development should be such that people actually want to live there, and stay there for the long term, rather than seeing it as a jumping-off point. This rather goes against the notion of affordable housing built on a flexible tenure basis, where presumably once incomes have risen above a given level, the tenancy will be determined; thus the area risks becoming an economic ghetto.

How do the three sustainabilities fit together?

There is an obvious link between the three types of sustainability, and it is hard to envisage a truly sustainable development in the absence of one of them. So economic sustainability, in ensuring that dwellings are affordable, helps to bolster social sustainability where people feel they wish to remain. Similarly, environmental sustainability boosts the image of the area and if properly engineered, will complement economic sustainability through (for example) the deployment of cheaper renewable heating supplies. And social sustainability will bolster economic sustainability through people respecting their dwellings and environment because it is their valued home, thus stabilising M&M costs.

The importance of planning

At its best, the function of planning is to ensure that land uses fit together in a compatible way and that negative externalities are minimised. For example, it should not allow heavy industrial plant to be developed next to residential land, nor should it permit the destruction of natural habitats in favour of concrete. You can probably think of other incompatibilities, for example locating a busy road or intersection next to a school, or a sewage station or waste transfer facility next to residential property. Planning has a number of objects, of which compatible land-use management is one. Other include:

- Management of density – often expressed as minima rather than maxima;
- Ensure that building styles are compatible with existing ones to preserve continuity, where the existing building style is of value (for example of historic significance, or forming a group);
- Integration of natural with artificial properties – for example parkland with residential;
- Conservation – of the natural environment and historic areas;
- Specifying quantities of housing or other objects of development for an area and within areas;
- Preventing overlooking – for example of residential by industrial, or residential overlooking residential (through windows);
- Ensuring that there is a correct mix of dwellings according to statutory guidance or local aspirations as set out in planning policy;
- Preventing polluting activities, especially where they would be sited close to residential areas;
- Ensuring that workplaces are within easy travel distance to residential areas;
- Integrating recreation uses into schemes, and specifying where recreation can be developed;
- Preventing the destruction of wildlife habitats;
- Preventing residential development on 'redfield' (highly industrially polluted) land without due precautions.

There are other objects, but the above illustrate the main purposes which can be summarised as ensuring that the right functions occupy the right spaces.

Core strategies and planning guidance

A core strategy is a compulsory planning document which sets out the principles of planning in a given area. It is the principal development plan document, and is a strategic-level document which will provide the spatial planning vision and strategy that will shape the future of the area to which it relates. It relates to a period of years – for example, 2012–2020, and sets out the long-term spatial vision for areas and the overall strategy for delivering that vision. It will typically identify the overall level of different types of development (including housing, employment and retail functions) which are required over the lifetime of the strategy, and how development will be distributed. It will also identify the main improvements in infrastructure that are required to support that scale and distribution of development – for example, new road and rail links to bind areas together. It will also set out a number of strategic planning policies for the area, including the key policies for determining planning applications. At the heart of such a strategy is a diagram which illustrates its main provisions. It is important that the strategy does not sit in isolation – it should support the delivery of other key strategies and plans, including sustainable community strategies. It is supported by a database of supporting evidence, for example population growth and migration trends, changes in land use over a period, economic development trends in the area and traffic counts.

Such strategies are relatively broad-brush, but are subject to consultation with stakeholders including local residents. Once consultation is through, the core strategy is submitted to the secretary of state for the environment, or whoever has planning policy as part of their portfolio along with the supporting evidence. Core strategies are then subjected to scrutiny by a planning inspector appointed by the secretary of state to conduct an independent examination of the document. Following the examination hearing sessions, the inspector will write a report concluding whether or not the core strategy is considered to be legally compliant and sound, or can be made sound with some changes. If the document is found to be legally compliant and sound, or can be made sound, the local authority can adopt the core strategy. It will then form the main document used to determine planning applications, following adoption by the authority.

Development planning – post-localism

Localism has affected the planning process, about which more will be said in the next chapter. In relation to core strategies and other development plan documents, there is now a far greater emphasis on local community input through parish councils and local neighbourhood forums who can publish their own local development strategies as long as they are broadly conformant with the overall core strategy. Regional spatial strategies, to which core strategies had to have regard, have been abolished, despite attempts by developers (notably Cala Homes) to retain them in the lead-up to the passing of the Localism Act (England and Wales High Court, 2011). There is also the intention that core strategies should be influenced by 'bottom-up' deliberations from local community groups (parish councils and neighbourhood forums principally). It is most important that authorities develop coherent core strategies as the presumption following the Localism Act is that local planning authorities should 'grant permission where the plan is absent, silent, indeterminate or where relevant policies are out of date' (Draft National Planning Policy Framework (NPPF), DCLG, 2011a).

Brownfield and greenfield development

Brownfield development means development on land which has previously been built on, and is mainly within urban areas. Greenfield development is that which takes place on previously undeveloped land (for example agricultural land), and redfield development is that which takes place on heavily polluted industrial sites. There are pros and cons of developing in each of these contexts. Brownfield and redfield sites may well be close to existing infrastructure and dwellings, which may be a good thing in terms of employment opportunity, if the development is commercial, but the site may need extensive and expensive clearance – and in the case of redfield land, comprehensive depolluting can be very costly, although such an outlay may be wholly or partially reflected in the price of the land. Greenfield land is almost always easier to develop that the other categories, but there is the opportunity cost in terms of loss of scenic attraction, agricultural land and wildlife habitat and biodiversity, although some of this may be reinstatable elsewhere.

Design matters

Layout and dwellings

The layout of dwellings is an essential aspect of good development briefing. Thought must be given to the actual function that a dwelling has and to the uses which take place within in. Consider a typical day in a dwelling. You emerge from sleep: a good night's sleep can be aided by spacious, aired sleeping accommodation, and can be impeded by small rooms which abut potential noise sources. You then wash or shower: the facility should be close to the bedroom to minimise travel distance and to avoid disturbing other users. You then eat breakfast: the kitchen should be arranged so that there are a minimum of hazards such as trailing flexes and units which are easy to trip over, and large enough to take cooking and washing facilities, as well as to eat in, given the size of the household occupying the home. We then move to the rest and communal area, the living room: which should be large enough to take entertainment equipment (TVs, etc.) as well as to accommodate all residents communally. There should be adequate space outside the dwelling, if a house, to enjoy private space for relaxation in the fresh air, so gardens need to be designed with privacy in mind as well as ease of maintenance. Finally, we exit through the front door, which raises the issue of whether there are steps down to the outside area and their gradient.

Much valuable work was done by the parliamentary Parker Morris Committee (1961) in its publication Homes for Today and Tomorrow', which made recommendations on size and layout resulting from an extensive user survey. It is worth visiting this publication, if only to find out what households in the early 1960s expected from their homes. It is also worth consulting the *London Housing Design Guide* for a contemporary view of interior and exterior design (LDA, 2010).

Density

There is much debate about what density dwellings should be built at. Density can be expressed as the number of habitable rooms per square hectare, or the number of dwellings per square area. An article in the *Local Government Chronicle* (Drillsma-Milgrom, 2009) suggested that land use change statistics for 2008 showed that new dwellings were built at an average density of 46 per hectare, whereas the figure for 2007 was 44 dwellings per hectare. This may have been caused by the previous government's guidance that new housing developments in each region should be encouraged between 30 and 50 dwellings per hectare. This guidance has now been abolished (see PPS3 in DCLG, 2011b). Unsurprisingly, an inner London borough, Tower Hamlets, had the highest recorded new-build density at an average of 254 dwellings per hectare, contrasting with Test Valley Borough Council in Hampshire and Richmondshire District Council in North Yorkshire, which had the two lowest average densities at 16 dwellings per hectare. This is largely due to the cost of acquiring land.

There is no evidence that high-density dwellings are any worse for much depends upon interior layout and soundproofing, and it makes sense to build at high densities in cities to conserve the natural environment and prevent the wholesale spread of dwellings into the countryside. It also makes sense in terms of reducing the per unit cost of land, which is essential in producing affordable rented and for-sale accommodation.

Focus on lifetime homes

A lifetime home is a home which is suitable for occupants throughout their lifecycle, and many planning authorities have adopted the view that, as far as possible, homes should be designed to these standards. In *Lifetime Homes, Lifetime Neighbourhoods: A National Strategy for Housing in an Ageing Society* (DCLG, 2008), it is stated that:

> Lifetime Homes Standards will be made a mandatory part of the Code for Sustainable Homes to encourage progressively increased take-up in new build projects. Our aspiration is that by 2013 all new homes will be being built to Lifetime Homes Standards. We will review take-up of the standards in 2010 with a view to bringing forward regulation in 2013 if take-up has not matched expectations.

Sixteen criteria for lifetime homes were set out in that publication, and they are reproduced here in summative form:

- Car parking width: where car parking is adjacent to the home, it should be capable of enlargement to attain 3.3 metre width;

- Access from car parking: the distance from the car parking space to the home should be kept to a minimum and should be level or gently sloping;
- Approach gradients: the approach to all entrances should be level or gently sloping;
- External entrances: all entrances should be illuminated, have level access over the threshold and have a covered main entrance:
- Communal stairs and lifts: communal stairs should provide easy access and where homes are reached by a lift, it should be fully accessible;
- Doorways and hallways: the width of internal doorways and hallways should be 900 mm rather than 800 mm. There should be a 300 mm nib or wall space to the side of the leading edge of the doors on entrance level;
- Wheelchair accessibility: there should be space for turning a wheelchair in dining areas and living rooms and adequate circulation space for wheelchairs elsewhere;
- Living room: the living room should be at entrance level;
- Entrance level bed space: in houses of two or more storeys, there should be space on the entrance level that could be used as a convenient bed space;
- Entrance level toilet and shower drainage: in houses with three or more bedrooms, and all dwellings on one level, there should be a wheelchair-accessible toilet at entrance level with drainage provision enabling a shower to be fitted in the future;
- Bathroom and toilet walls: walls in the bathroom and toilet should be capable of taking adaptations such as handrails;
- Stair lift/through floor lift: the design should incorporate provision for a future stair lift and a suitably identified space for a through the floor lift from the ground floor to the first floor, for example to a bedroom next to the bathroom;
- Tracking hoist route: the design and specification should provide a reasonable route for a potential hoist from a main bedroom to the bathroom;
- Bathroom layout: the bathroom should be designed for ease of access to the bath, toilet and wash basin;
- Window specification: living room window glazing should begin no higher than 80 0mm from the floor level and windows should be easy to open/operate;
- Controls/fixtures and fittings: switches, sockets, ventilation and service controls should be at a height usable by all (i.e. between 450 mm and 120 0mm from the floor).

Additionally, DCLG (2008, p. 96) sets out a standard for lifetime neighbourhoods:

> The concept of the lifetime neighbourhood is simple. It is linked to the concept of the Lifetime Home, and it is designed to be welcoming, accessible, and inviting for everyone, regardless of age, or health, or disability. In some places these ideas are linked to 'Age-Friendly Cities'. The lifetime neighbourhood is sustainable in terms of changing climatic conditions, but it also means that transport services, housing, public services, civic space and amenities, all make it possible for people, to have a full life and take part in the life of the community around them.

If homes are designed to lifetime standards, the need to move between dwellings at crucial points in the lifecycle (for example when the occupants loser some mobility or family sizes grow or decline) can be reduced, so that the use of dwellings is more efficient and effective than those without such a solution.

Form of building contracts and contract management

The principal forms of contracts are the JCT (joint contract tribunal) contract with quantities and design and build contracts. The JCT is in a format with or without quantities. The current (2005) models are with quantities, with approximate quantities and without quantities. 'Quantities' refer to building materials and labour. There are also minor works, intermediate and standard works models; and around 90 per cent of UK construction projects are carried out on JCT terms. The JCT (20) 05 Contract with quantities is used for larger works designed by the employer (client), where detailed contract provisions are necessary, and in this case the employer provides the contractor with drawings and bills of quantities to specify quantity and quality of the work; and an architect/contract administrator and quantity surveyor administer the conditions of the contract.

JCT 05 without quantities is also a relatively common form of building contract. It applies to larger works designed and/or detailed by or on behalf of the employer, where detailed contract provisions are necessary and the employer is to provide the contractor with drawings; and with either a specification or work schedules to define adequately the scope and quality of the work and where the degree of complexity is not such as to require bills of quantities; as with the former contract, an architect/contract administrator and quantity surveyor administer the conditions.

Then there is the JCT 05 with approximate quantities. This is a contract for larger works designed and/or detailed by or on behalf of the employer, where detailed contract provisions are necessary and the employer is to provide the contractor with drawings; and with approximate bills of quantities to define the quantity and quality of the work, which are to be subject to re-measurement as there is insufficient time to prepare the detailed drawings necessary for accurate bills of quantities to be produced; and (again) where an architect/contract administrator and quantity surveyor are to administer the conditions.

There are four main JCT sub-types which are used:

1. Lump sum contracts – where the contract sum is determined before construction work is started.
2. Contracts 'with quantities' are priced on drawings and firm bill of quantities. Contracts 'without quantities' are priced on a specification or work schedules.
3. Measurement contracts – where contract sum not finalised until after completion, but is assessed on re-measurement to a previously agreed basis.
4. Cost reimbursement contracts – where the sum is arrived at on the basis of prime (actual) costs of labour, plant and materials, to which there is added an amount to cover overheads and profit.

Design and build contracts

These are sometimes known as pattern-book contracts, where designs are picked by the client form a portfolio, and the developer then works to this design and produces the development, with all supervision being undertaken by the contractor. There are essentially three variants:

1. Package deal or 'turn-key' contracts – where the client settles on a complete package, usually to some standard specification.
2. Design and build contracts – where project documents will be written (for the client on a bespoke basis) with the contractor's design obligations relating to the whole of the works in mind.
3. Contractor's design for specific elements only – these are not strictly design and build contracts at all but traditional 'work and materials' contracts which include for limited design provision relating to a specified bit of the work, for example a specific architectural feature.

Payments under JCT 05 take place at various stages of the contract, as follows: start on site; interim payments – as the work progresses, on the basis of monthly valuations; and at practical completion. Also 2.5 per cent of the contract sum is then generally retained for final payment after a snagging period (6–12 months after practical completion). Over-runs and extensions are generally allowed for in the contract, which may affect the contract sum.

Dealing with defects after completion

Construction contracts usually include a defects liability period. This is a period during which the contractor is responsible for repairing or rectifying defects that appear in the works. It usually starts on practical completion of the works and runs for a specified timeframe (the 'maintenance period'). The contract sets out how and when the contractor must remedy defective work which becomes apparent during the defects liability period – usually 6–12 months. There are no obligations to repair defects which occur as a result of fair wear and tear.

Resident involvement

It is essential, or at least good practice, to involve residents at all stages of the development process. This is because they are ultimately the experts – the end users of the dwellings they inhabit, and therefore a valuable source of good practice design intelligence. They can be involved in planning for real, design and estate-layout views, as 'eyes and ears' on site during contract, as part of a check for defects at snagging/ defects liability period, and satisfaction surveys are valuable resources to learn from mistakes to inform the next scheme. As already stated, the 1961 Parker Morris *Homes for Today and Tomorrow* standards were based on a consumer survey of lifestyle requirements, and these standards were not bettered for at least 30 years.

Other drivers to resident involvement include the Home Standard and associated local offers. The Home Standard (TSA, 2010) states that:

> registered providers shall:
> - ensure that tenants' homes meet the standard set out in section 5 of the Government's Decent Homes Guidance by 31 December 2010 and continue to maintain their homes to at least this standard after this date;
> - meet the standards of design and quality that applied when the home was built, and were required as a condition of publicly funded financial assistance, if these standards are higher than the Decent Homes Standard;
> - in agreeing a local offer, ensure that it is set at a level not less than these standards and have regard to section 6 of the Government's Decent Homes Guidance.

Conclusion – the future of development

It will always be necessary to develop dwellings to cater for a growing population with changing lifestyles and aspirations and to try to balance conservation and ecological issues with the need to accommodate a growing population. It is likely that existing developments will be reworked and even relocated as global warming kicks in, with rises in sea level making some sites unviable. Whatever the form of new development, it is essential that intelligence is gathered and used from existing projects, so that mistakes from the past can be learned from, and the views of residents will be paramount in guiding new development to ensure that it remains relevant to need and demand. The issue of affordability means that there will always be some form of compromise between ideal forms and what can be provided, but it is essential to ensure that dwellings are fit for purpose at the outset with minimal built-in obsolescence to ensure that we do not build the slums of tomorrow.

References

Business in Glasgow (no date). Glasgow's economic strategy, available at: www.glasgow. gov.uk/en/Business/Businesssupport/Research_statistics/glasgoweconomicstrategy.htm, viewed 27 June 2012.

DCLG (Department of Communities and Local Government), (2005a) *Town and Country Planning Act 1990: Section 215, Best Practice Guidance*. London: Office of the Deputy Prime Minister.

DCLG, (2005b) Circular 05/05: Planning Obligations – B5, available at: www.communities. gov.uk/archived/publications/planningandbuilding/circularplanningobligations, viewed 27 June 2012.

DCLG, (2008) *Lifetime Homes, Lifetime Neighbourhoods: A National Strategy for Housing in an Ageing Society*. London: DCLG.

DCLG, (2011a) Draft National Planning Policy Framework: Consultation. London: DCLG. Available at: www.gov.uk/government/uploads/system/uploads/attachment_data/file/11802/1951747.pdf

DCLG, (2011b) *Planning Policy Statement 3 (PPS3): Housing*. London: DCLG.

DCLG, (2012) Definition of general housing terms, available at: www.communities.gov.uk/

housing/housingresearch/housingstatistics/definitiongeneral/, viewed 27 June 2012.

Drillsma-Milgrom, D., (2009) Housing Density in England Grows. *Local Government Chronicle*, 4 June. Available at: www.lgcplus.com/housing-density-in-england-grows/5002193.article, viewed 27 June 2012.

England and Wales High Court, (2011) [2011] EWHC 97 (Admin), England and Wales High Court (Administrative Court) Decisions. Available at: www.bailii.org/ew/cases/EWHC/Admin/2011/97.html, viewed 27 June 2012.

LDA (London Development Agency) (2010) *London Housing Design Guide*, Interim Edition. London: London Development Agency/Palestra.

London Assembly, (2008) *Who gains? The operation of section 106 planning agreements in London*, March. London: Planning and Spatial Development Committee. Available at: www.london.gov.uk/assembly/reports/plansd/section-106-who-gains.rtf, viewed 27 June 2012.

Mayor of London, (2010) The Mayor's Housing Strategy, London: GLA.

Ove Arup, (2007) RENEW North Staffordshire: Area Regeneration Framework For Northern Stoke, Draft 2. Manchester: Ove Arup & Partners Ltd.

Parker Morris Committee (1961) *Homes for Today and Tomorrow*, Report of a Committee of the Central Housing Advisory Committee. London: HMSO.

Relph, E., (1976) *Place and Placelessness*. London: Pion.

TSA (Tenants Services Authority), (2010) *The Regulatory Framework for Social Housing in England from April 2010*. Manchester: TSA.

7   Localism

Keywords: *introduction – all in it together; a short history of localism; Coalition policies and cross-party enthusiasms; the Localism Act – legislation and guidance; localism and planning policy; localism and housing development; localism and housing tenure; involvement of communities in planning and housing development; evaluation of the impact of localism on planning policy; evaluation of the impact of localism of housing policy; the future of the localist approach.*

Introduction

Localism means the devolution of power to local people in a variety of contexts. There are undoubtedly some aspects of governance that are best left to locals, notably those relating to the protection or betterment of their surrounding environment, the choice of local democratic representatives and to a certain extent the level of services provided to them at the local level by their councils. This seems fair, since they pay for such services in part through a local tax – the council tax in the UK. There are other functions – for example the defence of the realm – which are arguably best left to the collective state representing everyone in the country. The line is not always easy to draw. Take housing provision. It is important to try to cater for anticipated demand and need in housing strategies – from people who are not yet locals, balanced with the needs of existing communities, so there are localist and non-localist pressures here which need to be taken account of and mediated. A good test seems to be what is enjoyed locally.

What do you enjoy locally? Services to your home – for example, rubbish collection, electricity and gas, the roads in your neighbourhood, local employment and leisure and recreation. The quality of each of these affects your daily life, and any diminution in their quality would impact on your life experience. It would therefore seem correct that you should have some input into deciding on the level of provision of these things and have a chance to monitor their quality. To a certain extent this is already done through local democracy. But what else could be devolved to you, as a citizen of a local state?

Much depends upon equity and finance. A collective decision to reduce expenditure on policing would have potentially serious consequences to the community, and would result in a postcode lottery of security which would probably not be acceptable, even though money would be saved, so the level of policing is probably not best decided at a local level, even though it affects citizens at the locality. Another example is the provision of libraries. It is conceivable that local people might decide collectively that library provision should be reduced in favour of spending on leisure centres. A number of issues arise here: the level of vote needed to enforce such a decision is one. It is hardly likely that such a mandate would be universal, and likely that only those with well-stocked book-shelves would vote in this fashion. Therefore the outcome would be inequitable. Another area is schooling. It may be permissible to allow local people to decide on the level of schooling beyond a base level, subject to finance, but not to decide to reduce the acceptable national base in the locality, as this would be inequitable as regards incomers and children who would not have the vote and who might be disadvantaged as a consequence of such decisions.

It may, therefore, be correct to enable local people to decide to increase provision above a nationally acceptable baseline, and to allow choice where there would be no overall detriment to the community. So, in terms of housing, a local community might decide that there should be more affordable housing in the area, but it would surely be wrong to enable them to choose not to have any new affordable housing whatever, because this would tend to work against community coherence and sustainability.

What of local allocations policies? Localism has engendered the right for local communities to decide to prioritise local people in the allocations process over incomers. It might be argued that this is inequitable, since it tends to deny essential resources to incomers who may make a very positive contribution to the local economy, and means that some other area (where local people presumably could exercise similar rights) would take an 'excess' of incomers. There is also the issue of future choice – the choice of those who have yet to become locals because they have not yet been born or because they have not reached the age at which they can vote or are not yet in the area. By making decisions today, future choice may be denied to these groups, and this may be seen as inequitable. At some time in the future, decisions will become those of a past (or passed) community, which will in some way curtail the choices available to present ones. Care must therefore be taken in deciding which decisions should be taken locally, and which nationally or regionally. There is, of course, no guarantee that decisions taken nationally or regionally would be any better in terms of outcome than those taken locally, and they still constrain future choice, but at least they have an overall effect and do not penalise one spatially defined community at the expense of others.

Localism, then, is far from an easy option. There is a horizontal and vertical effect to be taken account of. The horizontal effect is the creation of a patchwork effect of policy depending on which neighbourhoods decide to do what, and where some areas might fall below nationally accepted minima unless there is effective monitoring and a modicum of central regulation and law. Indeed it could be argued that this is the purpose of the law – to ensure than minima are respected. A postcode lottery may be very unhealthy – literally, if localism is to apply to health provision below a minimum standard. There is also a vertical effect. Decision-makers at the local level tend to be the articulate middle class, those with wealth and power. If they decide to limit the provision of affordable housing on the basis of preservation of property values, this decision has a vertical negative effect on those with lower means who have to resort to subsidised or lower-cost housing provision. It therefore seems reasonable that vertical and horizontal inequities should be guarded against in the pursuit of local solutions.

Localism as a philosophy arose because some thinkers believed that the state had become too large, that it encroached on daily lives to a greater than permissible extent. It is quite instructive to consider the foreword to *A Plain English Guide to the Localism Act* published by the UK government, which outlines the basic tenets of localism, and perhaps to challenge aspects of this thinking before moving forward (DCLG, 2011).

The first sentence asserts that 'The time has come to disperse power more widely in Britain today' and this is part of the prime minister's and deputy prime minister's Coalition Agreement of May 2010. By 'widely' is meant, to local communities. Why might this be thought to be the case? The philosophy is that:

> For too long, central government has hoarded and concentrated power. Trying to improve people's lives by imposing decisions, setting targets and demanding inspections from Whitehall simply doesn't work. It creates bureaucracy. It leaves no room for adaptation to reflect local circumstances or innovation to deliver services more effectively and at lower cost. And it leaves people feeling 'done to' and imposed upon – the very opposite of the sense of participation and involvement on which a healthy democracy thrives.
>
> (DCLG, 2011, p. 1)

It could be argued that central government 'does' things to people precisely because it has a democratic mandate through the national elective process. A bureaucracy exists to enforce those democratic decisions – how else could they be enforced? However, the idea that services can be provided more effectively and at lower cost through local democratic specification and involvement complies with the requirement set out earlier that standards should not be allowed to fall below a minimum level, although there is the risk that they might – which is why national targets are set and why inspections take place – to safeguard the rights of local communities.

Moving on, the then Minister of State for Decentralisation Greg Clark states in the same document that:

> Today, I am proud to be part of a Government putting this vision into practice. We think that the best means of strengthening society is not for central government to try and seize all the power and responsibility for itself. It is to help people and their locally elected representatives to achieve their own ambitions. This is the essence of the Big Society.

We have already begun to pass power back to where it belongs. We are cutting central targets on councils, easing the burden of inspection, and reducing red tape. We are breaking down the barriers that stop councils, local charities, social enterprises and voluntary groups getting things done for themselves.

(DCLG, 2011, p. 2)

Now, this presents a rather odd view of government and an inherent contradiction. The phrase 'seize all the power and responsibility for itself' suggests that government is an organ at distance from those who have elected it, whereas it has come into being through the democratic process – and so the idea of seizing power for itself needs to be qualified. It could be argued that it has 'seized' power and rightly so on behalf of those who it represents, which is not a bad thing, and surely better than it being seized by an undemocratic organisation. What is in fact meant is that the balance of power between local and central democratic institutions has tipped towards the central too far and that some form of redress is needed.

However the term is interpreted, localism is here to stay, and the housing world will never be the same again on account of it, although some aspects are something of a blast from the past. Before the 1980s it was common to find councils imposing a local connection on housing waiting lists, and allocations policies were tailored to local needs. Who got what and where was often the preserve of local councillors sitting as a committee, considering medical and social priorities. Under the new regime it is unlikely that councillors will ever get so up close and personal in allocations, but there is definitely more scope for localist policies in deciding on allocations to specific groups of people, for example those in employment or undertaking training, and giving a degree of priority to those who have lived in the area for a given number of years. Some local authorities in England have started to do just that in the wake of the enabling legislation.

Coalition policies and cross-party enthusiasms

Localism is not the preserve of the Coalition. For some years, there has been a degree of devolution to local councils in allocations, with a number of key test cases confirming their ability to select preference groups for special consideration, following the publication of *Fair and Flexible* (DCLG, 2009). There has been broad cross-party agreement on housing policies for some years, and it is likely that some form of localist agenda may have been promulgated had the current incumbents not won the day in 2010. There has been an undercurrent favouring voluntarism, which is a major plank of localism, since the mid-2000s, encouraging young people without work to undertake tasks which would strengthen their employability. Tenant management organisations were encouraged, as were resident service organisations. There has been a change in emphasis since 2010, and communities have taken up the challenge across the country in a number of areas, from parent-run schools to community-run post offices and shops. Housing is no exception, as will be demonstrated when the localism legislation is examined in detail.

The Localism Act – legislation and guidance

The Localism Act became law in November 2011, with its provisions gradually introduced over a period of a year. Some of the key aspects are major changes to the planning regime which will affect housing delivery and increase local (neighbourhood) input into planning strategies, policies and deliverables, and there will be a presumption in favour of development. Also there are changes to the Section 106 and Community Infrastructure Levy regimes. There are major changes to housing policy – homelessness, tenancy types, allocations, housing mobility, complaints systems and housing finance. Additionally, the act confirmed new models for local authority governance, moved the abolition of TSA and put in place major changes to the compulsory purchase order regime.

Chapter One of the act is concerned with plans and strategies. Section 109 abolishes regional planning strategies – apart from the London mayor's, and replaces over-arching strategies with (s. 110) a duty to cooperate in relation to planning of sustainable development (between local authorities and agencies, etc.). An important aspect to the planning provisions of the Localism Act is the introduction of local development schemes, under s. 111 which amended s. 15 of the Planning and Compulsory Purchase Act 2004. Essentially neighbourhoods – to parish council level – will be able to devise development strategies and planning policies for their areas. The intention is that they will not be able to counter the quantitative import of local plans devised by councils, but they will be able to influence the quality of development.

Chapter 2 concerns the Community Infrastructure Levy. The levy is essentially a local tax based on the difference between the value of the land without and with planning permission and available to support infrastructural needs, widely defined. Under s. 115, Community Infrastructure Levy funds are no longer limited to providing infrastructure, but can be used in any way to support the development. Section 115 (5)(g) – amends s. 219 of the Planning Act 2008 – power for local authorities to use levy funds to support anything in their area related to 'development' – not confined to projects on a list – which may means that they can use levy funds to support housing improvement and regeneration. Schedule 9 under 116 brings neighbourhood plans and neighbourhood development orders into effect, and charges for meeting costs related to neighbourhood planning. Section 120 enables financial assistance in relation to neighbourhood planning. The secretary of state can assist financially in relation to publicity and the implementation of neighbourhood planning.

Chapter 4 relates to the publicisation of planning applications; the person must publicise the proposed (planning) application in such manner as the person reasonably considers is likely to bring the proposed application to the attention of a majority of the persons who live at, or otherwise occupy, premises in the vicinity of the land; and under 61X (2) the person must, when deciding whether the application that the person is actually to make should be in the same terms as the proposed application, have regard to any responses to the consultation that the person has received.

Turning to housing matters, Chapter 1 concerns allocation and homelessness. Section 145 concerns the allocation of housing accommodation, with an amendment to s. 159 Housing Act 1996. This removes existing council tenants from the allocations rules: it is no longer necessary to treat transfer applicants in the same way as waiting-list applicants, and s. 4B reinforces the importance of abiding by the reasonable preference categories in allocations schemes. Section 146 states that allocations in England should only be to eligible and qualifying persons. There is an insertion in the Housing Act 1996 before s. 160A to the effect that a local housing authority in England shall not allocate housing accommodation to a 'person from abroad' who is ineligible for an allocation of housing accommodation by virtue of subsection (2) or (4). Additionally, a person subject to immigration control within the meaning of the Asylum and Immigration Act 1996 is ineligible for an allocation of housing accommodation by a local housing authority in England unless he is of a class prescribed by regulations made by the secretary of state.

Localism and allocations

Allocations policies have rightly been regarded as highly sensitive over the years: after all, they constitute the major gateway to social and affordable housing, and restricting them to certain classes of people means impacting on life chances. In many ways, they answer the question 'what is social and affordable housing for?' at the local level.

There are several answers to this question. The most obvious one is that this form of housing is for people who cannot compete in the market place to satisfy their housing requirements, or where there simply is not a market product to cater for their needs, even if they could afford it. If everyone could satisfy their housing need through the market, there would not be any need for social or affordable housing, and it is largely because of market dysfunctionalities that it came to be in the first place. Other purposes are arguably subsidiary to the main reasons. Such housing can be instrumental in attracting lower-paid workers to an area where their presence is needed to service needs such as cleaning, lower-paid retail functions and office administration, etc. Since the tightening of benefit restrictions following the welfare reform changes in the UK since 2011, the question how to ensure a reasonable supply of lower-paid workers has become more acute, and the need for lower-rent housing has also become more acute since then.

It is also reasonable to assume that a person's housing need will not be constant over their lifecycle. This is verified through the right to buy system, now made more generous through discounts of up to £75,000. Patently, if you can afford to buy the home in which you live, even with a discount, you have no need to rent at below market levels. There are also those in council and housing association housing who could well afford to buy or rent privately if they wished to, but prefer to 'bed-block' housing oriented at meeting need rather than effective demand because the lower rent is a very good deal indeed. Arguably, therefore, social or affordable housing should not be available over the lifecycle of individuals, but only when they actually need it and demonstrably are unable to resort to market products. Naturally it would be necessary to take a medium- to long-term view of income and savings before removing tenancies, but the principle seems to be sound. This form of thinking has led to flexible five-year fixed term tenancies offered by many councils and housing associations, reviewable in the basis of savings and income, and council and housing association housing is fast becoming housing of last resort, as it was when it was first developed. Following this argument through, such housing should be earmarked only for those who need it and cannot find housing elsewhere, both at the point of entry and during their housing career.

Allocations approaches following localism follow this line. The act restates the importance of the reasonable preference categories as a guideline to allocations, albeit stressing the importance of choice. This is consistent with the argument above, as the categories represent areas of housing need.

In more detail, Chapter 1 – Allocation and Homelessness – makes some important changes, such as removing existing council tenants from the allocations rules: it is now no longer necessary to treat transfer applicants in the same way as waiting-list applicants. This is because their need has already been satisfied, whereas that of applicants has not (s. 4A). However, s. 4B re inforces the importance of abiding by the reasonable preference categories in allocations schemes.

In a direct challenge to housing recent immigrants and those with no national connection with the UK, s. 146 says that allocation should only be to eligible and qualifying persons, that is, people with a right to live and/or work in the UK. A new section (before s. 160A) is inserted into the Housing Act 1996 which says that a local housing authority in England shall not allocate housing accommodation to a person from abroad who is ineligible for an allocation of housing accommodation by virtue of subsection (2) or (4), or (b) to two or more persons jointly if any of them is a person mentioned in paragraph (a); or to anyone subject to immigration control within the meaning of the Asylum and Immigration Act 1996, unless in a class prescribed by regulations made by the secretary of state. The drawbridges are well and truly being pulled up, and the resource is effectively ring-fenced in a nationwide expression of local connection. This is partly due to ideology and partly down to the scarcity of the resource. Allocating council housing to recent workless immigrants with no connection to the UK has never been a vote winner.

Under s. 166A (allocation in accordance with allocation scheme: England), councils must have an allocation scheme for determining priorities and a set of procedures to be followed in allocating housing accommodation. For this purpose 'procedure' includes all aspects of the allocation process, including the persons or descriptions of persons by whom decisions are taken. It must also include a statement of the authority's policy on offering a choice of housing accommodation to people who are to be allocated housing accommodation or giving them the opportunity to express preferences about the housing accommodation to be allocated to them.

As stated before, the reasonable preference categories are paramount in deciding allocations schemes, although the act does say that it may also be framed so as to give additional preference to particular descriptions of people within this subsection (being descriptions of people with urgent housing needs). This includes working people – so additional preference could be given to working people occupying insanitary conditions, for example. The act also explicitly states the factors which can be taken into account when allocating accommodation, which include the financial resources available to a person to meet their housing costs; any behaviour of a person (or of a member of his household) which affects his suitability to be a tenant; and any local connection (within the meaning of s. 199) which exists between a person and the authority's district – for example, length of residence or employment. Notably, the secretary of state can frame additional factors by regulation. Some authorities have begun to implement local connection policies in connection with allocation schemes: for example the Royal Borough of Greenwich in London insists that applicants have had a residential or work connection with the borough for at least five years before being eligible to join the housing register. There is a risk that this entails treating certain equalities groups less favourably than others, since more white UK people can satisfy the criteria than non-white UK citizens, but the policy has been legally tested. A problem with this approach may be that people who have something to contribute to the borough may be excluded from affordable housing, whereas those living in the borough who do not intend to make a social or economic contribution to borough life and wellbeing may find themselves more favourably treated. There are rights to information about the scheme and to a review of decisions in the act, but these are powers and duties which have been transferred from other law and in any case represent existing good practice.

Section 147 spells out what local authorities must have regard to in framing their allocations policies, and this includes their current homelessness strategy under s. 1 of the Homelessness Act 2002, their current tenancy strategy under s. 150 of the Localism Act 2011, and in the case of London borough councils, the London housing strategy. They must consult with other registered providers, and finally must abide by their adopted allocations scheme. This tends to reinforce the role of need in allocations, as it refers to the greatest form of need which is homelessness. The reference to tenancy strategies is important here: if a council has decided to go for fixed-term flexible tenancies in addition to or instead of regular secure tenancies, then it makes sense to refer to reassessment criteria based on examining savings and income in relation to the housing area at the allocation stage as well as at review.

The act also serves to stimulate the private rented sector market in the locality by enabling people who have been housed as homeless with a private rented sector offer to be housed once more under these conditions even if they no longer have priority is made homeless again (for example through a s. 21 notice plus court action in relation to an assured shorthold tenancy. However, this may not be a realistic option given the lowering of housing benefit caps and attendant restrictions brought in through welfare reform policies.

Localism and tenure reform

Tenancy strategies

Section 150 of the act states that local housing authorities in England must prepare and publish a strategy (a 'tenancy strategy') setting out the matters to which the registered providers of social housing for its district must consider when devising policies relating to the kinds of tenancies they grant, the circumstances in which they will grant a tenancy of a particular kind, where they grant tenancies for a fixed term, the lengths of the terms, and the circumstances in which they will grant a further tenancy on the coming to an end of an existing one. It also says that a local housing authority must have regard to its tenancy strategy in exercising its housing management functions, and that it must keep its strategy under review, and may modify or replace it from time to time.

What is the reason for and effect of such a direction? It really goes to the heart of how the authority considers itself as a landlord but also as a housing enabler, in the sense that it has a number of options as to the sequence and type of tenancies it can grant. For example, it may decide to test tenants by using an introductory tenancy and then moving straight to a fixed-term tenancy once the tenant has proved that they are capable of sustaining the contractual arrangement, on the assumption that many tenants will have the wherewithal to move out of affordable housing at the end of the fixed term and into owner-occupation or even possibly private renting. This would serve to reinforce the view that council tenancies are not for life, but are a stepping stone to something else. Other authorities might prefer not to use the flexible tenure form but instead to grant secure tenancies after use of introductory tenancies to help them judge whether the tenant is likely to be able to sustain that arrangement in the longer term. Yet others might prefer the higher-risk strategy of granting secure tenancies as a matter of course, ignoring introductory or flexible tenancies. This is higher risk as most of the grounds for possession of secure tenancies are discretionary, whereas an introductory tenancy can be ended without any grounds, as can a flexible tenancy, giving the landlord more control over the asset.

Tenancy strategies must be transparent and published, so that objections can be raised or questions asked. The documents are frequently controversial, as including flexible tenure means that the authority is set on regarding its housing offer as a piece of social engineering. Why has this assertion been made? The reason is that flexible tenancies can be ended for a variety of reasons, including a judgement that the tenant can now afford to move on to another form of housing. This is nothing to do with classical tenancy law, which majors on rent payment history, abiding by terms of a tenancy, etc. The flexible tenancy form is similar to the assured shorthold tenancy, and that was introduced to enable landlords to gain possession in order to create a new tenancy with a higher rent, among other reasons, but this is not the preserve of a local authority.

Flexible tenancies

Section 107A inserts a new s. 106A of the Housing Act 1985, which has the effect of defining a flexible tenancy as a secure tenancy, and as one which is granted by a landlord in England for a term certain of not less than two years. The landlord must, before it is granted, state in writing that the tenancy is a flexible tenancy. It may be granted on the cessation of a family intervention tenancy, granted so that the landlord may observe the behaviour of a household. It also applies after the end of a demoted or introductory tenancy.

As with other forms of tenancy, the landlord can only end the flexible tenancy through a court order, and the court must make an order for possession of the dwelling-house let on the tenancy if it is satisfied that the following conditions are met. The conditions are as follows: condition 1 is that the flexible tenancy has come to an end and no further secure tenancy (whether or not it is a flexible tenancy) is current, other than a secure tenancy that is a periodic tenancy. Condition 2 is that the landlord has given the tenant not less than six months' notice in writing stating that the landlord does not propose to grant another tenancy on the expiry of the flexible tenancy, and setting out the landlord's reasons for not proposing to grant another tenancy. The landlord must inform the tenant of his or her right to request a review of the proposal and of the time within which such a request must be made. Condition 3 is that the landlord has given the tenant not less than two months' notice in writing stating that the landlord requires possession of the dwelling-house.

Analogous conditions are also made which allow housing associations to grant assured shorthold tenancies more widely than hitherto, when they were only permitted to create them if housing homeless households in temporary accommodation. It would seem odd if one regime were to apply to local authorities and another to associations, and s. 164 of the act deals with these matters. The tenancies must be for not less than two years. There is a requirement for housing associations to give not less than six months' notice in writing to tenants before the end of the fixed-term tenancy, and to give advice about the notice or any other advice which they may be able to offer, including on alternative accommodation.

It is now possible for landlords to make payments to tenants to assist them to become home owners. This is under s. 177 of the act, but the power must be within the constitution of the registered provider. No doubt very many such providers have now changed their constitution to enable this possibility. This is a response to the certainty that there is a shortage of social and affordable housing for rent in many areas, and also underlines the philosophy of affordable housing as a hand-up rather than a hand-out, a route to a destination rather than the destination itself.

What sorts of payments have been made? In 2012, Guildford City Council made bridging grants available to tenants who could afford a mortgage but needed help to bridge the gap between that and the purchase price, up to a limit, though it does not apply to shared ownership purchases (Guildford Borough Council, 2012). A similar scheme by Runnymede District Council offered a maximum of £20,000 to tenants to help them buy a private property, and one condition is that they will be unable to apply to the council for housing for 50 years! (Runnymede District Council, 2012).

All in all, localism is set to have an indelible effect on social and affordable housing, and many policies and strategies will have to be altered to accommodate its import.

Localism and planning policy – the involvement of communities in planning and housing development

One of the most significant features of localism is its effect on planning and the devolution of some planning and enforcement matters to local communities. Section 111 of the act – local development schemes – amends s. 15 of the Planning and Compulsory Purchase Act 2004. Essentially, neighbourhoods – at parish council level – are now able to devise development strategies and policies for their areas. Section 116 and Schedule 9 bring neighbourhood plans and neighbourhood development orders into effect. There are two routes to influence: neighbourhood forums and existing or newly formed parish councils. A neighbourhood forum has to have a constitution, and must be recognised by the local authority before it can help to develop local plans. A neighbourhood forum also must be formed of at least 21 local people, and interestingly local businesses as well as residents can be involved. It has become clear that where groups can be defined as resident in an area, willing to work with each other and neighbouring communities, council support should be forthcoming. However, plans must be in conformance with existing local plans, and they are subject to referenda. If 51 per cent of local residents can be shown to be in favour of the locally devised plan, then it can be adopted. Time will tell as to whether neighbourhood forums and parish councils make noticeable changes to planning policy and practice – it is too early to evaluate this – but there is potential for local people to make a real difference to the scale and appearance of developments.

A community right to build

The act has also brought in a community right to build. Again, it is too early to evaluate the success or otherwise of this policy as it was introduced only in April 2012. The idea is that communities will be able to build family homes to sell, affordable housing for rent, sheltered housing for older local residents or low-cost starter homes for young local families who might otherwise find it hard to get on the housing ladder. At the heart of the proposal is that properly constituted local interest groups need to devise a community right to build order, which will enable to the community to grant planning permission for the developments they wish to go ahead, without developers applying separately for planning permission to do so. Consultation and conformity with local, national and EU planning policy are a must, and an independent examiner needs to check that the right basic standards will be met. Following this, the council must organise a referendum on the order, and it will only go forward if a majority of local residents who are registered voters agree that it should. Once these hurdles have been overcome, the council must grant planning permission. The community body will then oversee the development, and any profits made will be recycled for the community's benefit (DCLG, 2012). The classes of development possible under these provisions include family homes to sell on the open market, affordable housing for rent, sheltered housing for elderly local residents, low-cost starter homes for young local families struggling to get on the housing ladder, facilities such as a new community centre or a children's playground, or to convert disused farm buildings into affordable homes. Widespread use of these powers could see quite a significant amount of local control being exercised over the development of affordable homes provided that the money and land is available to enable it.

The future of the localist approach

It is too early to say whether localism, as discussed in this chapter, will hold the day or whether here will be a drift back to big government, but there are already encouraging signs that local people are making a difference by getting involved in neighbourhood forums and parish councils. At best, localism will see allocations policies tailored to local needs without excluding incomers, who may be a valuable source of income generation for communities, bolstering local workforces and helping to escape the worst ravages of the recession. It will see local planning which is more responsive to local sentiment than hitherto, without strangling local affordable development, and it will see local groups taking a proactive rather than a reactive stance on affordable and for-sale housing development. The evaluation of a set of policies designed to enhance local influence in planning and housing will have to wait until the next edition, but early signs are fruitful indeed.

References

DCLG (Department for Communities and Local Government), (2009) *Fair and Flexible: Draft statutory guidance on social housing allocations for local authorities in England*. London: DCLG.

DCLG, (2011) *A Plain English Guide to the Localism Act*. London: DCLG.

DCLG, (2012) *An Introduction to the Community Right to Build*. London: DCLG. Available at: www.communities.gov.uk/documents/communities/pdf/21261671.pdf, viewed 25 July 2012.

Guildford Borough Council, (2012) Cash Incentive Scheme, available at: www.guildford.gov.uk/CHttpHandler.ashx?id=9709&p=0, viewed 25 July 2012.

Runnymede District Council, (2012) Tenants' Incentive Scheme, available at: www.runnymede.gov.uk/portal/site/runnymede/menuitem.d6f5346fbba12d2bba13bf13af8ca028/, viewed 25 July 2012.

8 Summary of key themes

This book has endeavoured to outline and explore the key themes in social and affordable housing. Several key themes have emerged. First, there is very little that is new in housing policy: it started as a reaction to public health issues, and this continues as an enduring theme. Social housing started out as most definitely earmarked for the respectable poor, and this is still a feature of the general approach to housing in the UK. It began as a reaction of local communities to housing need, and this theme has been revisited in consequence of localism in the planning and housing arenas.

The economic concept of supply and demand was examined, and its application to housing markets. It became clear that dysfunctions in the market economy are pervasive, and that this supplies much of the rationale to provide social and affordable housing. This leads to the justification for someone – in this case, local authorities – to assess the quantum of housing need, and endeavour to distinguish between general and acute housing need, and the breakdown of tenure required. It was concluded that planning reforms in themselves cannot solve the problems of supply and demand.

This led logically to a consideration of the development of consumer and customer cultures generally. Social and affordable housing is more than just housing: it contains customers who have a range of wants and needs, and who are experts in respect to the product. There are political, social and economic drivers to customer empowerment, and this reflects the complexity of the product as well as more general trends towards customer involvement in the wider arena. This is shown in the rise of the customer in housing, from the Citizens' Charter to co-regulation. Taking the customer seriously almost came off, with the TSA and its regulatory standards and local offers. Recent developments such as localism have prompted a re-examination of tenant management organisations, perhaps the clearest exposition in the housing world of said localism.

The question of 'What is housing management?' was answered by considering the its role as social engineering versus the rights and responsibilities approach, and it is likely that both elements subsist within the task, since all tenancy management involves imposing strictures on households and penalising them if they do not tow the line, as well as catering for their needs contractually, for example providing a fit-for-purpose repairs service. It was argued that there should be a seamless continuum from so-called general needs housing management through to special needs containment, and that alternative management strategies – in-house and arms' length – should be regularly tested against each other to ensure that customers receive value-for-money services, providing a link to Chapter 4 on housing finance.

Attention was drawn to the fact that there are many and varied reasons why households cannot engage with the market effectively, and that these make managing the patch particularly complex. The management task embraces special-needs housing management, dealing with special consideration groups, those who suffer economic and social discrimination and disadvantage through racial, ethnic or cultural status, those with unfavourable medical or related conditions, and others possessing other characteristics meeting with social disapproval and marginalisation. Sensitivity is therefore needed in considering how best to manage tenancies in the social and affordable sectors. The drive towards decent homes was examined, as were the pivotal roles of asset management and repairs and maintenance systems in achieving this aim, and ensuring that homes remain fit for purpose.

Housing finance was set in context. It has to be remembered that housing subsists within an economic envelope, specifically within government macroeconomic controls. The spending review and the budget are crucial in controlling the amount of capital and revenue finance directed towards the sector, even in the context of notional independence – the post-2012 approach to capital finance resourcing, spending allocation and control, borrowing and spending limits. There is still scope for reform in housing finance, and it is unlikely that we have seen the last of this in even the medium term. Meanwhile, it remains to be seen how housing associations will implement new affordable rents while ensuring that their homes remain accessible to their target markets, especially in the light of swingeing welfare reforms and caps on housing benefit in particular.

Housing law was placed in its context, as an important part of English and other UK legal systems, with especial reference to homelessness and allocations systems, where the law has changed significantly in the past decade. Special attention was paid to the law relating to decent homes and the 2004 Housing Act fitness system, since disrepair and urgent action regarding unfitness have rightly been highlighted time and time again in the housing press, and these again, correctly, are the main concerns of tenants. The major changes brought about by the Localism Act in the UK were highlighted, leading into the final substantive chapter.

Housing regeneration and development were introduced, at a time when local authorities are coming back into their own as affordable housing developers, and when regeneration is up there on the agenda following the 2012 Olympics in the UK. It is important to understand that true regeneration entails a four dimensional approach and must encompass social, economic, physical and environmental aspects to be truly successful – and that it is totally invalid unless there is meaningful consultation and engagement with communities who will be affected, linking this chapter in with that on participation and housing management. Housing development was examined as entailing the enabling and production of new build housing for rent and for sale, which crucially depends on the assessment of need and a sound planning system, all of which has changed through the Localism Act, leading logically to the final chapter which examined the way in which localism has had a root and branch influence on the provision and management of social and affordable housing.

In endeavouring to integrate the key themes of social and affordable housing, albeit in distinct chapters, it is hoped that this book has made the key issues which face housing managers and developers clear, and may even help practitioners to cope with the ever-changing worlds which social and affordable housing offers. The agenda is constantly changing, but at root, effective housing development and management relate to very simple themes: the production of decent, affordable homes and humane and non-intrusive management which responds to the views of occupants rather than imposes strictures on those who are fortunate enough to live in them in the early twenty-first century.

Glossary

Active citizen The citizen who takes responsibility for his or her wellbeing and who is unwilling simply to be the passive recipient of public or semi-public services.

Affordable housing Housing which is let by local authorities or housing associations at up to 80 per cent of market rents, and not governed by the rent restructuring formula.

Affordable Housing Programme A four-year budget in England to part-fund affordable housing development through government subsidy. The current round is 2011–2015, to help finance the construction of affordable homes for rent and for sale. The current AHP is £4.5 billion and is targeted to deliver 80,000 new homes for rent and for sale in England, added to the unfulfilled target amount from the previous National AHP (2008–2011).

Annually managed expenditure The budgets which the government makes available to pay for volatile social expenditure items such as housing benefit and other forms of social security, as opposed to sums made available for capital works and major procurement over a period of time, which can often be planned over four years.

Arms' length management organisations Bodies set up to manage local authority housing in England and Wales in the 2000s to provide a more focused housing management service. Also used to focus investment on homes to achieve Decent Homes status.

Assured shorthold tenancy The default type of tenancy granted in England and Wales in the private rented sector.

Biodiversity value The value of having a variety of plant and animal species in an ecosystem.

Brownfield sites Housing sites which have previously been developed. They can subsequently be cleared for building.

Capital development The development of fixed assets (e.g. homes) or the improvement or enhancement of assets.

Care in the community A system of bringing care and support services to the client in their own home, rather than warehousing them in a geriatric ward or Part Three accommodation.

Case law   In England, the principles which emerge from 'case law' must be taken account of when similar cases are heard at that level.

Choice-based letting   A system where applicants for council and housing association lettings bid against others to secure a property, using their housing needs score (often their position in a needs band) as currency.

Combinatorial modelling   A model which contains very many variables which have a mathematical relationship between them.

Compulsory competitive tender   A regime introduced in the UK in the mid 1980s to force local authorities to put many of their services out for tender with the private sector as the key competitor. As a result, many services once run by councils (e.g. refuse collection) are now run by private companies.

Controlled tenancies   Pre-Rent Act tenancies let on a controlled (very-low) rent.

Core functions   Activities which relate directly to the housing management landlord function such as tenancy enforcement, rent collection and allocations.

Co-regulation   The idea that landlords and tenants can together determine the way in which an organisation's performance can be judged and improved.

Credit crunch   A phenomenon which existed between 2007 and 2009, whereby banks ceased to lend to each other due to liquidity problems brought about by questionable lending policies. One result was the shrinkage of the mortgage lending market. In the UK, this was eased by the state pumping money into the lending system.

Cumulative need   Where housing need has more than one aspect – for example, someone may be living in overcrowded accommodation (need 1) and also be suffering from poor health as a result of dampness in the accommodation (need 2) and also be subject to a notice to quit (need 3).

Decanting   Moving tenants from their home to another property, often as the result of improvement or major repairs work, on a temporary or permanent basis.

Decent Homes   The aim of ensuring that social housing is in a fit for purpose state with reasonably modern facilities by a target date, initially set at 2010.

Doctrine of binding precedent   A decision made by a judge in one court ('case law') may bind future decisions in a court of the same level. The decision is generally referred to in court when similar cases are heard.

Dysfunction   An operational or organisational problem which causes a system to malfunction.

Economic sustainability   Ensuring that developments are located closed to sources of employment.

Economies of scale   A situation whereby the cost of producing the next unit is lower than the cost of producing the preceding one. This is due to a number of factors, including absorption of the capital cost of machinery over time, and reducing the ratio between labour and output over time. An example is housing administration which is heavily IT dependent. It does not cost 1,000 times the cost of storing one record to store 1,000, due to the fact that computers have large memory capacities and can perform multiple calculations at roughly the same rate as individual calculations. A very large organisation can borrow at cheaper rates than a small one due to the size of the collateral it can put up and also due to the better guarantee of repayment due to large incomes – the lower loan rate is down to increased certainty of repayment.

Empowerment   To enable someone or something to do something which they wish to do, or to take advantage of an opportunity which is presented.

Equilibrium price   The price of a good where the amount that consumers are prepared to pay meets the amount at which the vendor is prepared to sell it for.

Financial instrument   A document which represents a legal agreement to trade. They can be equity or debt based. For example, an equity-based instrument could be an agreement to transfer the ownership of an asset to another party at a time in the future for a price determined at the time that the instrument is issued. A debt-based instrument could be a loan made to the owner of an asset with a repayment date set at some time in the future.

Flexible tenancy option   Fixed-term tenancies offered for less than five years, but no less than two years, by public sector and not-for-profit landlords, which came in as a consequence of the Localism Act 2011.

Foyers   Accommodation provided usually in a block for young people, with work opportunities as part of a package of support.

Garden cities   Cities built to combine the advantages of country and town living, with attention paid to public open spaces, large gardens and allotments, e.g. Welwyn Garden City. Ebenezer Howard (1850–1928) is usually regarded as the founding father of the movement. See his *Garden Cities of To-morrow* (1898).

Gearing ratio   Capital compared to borrowed funds. For example, if my total debt is £10,000 and my total capital (including the value of assets) is £1,000, the gearing ratio is £10,000/£1,000 = 10:1. The ratio between debt and capital is often used as an indicator of financial health, and ratios are compared between companies which undertake similar operations.

Gemeinschaft   The ethos of a community which looks after its members as human beings and who are not subservient to financial exchange. A concept of 'shared space'.

General fund   The account of a local authority for spending on general services to all citizens, e.g. rubbish collection, parking, environmental health and housing advice.

Greenfield sites   Sites which have not been previously developed.

Hard and soft landscaping   Hard landscaping – built features such as walls, and raised features (mounds, etc). Soft landscaping – hedges, trees and plants.

Homes and Communities Agency   A non-departmental public body which funds new affordable housing in England and regulates the social housing sector.

Housing benefit   A personal subsidy paid by local authorities in England and Wales to help social housing tenants pay their rent. Local housing allowance is the equivalent term for personal subsidy paid to private-sector tenants. The regimes will be abolished from 2013 when the Welfare Reform Act becomes effective.

Housing Corporation   A quasi-autonomous non-government organisation which regulated housing associations and made available grant finance to assist them in building for social rent and for-sale housing from a budget voted annually by parliament. Abolished in December 2008, its regulatory functions were transferred to the TSA, since abolished, and its funding powers to the Homes and Communities Agency, which contains most of the functions of the Housing Corporation, except that it now makes funds available to local authorities to build.

Housing need   The total number of households who cannot afford to satisfy their housing requirements through the market. To stand in housing need is to require housing but to be unable to afford to compete in the owner-occupied or private rented market.

Housing requirement   The state of being in need of housing whether or not you can afford to compete for it in the market. The total housing requirement is the number of households who need their own accommodation but do not currently have it.

Housing revenue account   Often abbreviated as HRA, the current account showing housing income and expenditure in respect of local authority housing in the UK.

In-kind subsidies   Non-monetary subsidy, including free or discounted land, which reduces the cost of development.

Joint service vehicle   A body set up by partners to achieve a jointly desired aim, for example where councils and housing associations get together to pool management and maintenance and/or administrative resources to achieve economies of scale, or jointly procure ICT services to achieve the same effect.

Joint venture company   A company formed between two or more companies to undertake a programme to mutual benefit – for example, a council may form a construction company together with a commercial developer to take advantage of cheap or free land in the ownership of the authority and pass on some of the development profits to the private sector partner in return for properties acquired by the authority at cost.

Key multiplier industries   Industries which generate and support others e.g. ship-building which generates demand for components, steelmaking, fuel etc. Another example is oil refining which provides key input for petrochemical industries. Removing a key multiplier industry often has the effect of regional economic melt-down, as the businesses which rely upon the key industry close down, with catastrophic job losses.

Keynesian intervention   Intervention by government to correct dysfunctions in the market – for example creating jobs backed by public money to reduce unemployment and increase tax yields, and to grow new industries. Grant-funding housing organisations to produce affordable homes to plug gaps in between the national housing requirement and production/availability through the market place is arguably a Keynesian intervention. John Maynard Keynes (1883–1943) was an influential British economist who advocated government intervention to reduce the effect of recession and depression, and who is widely credited as the father of macroeconomics.

Lean A version of systems thinking applied to management systems.

Lifetime homes Homes designed to ensure that the occupants can live there throughout their lives, typically incorporating doorsets capable of wheelchair access, level thresholds and kitchens with circulation space to enable wheelchair users to use the facilities.

Limited liability partnership A limited partnership has two classes of partners. The general partner or partners have full management and control of the partnership business but also accept full personal responsibility for partnership liabilities. Such partners do not have personal liability beyond their investment in the partnership interest.

Liquidity ratio This shows the number of times that short-term borrowing is covered by cash. For example, if I have borrowed £1,000 short-term and have £1,000 cash, the liquidity ratio is 1:1. If I have borrowed £1,000 and have £100 cash available, the ratio is 1:10. The formula is liquid assets divided by short-term liabilities.

Local exchange and trading schemes Schemes where individuals in the scheme perform services for others and bank points in return, which can be used to procure services from others in the group. An excellent way for those with few means to obtain services which are frequently expensive, and a stimulus for training for a new career which may lead to paid work.

Logical soundness A situation which exists where an argument does not lead to a contradiction in terms, and where the conclusion is fully supported by the premises of the argument.

Macroeconomics The study of the way in which national economies function.

Malthus, Thomas (1766–1834) A pessimistic clergyman who believed that population growth tends to outstrip the means of supply. He believed that population grows geometrically, in comparison with resource production which increases arithmetically.

Market dysfunctionalities Allocation problems which exist due to market forces for example, household being priced out of the homes market.

Marginal effective demand What consumers with lower-income levels can afford to pay for market housing.

Master planning The act of creating an overall template for an area's development, for example, street layout, relative location of land uses, provision of leisure and recreational facilities, positioning of retail facilities, etc.

Mobility of labour The extent to which labour can move to available work.

Monetarism   An economic theory popularised by Milton Friedman (1912–2006) which suggests that inflation is caused by an oversupply of money in circulation, and that it will increase in proportion to the velocity of its circulation. One way of controlling inflation is therefore to restrict the money supply, e.g. through increasing interest rates or reducing public expenditure.

Negative externalities   An output of a development which results in a cost to the community, for example pollution associated with a road development.

Net expenditure   Expenditure less support received, e.g. expenditure on providing housing services net of subsidy from some other source, or the cost of development less any grant applied to the operation.

Net migration   The difference between immigration into and emigration out of an area during a year.

Non-core functions   Activities which are performed as part of, but which are not essential to, housing management, such as debt advice, housing strategy work and arguably resident participation.

Normative system   A 'norm' is an accepted value, so a normative system is a system of values, of which legal systems are an example.

Part Three accommodation   Supported housing provided for usually elderly and infirm people under Part Three of the National Assistance Act 1948, with intensive management. Phased out in most areas in favour of supported housing schemes with an emphasis on independent living.

Personalisation agenda   An initiative to pay people who previously benefited from services provided under Supporting People a sum of money, or to organise a budget for them, to commission their own services, sometimes with the help of an adviser.

Planning for real   An exercise where individuals who have some connection with a scheme take part in a planning scenario, typically placing model dwellings on a board and locating hard and soft landscaping as well as other infrastructural items with the assistance of planners and architects.

Price to income ratio   The ratio between house prices and income necessary to purchase or rent. For example, if the average price of owner-occupied housing in an area were £300,000 and the average wage were £30,000, the price income would be 10:1 (£300,000 is 10 x £30,000).

Primary data   Data collected first-hand by a researcher e.g. shopping survey information direct from the consumer.

Real house prices   The price of housing adjusted for inflation.

Redfield sites   Heavily polluted sites which need considerable sums of money spending on them to make them fit for redevelopment.

Regeneration   At its best, a comprehensive scheme which has the effect of improving the social, physical, environmental and economic condition of an area with the consent and involvement of local residents.

Residualisation   In a housing context, the result of needs-based allocations policies which have resulted in herding poor households into the same area in social rented accommodation, aided and abetted by sales under the right to buy scheme which has reduced the stock of the most desirable housing.

Retail bonds   An interest bearing financial instrument which usually have a duration of more than one year, and can be traded. At the end of the term (when they mature) they can be redeemed for the face value of the bond plus interest accrued.

Revenue finance   Financing the running of a housing organisation through income from rent, service charges and interest on accounts.

Right to buy   A policy of selling council houses to sitting tenants in the UK which came about as a result of the Housing Act 1980.

Secondary data   Data which have already been collected and analysed and which are then used by a researcher e.g. population growth trends.

Secondary surveys   The analysis of survey data which have already been collected.

Secondary, tertiary and quaternary sectors   (of industry) Manufacturing is secondary sector, retail is tertiary sector, and banking is quaternary.

Snow, Dr John   (1813–1858) A physician and social reformer best known for his work in epidemiology, especially cholera prevention.

Social housing   Housing rented by local authorities and housing associations in England and Wales which is rented at levels informed by the rent restructuring formula.

Social engineering   The art of manipulating people into performing actions. The practice of trying to achieve an overriding social objective by manipulating people to act in a certain way and/or hold given views so that they are compliant with the ends desired and the means to be used.

Societal dysfunctionality   A society which does not or cannot support some or most of its members with welfare support, education, health care, etc.

Special consideration groups   Groups which are singled out for specific housing management interventions, for example, young homeless persons who may have a degree of priority in allocations systems, and who may be provided with a package of work training. Other groups include travellers, asylum seekers and even students. The common factor is that they are otherwise disadvantaged by the market.

Stagflation   A situation where inflation is high but where economic productivity is very low and unemployment is high. Efforts to reduce inflation may well increase unemployment, as businesses suffer revenue losses and cannot afford to keep workers on.

Stock conditions surveys   Evaluations of the physical state of housing stock, often carried out prior to valuations, designed to highlight the need for modernisation, improvement and repairs and maintenance programmes.

Strategic housing market assessment   An evaluation of the housing market, looking at all dimensions including private rented and owner-occupier markets in an attempt to define the quantum of housing requirement and need.

Supported housing   Housing provided with a sheltered scheme manager on site or with peripatetic support.

Sustainable wealth   Long-term provision to ensure wellbeing, such as long-term employment.

Systems thinking   A way of analysing the flows and stores of any system, and evaluating the most efficient and effective way in which a system can work.

Tenant management organisation   A housing management body run by tenants and leaseholders living on an estate or with a property of 25 or more secure tenancies.

Tenant Services Authority   A now-disbanded non-governmental body which was formed in 2008 to ensure that tenants' views are taken into account in housing management decision-making and that housing providers adhered to standards set by the government and by themselves. The functions have been transferred to the Homes and Communities Agency.

Tenant Services Authority Home Standard   One of six standards published by the now-defunct Tenant Services Authority, in force since 1 April 2010. It required housing providers to set standards for repairs and maintenance, and the quality of accommodation. It came with a 'local offer' – an agreement to abide by certain standards in relation to these services, to be validated by tenants, and devised through consultation.

Ultra vires   Literally 'beyond the powers'. If a local authority makes a decision which is outside the powers laid down by statute, it is said to be acting *ultra vires*. Actions which are within the powers prescribed by law are known as *intra vires*.

Value added tax   A tax on the purchase price of an object or service. It is an indirect tax, paid to the government by the vendor, having collected it from the buyer.

Index